A Pinch of This and A Pinch of That

~ A Story~Cookbook ~

~ ~ ~ ~ ~ ~ ~ ~

A Pinch of This and A Pinch of That

The Cooking Treasures of Our Fairytale Italian Restaurant,

Mama Lena's Italian Kitchen

By

**Salvino and Margo
Madonna**

~ ~ ~ ~ ~ ~ ~ ~

A Pinch of This and A Pinch of That

The Cooking Treasures of Our Fairytale Italian Restaurant,

Mama Lena's Italian Kitchen

Copyright 1998, Library of Congress
Salvino Madonna and Margo Madonna
Co-Authors and Creators
Copyright TXu 876-771

First Printing, Fall, 1999

For Further Information, Contact ~
MarSala's Enterprises, Ltd.
Two Elm Creek Drive ~ Suite # 501
Elmhurst, Illinois   60126

Library of Congress
Catalog Card Number 99~96110

ISBN 0~7392~0457~2

Printed in the USA by

MORRIS PUBLISHING

3212 East Highway 30 • Kearney, NE 68847 • 1-800-650-7888

Our
Dedication

We Dedicate This Book to the Very Loving Memory of

Our Dear Mama Lena and Her Mother, Grandma Anna

Two Very Special Angels to Each and Everyone

When on Earth, and Now to Everyone in Heaven

True and Special Inspirations to Us in

Writing our Treasured Book for You

~ May God Bless Both of Them ~

Table of Contents

Section I
Our Story Section

Section II
Our Cookbook Section of Treasured Recipes

Chapter One ~ The Appetizers

Chapter Two ~ Soups & Broths

Chapter Three ~ Salads & Dressings

Chapter Four ~ The Pastas

Chapter Five ~ The Sauces

Pages 107 ~ 127

~ Tomato Sauces, Basic ~

"Large" Recipe ~ Tomato Sauce
"Quick" Recipe ~ Tomato Sauce
" Meat~Style " ~ Tomato Sauce

~ Tomato Sauces, Special, and A Special Tribute to The Tomato ~

Marinara Sauce ~ ala Madonna
Tribute to The Tomato ~ Pomodoro Honore
Our "Velvet Cloud" Sauce

~ Clam Sauces ~

White Clam Sauce, Mushrooms & Pine Nuts
Red Clam Sauce, Mushrooms & Pine Nuts

~ Oil & Butter Sauces ~

Butter, Parsley, Oil & Garlic Sauce
Butter & Almond Caper Sauce
Oil & Garlic Sauce, Olives & Pine Nuts

~ Cream Sauces ~

White Cream Sauce Supreme
Red Cream Sauce Supreme

~ Variations for Tomato Sauces & Cream Sauces ~

Additions of
Vegetables, Meats, Cheeses or Wines

Chapter Six

Fish & Seafood Entrees

Pages 129 ~ 139

Lemon Oregano Tuna, Broiled

Mussels in Sherry Sauce

Shrimp and Scallops, Marinara

Swordfish in Lemon Sauce, Baked

Vermouth Sole with Sauteed Vegetables, Baked

Chapter Seven

The Chicken Entrees

Pages 141 ~ 151

Chicken in Marsala Wine

Chicken Breast, Eggplant Sauce

Chicken in Amaretto Rice

Chicken Oregano, Orange Sauce

Chicken Tarragon, Spumante Sauce

Chapter Eight ~ The Meat Entrees

Chapter Nine ~ Vegetable Entrees &

Vegetable Side Dishes

Pages 195 ~ 215

~ Vegetable Entrees ~

Eggplants Parmesan ~ Vegetarian Style & Meat Style

Peppers, Baked ~ Stuffed with Sausage

Artichokes ~ Sicilian Olive Filling

~ Vegetable Side Dishes ~

Mama Lena's Roasted Sweet Peppers

Asparagus & Sicilian Olives, Sauteed in Garlic Butter

Italian Green Beans, Onions & Tomatoes, Baked in Romano Cheese

Potatoes, Herb ~ Specially Baked

Potatoes, Parsley Cheese ~ Sauteed in Olive Oil

Spinach, Tomato & Green Olives, Baked in Cream Sherry Sauce

Zucchini, Breaded ~ Served with Orange Sauce

Chapter Ten ~ Homemade Breads

Pages 217 ~ 235

~ Dough for Italian Bread ~

**Mama Lena's Bread Dough &
Tips for Baguette~Style, Loaf~Style and Round~Style Breads**

~ Pizza Dough ~

**Traditional Thin~Crusted Pizza
Sicilian Pizza and Focaccio, Old~World Style**

~ Special Italian Breads ~

**Garlic & Sweet Onion Bread
Herbs & Spices Bread
Hot Cheese Bread
Mama Lena's Tomato Cheese Bread**

~ Bread Crumbs & Bread Sticks ~

**Bread Crumbs ~ Plain or Italian Seasoned Styles
Bread Sticks ~ Plain, Garlic, Salted & Seeded Styles**

~ Crisp Croutons ~

Croutons, Plain or Garlic Crisp Styles

~ Miniature Italian Toasts ~

Miniature Italian Toasts for Our Appetizer Spreads and Buffets

Chapter Eleven ~ Sweet Desserts

Pages 237 ~ 259

~ Cannoli & Cream Puffs ~

Sweet Cream Sicilian Cannoli
Cream Puffs ~ Amaretto

~ Cassata Cakes ~

Cassata ~ Amaretto ~ With Pine Nuts
Cassata ~ Chocolate & Vanilla Cake ~ Vanilla Rum Sauce

~ Fillings for Cakes & Cream Puffs ~

Ricotta Cheese Filling ~ The Basic Recipe &
Variation Fillings ~ Candy, Fruits, Nuts Or Wines

~ Zabaione ~

Zabaione ~ Marsala ~ With Fresh Fruit

~ Holiday Dough Treats ~

Sweet Dough Treats ~ Vegetable Or Plain Styles

~ Cookies ~ A Christmas Tradition ~

Biscotti ~ Anisette & Vanilla ~ Toasted Dessert Slices
Chocolate Spice Cookies ~ Papa's Favorite
Fig Cookies ~ Cucidati ~ Mama's & Grandma Anna's Favorite

Chapter Twelve ~ The Kitchen Essentials

~ The Contact Information Page ~

" A Pinch of This and A Pinch of That"
Contact Us to Order, Arrange Group Discounts
& Learn Future Projects
Our Sincere Thanks for Joining Us on This Journey Into
" Mama Lena's Italian Kitchen "

~~~~~~

Section I

Our Story Section

~~~~~~

Foreword

Sometimes you just have to take a chance in Life!   In 1967, the Leonard and the Madonna Families each took a chance and made decisions that were to really change their lives.   And although, we wouldn't meet for three more years to share our stories, our individual decisions turned out to be the best ones for each of us.

In the Fall of 1967, my wife, Sheila, who had never been West of the Hudson River, left our Wellesley, Massachusetts home with our six sons, ages one to twelve years, and joined me in Chicago where I had accepted a new job at WGN Radio & TV.

At about the same time, here in the Windy City, Salvino, the youngest of Frank and Lena Madonna's nine children, decided it was time for the rest of the world to sample the Magic that his Mother had been working in the Family Kitchen for years ~ It was now time to open the restaurant that he had dreamed of.

It didn't take long for Salvino's concept to catch on and become popular with the locals and the out~of~towners, as word quickly spread of the wonderful concept, the ambiance and the outstanding food being served!   And lucky for me, Chicago radio listeners seemed to enjoy the combination of movie, theatre and restaurant reviews, sprinkled with pop and jazz music that we offered daily on WGN Radio.

Now I don't have to tell you what a busy young mother of six boys, all under age 15, wants the most ~ "A Nice Night Out!" And what we both missed so much from our days in the Boston area was a small Italian restaurant on Beacon Hill that had been our favorite and where we had always felt "at home." One day in the Spring of 1970, as I was relating this to a new~found friend, he was amazed that we hadn't been to Mama Lena's Italian Kitchen Restaurant on Chicago's Near North Side ~ a place "Everyone" knew had a welcoming family atmosphere and "The Best Italian Food in Town!" Our call to Mama Lena's Italian Kitchen Restaurant for dinner reservations was promptly answered, but there was a wait for a table, a three~week wait!   Roy & Sheila Leonard were very willing to wait!

On Monday, June 8, 1970, Sheila and I walked underneath the Mama Lena's Italian Kitchen red canopy at 24 East Chicago Avenue for the first time. With a bottle of Verdicchio discreetly tucked under my arm, we entered Mama Lena's Italian Kitchen for the 8:30 Dinner Seating. It was just like "coming home," as we were led to our table in the intimate Dining Room that seated only thirty or so Guests. Salvino Madonna welcomed his Guests, and announced to everyone The Dinner Menu that he and Mama had prepared for that evening. The Memorable Evening at Mama Lena's was beginning!

Our Memorable Dinner that evening began with a Basket of Delicious Homemade Tomato Cheese Bread followed by a Large, Tasty Italian Antipasto Salad. We were served an "Unusual" Appetizer of Homemade Sausage and Sweet Peppers in a Wine Sauce, followed by the Evening's Entree ~ an "Unforgettable" Sicilian Lasagna!

After a "Very Satisfying" Dessert of Mama Lena's Sweet Cream Cannoli, we made our visit to The Kitchen to meet and thank Our Hosts. We had a Thoroughly Enjoyable Experience that fine evening, and there were Many Wonderful Visits to This Very Special Restaurant over the years. But, we're so sad to inform you, as you are reaching for your phone to make reservations that our Mama Lena's Italian Kitchen Restaurant is there no more. However, you can now get to know This Wonderful Story and Share in The Memories of Mama Lena's, as you leaf through the pages of "This Very Loving Memoir By Salvino and Margo Madonna." Most Importantly, you will have at your very own fingertips The Great Original Recipes from Mama Lena's Italian Kitchen to Enjoy just as their Guests did! And Mama Lena will know, from the Enthusiasm at your own dinner table, that Her Memory Lives On. Bon Appetito!

Roy Leonard Covered The Arts in Chicago for
WGN Radio & TV for More Than 30 Years.
Roy's "New Goal " in Retirement is To Dine At
"Every" Great Restaurant in The World!

Preface

Every child wants and needs a "Special Hero" to admire and to imitate ~ And, all these years, I have been truly blessed with my own "Special Hero" ~ My Mother, Mama Lena. Each time I looked into the face of my Mother, I could clearly see a woman who never stopped giving of herself ~ an extremely hard-working woman ~ the Wonderful Mother of Nine Children ~ whose caring and concern for each of us took her every waking hour.

I was the youngest child ~ her baby ~ always hanging on to her every move. It was, of course, just natural for me to be the one interested in her wonderful cooking, as I spent the most time alone with her as a youngster ~ All the other Children were already off to school, and out and about for awhile before me.

As a very young child, I watched and tried in my own little way to help as Mama cooked her special recipes daily and baked 10 loaves of homemade bread every other day. Mama really loved to cook! I remember how I loved to watch her and play at doing just the same as she did. Without even realizing it, I learned so much during these times ~ times that were some of the very happiest days of my young life. Little did Mama and I know, at that time, how we were preparing for the future ~ for our Fairytale Restaurant.

It was just a natural progression through the years that Mama and I cooked together for the Family, for parties and special occasions. We talked between ourselves for many years of opening a small restaurant, because we both loved to cook ~ We felt it would be a happy and rewarding experience to share our heritage and special expertise in cooking.

Then, Mama's and My Dream became a reality in 1967 ~ We opened a luncheon spot, and quickly, by popular demand, converted it into a full Dinner Restaurant, naming it Mama Lena's Italian Kitchen. The success came quickly and consistently ~ Mama was so surprised and thrilled at the fame she had really never sought. Best of all, Mama did feel fulfilled and proud of satisfying so very many appreciative guests. Needless to say, she was proud of her baby, too!

Our little Fairytale Restaurant brought such happiness in the form of many new and wonderful experiences. We had the opportunity to serve lovely people, some celebrities of fame and some celebrities of life ~ I am personally grateful for all the friendships cultivated during those times. And, I am most grateful for Mama's personal happiness and for the fulfillment of Our Dream together.

Next, I am forever grateful for meeting my angel, Margo, my wife & partner, who worked along side me for so many years to keep Mama's dream and mine alive. Margo and I wrote this Story~Cookbook to honor Mama, who had a special place in everyone's heart. We hope now to share with you this Most Wonderful Woman and Mother, Mama Lena, and Our Fairytale Story ~ the experiences, the heritage, and the cooking treasures of a very humble, but richly blessed, Mother and Son, Mama Lena and Salvino Madonna.

Please follow Margo through the Introduction, where she takes you on a Journey into Mama Lena's Italian Kitchen Restaurant. As she opens the door of Mama Lena's for you, a Journey starts from our humble beginnings through all "The Dreams Come True" Times, sharing the love, the recipes and the experiences that made all our lives so richly blessed.

Mama's Family, "Her Real Treasure," is a very special story, giving you insight into Mama's Very Loving Family. Glance through our Photo Memories, Celebrity Guest List & Stories, and Acknowledgments to a Kind Press. Review then ~ Our Table of Contents!

We truly want you to know Mama Lena and our Mama Lena's Italian Kitchen Restaurant! Then, as You work on The Cookbook Section, You will understand Our Treasured Recipes, Our Stories before Our Recipes, and know The Wonderful Way It Was At Mama Lena's!

Mangia Buona Salute,
Salvino,
Loving Son & Protege of Mama Lena

Introduction

Once, there was a "Magic" ~ It was known and loved by all, simply as ~ " Mama Lena's." Mama Lena's Italian Kitchen, our intimate and romantic restaurant, which was dedicated by name to my husband Salvino's Mother, was the nightly meeting spot for over 14 years for people from every walk of life. It also was a place of many "Dreams Come True" for Salvino and Mama Lena ~ a spot that brought much happiness to Her and Her Family. And ~ It was well known for making thousands of Mama Lena's Guests very happy, too !

We hope for you to fully enjoy Our Story~Cookbook, know what was so very special about Mama Lena's Italian Kitchen, and understand the Treasures that Our Recipes are to us and were to our Guests. We hope the Journey that follows will Inspire You to create your very own "Mama Lena's~Style" Dining Experience! Let's Begin Our Story and Journey!

Nestled on the Near North Side of Chicago, stood a one~story building with a long red canopy outside. The building had been a former four~story brownstone and still had a very special charm. Inside this charming building, Mama Lena's resided, in the center of a unique neighborhood where energy and life was always abounding, adjacent to a variety of Rush Street nightclubs and restaurants, and only two blocks from the famed Magnificent Mile of Michigan Avenue. Here in the midst of the clubs, restaurants, shops, brownstones and sleek highrises, this "Little Spot," known and loved as "Mama Lena's" welcomed its Guests each evening for many happy years.

As a Mama Lena's Guest, you would have stood under the red canopy or sat on the cement benches outside waiting for the door to open promptly at ~ 6:00 PM or 8:30 PM ~ one of the two nightly Seatings you would be able to reserve. As the red~curtained door opened, the robust sound of Italian opera music and the magnificent smell of Sicilian cooking immediately struck your senses. Just then, a warm hand stretched out to you, and with a smile, Salvino said, "Welcome to Mama Lena's ~ We are happy to serve you!"

The "Preliminary Welcome" over, the place to hang your coats and hats was just four steps down the wine red carpeting, prior to entering the Dining Room. The Dining Room, with its inviting warmth, extended before you like a long L-shaped hallway, which is exactly what it was ~ the splendid entrance of former brownstone!

Now, as you entered the Dining Room for seating, the entire atmosphere was starting to become known to you. The Venetian glass church windows that lined the east wall were covered with fishnet and clusters of Italian Chianti bottles, as miniature Italian Lights softly twinkled in and out of the fishnet, casting a glow over the room. The west wall held gold~leafed mirrors, and between them were photos of a Grand Cathedral in Monreale, Sicily, where Papa Frank, Salvino's Father, was baptized at the turn of the 20th Century.

As your eyes moved to the left, around the west wall, and to the L-shaped alcove, the walls there were covered with hand~painted gondoliers and a framed regional map of Italy and Sicily. Surrounding the map, were photos of Sinatra, Como, Martin, Caruso, Lanza, and Salvino ~ "All" Wonderful Italian Singers! Across from the photographs of these great Italian Singers was the entrance to our small and intimate Kitchen. Directly above that special Kitchen entrance was an large life-like photo of Salvino's son, Frankie, with his chin resting on his hands ~ Frankie gazed out at the Dining Room, just sort of personally visiting with each Guest! From this alcove area, you would be facing a raised stage area where a table for eight sat, with a background of red silk draperies. Centered on these silk draperies was a beautiful portrait of our Mama Lena, with a beautiful smile, always watching out over the entire Mama Lena's Dining Room.

Just next to this stage, hanging on the east wall were two "special" items ~ one was a large dinner bell, and the other ~ a lovely wooden frame holding an original photo of Enrico Caruso as Canio in I~Pagliacci and the white silk clown hat he wore while performing in I~Pagliacci. Salvino lovingly presented this particular treasure personally to Luciano Pavarotti, who had performed, along with the Chicago Symphony Orchestra, at Holy Name Cathedral before Pope John Paul II during his first papal visit to America.

23

As you stepped down from the stage, the Dining Tables, with their shiny red, white and green tablecloths, and topped with crisp white napkins and softly flickering red candles, and some fresh fragrant flowers just seemed to be inviting you to be seated and relaxed. Mama Lena's Italian Kitchen Restaurant could accommodate 35~40 Guests each Seating. Often, for Private Parties, we rearranged tables to accommodate more Guests.

Cozily seated, the "Official Welcome" would begin. Salvino would step out of the Kitchen, located to the west of the stage area and step onto the stage. He would reach up and ring the large dinner bell. After the laughter subsided, he performed the Evening's Menu. Note, I said, "Performed The Menu" ~ as Salvino involved a good deal of entertainment in his description of the wonderful five-course meal to be served! Salvino promised to return on stage at dessert~time to share a few Family Stories. Officially welcomed and relaxed, Guests were ready to enjoy the ambiance and experience a night and meal made by Love!

The Love, known as the Evening's Menu, began with Mama Lena's delightful Antipasto Salad, a Basket of Specially~Baked Tomato Bread, one of Our Light and Delicious Pasta Dishes, and a Glorious Main Entree to match the Wine of the Evening. This was always an exciting time for us, as we listened to Guests marvel at the tastes and aromas as each course was presented to them. Their comments meant so very much to us, as we had such pride in the recipes, the preparation of the food and the room for this moment ~ it was a true reward for all our efforts. Mama, who was rarely at the restaurant in the evening, looked forward each morning to hearing the stories of how satisfied Guests had been the night before. We were thrilled when Guests appreciated a Mama Lena's evening.

After the Entree Service was completed, we served these happy and satisfied Guests a Special Coffee and presented a large tray of our Homemade Cannoli Desserts for their individual selection. Guests, now nicely relaxed, were ready to receive Salvino on stage as he skillfully delivered several delightful stories. Laughter always rang throughout the Dining Room! At our 6:00 Seating, the crowd was off to the theatre or a nightclub show. But, at the 8:30 Seating, the Guests enjoyed lingering and visiting after the dinner and Salvino's entertainment. Salvino and I and Any of The Family would be happy to sit and visit with Our Treasured Guests. This was truly a satisfying end to a long, but lovely day!

We immensely enjoyed visiting with each and every Mama Lena's Guest. Our Guest List was varied and extensive ~ Many were celebrities from the entertainment world who were in town to film a movie or for a personal appearance; Some were corporate groups who hosted their clients for the trade shows every year; Others were local celebrities from sports, broadcasting, news, or political fields; and Then there was the very special blend of new and old friends, couples and families out for a special evening. From all walks of life they came, again and again for 14 years, and each time, we shared a night of warm hospitality and of Mama Lena's Love ~ Every Guest was A Favorite of Ours!

Now, we happily share with you Our Treasured Recipes of Mama Lena's Italian Kitchen! Prepare as Salvino does, the way Mama taught him and the way Mama's Mother, Anna, taught her. Work on these special treasures with the Love we all worked on them with. Serve these treasures with the same hospitality and manners that we served them with. And certainly, you will create a Mama Lena's~style experience for you and your guests!

We hope the Journey into Mama Lena's Dining Room and getting acquainted with the Mama Lena's Story has filled you with the same wonderful feeling we all experienced at Mama Lena's. We hope you are truly inspired to create "Love" each time you use one of our treasured recipes. Whatever your occasion, always make it an Enjoyable One!

Now Our Journey continues from the Charm of our intimate Mama Lena's Dining Room ~ As you will step into our small Mama Lena's Kitchen ~ Section II ~ Our Treasured Recipes. Learn Our Original Recipes ~ The Wonderful Food that satisfied our Guests for years!

We know you enjoyed Roy Leonard's Foreword. Salvino's Preface gave you good insight. Now, do as Salvino suggested, read on about Mama Lena's Family ~ Her Real Treasure ~ and glance over our Photo Memories, Celebrity Stories & List, and our Acknowledgments. Then, go on to work "Your Magic" on our recipes! Mama would be first to cheer you on!

Thank You for Joining Us on Our Journey ~ A Very Loving Memory of A Very Special Time in The Lives of All of The Mama Lena's Family! Always Remember ~ Enjoy !

Lovingly Presented
By
Margo Madonna

25

Mama's Family Story

Always and ever, Mama's First Love ~ Her Real Treasure ~ was her Very Own Family. She spoke so lovingly of her childhood days and of the days of raising her Own Children. Family was what Mama's Life was all about ~ you knew this the moment you met her.

Mama had a very happy childhood ~ She was the only daughter of her Sicilian-born parents, Matteo and Anna Cardella.   Mama's Mother and Father came to America in the early 1900's from the town of Altavilla Milicia, Sicily. Their first-born, a Lovely Daughter, arrived in 1905. Shortly after Mama's arrival, two younger brothers ~ Carl and Marty ~ came along and she delighted in growing up with them. Grandpa Matteo supported his family with the knowledge of fresh fruits and vegetables he had learned in Sicily. Each day, Grandpa took his Vegetable Wagon, led by his horse, Giuseppe, to market to pick only the best for customers. He steadily built a regular clientele with quality and service.

Grandma Anna was a Dear, Loving Mother and a Fabulous Cook. Grandpa Matteo was a Loving and Hard-Working Man, devoted to his Family and his regard for great quality in his food business. With Great Love, Mama was taught their Special Values and Talents ~ ones that made her ~ A Dear Wife, A Devoted, Loving Mother, A Careful, Excellent Cook., and An Exceptionally Good, Loving Person and Friend ~ All things she delighted in being!

Papa Frank had been born in 1898 in Monreale, Sicily. In the early 1900's, Papa's Mother and Father, Antonio and Antonnina Madonna, brought Papa, his brother Angelo and his five sisters, Giovannina, Nannina, Jennie, Mary and Angelina to America. They settled in Chicago. In time, Papa's Family became acquainted with Mama's Family.

Together, Mama Lena & Papa Frank raised a Wonderful Family of Nine Loving Children~ Three Daughters and Six Sons ~ This Very Special Family was nourished with the Love and Values Mama and Papa had learned growing up with their hard-working and proud parents. Mama was a wonderful and happy young Mother and later a loving and happy Mother-In-Law, Grandmother, Great Grandmother and Great-Great Grandmother.

Mama Lena's & Papa Frank's Family Grew To Their Special Delight As Follows:

Daughter, Annie ~ Husband, Vincent ~
3 Children, 7 Grandchildren, and 2 Great Grandchildren

Son, Anthony ~ Wife Jeannette ~
3 Children and 8 Grandchildren

Daughter, Jennie ~ Husband, Ernie ~
3 Children and 2 Grandchildren

Son, Angelo ~ Wife, Sarah ~
3 Children and 1 Grandchild

Son, Martin ~ Wife, Mary ~
5 Children and 4 Grandchildren

Son, Calogero ~ Wife, Virginia ~
8 Children, 3 Grandchildren and 2 Great Grandchildren

Daughter, Bernice ~ Husband, Jerry ~
5 Children, 13 Grandchildren and 7 Great Grandchildren

Son, Frank, Jr. ~
Named after Papa Frank ~ Grandchildren's Favorite Uncle

Son, Salvino ~ Wife, Margo ~
Son, Frankie ~ Also Named after Papa Frank!

Mama's Family ~ Her Real Treasure ~ Was the "True" Enjoyment of Her Life ~
Each One of Her Nine Loving Children Held A Very Special Place in Her Heart.
Both Mama Lena & Papa Frank Were Very Proud of Each of Their Nine Children!

Mama had come from a very loving Family and that is really all she wanted for herself for the rest of her life. She had an enormously happy life and she spread happiness first to her own Cherished Children and then to anyone whose life she touched along the way. Mama just kept finding room in her heart for everyone.

The Restaurant was an added blessing to Mama's life ~ Her Family was always the first. But, the Restaurant actually gave her a nice chance to visit personally with all her grown Children, as each day one of her Sons or Daughters would drive Mama downtown so she could start cooking with Salvino, or take her home each afternoon. We still smile when we remember how she had to stop all Dinner Cooking to make a special lunch for any of her Children that may be in the neighborhood and stop into the Restaurant to see her. Mama knew each of her Children's favorites and always made sure she prepared them.

In the earlier years, Mama's Sons ~ Angelo, Marty, Carl and Frankie ~ would come back to the restaurant to help serve Guests in the evening, giving them a chance to see Mama before she headed home for that evening. Son, Tony would help with any electrical needs. While Daughters Annie, Jennie or Bernice would stop at the market for any items that Mama & Salvino might need for their cooking. Everyone loved to be around Mama ~ and that was perfect for her too! There was no doubt ~ Mama was happiest with Her Family!

Early afternoon when Mama was having her "Coffee and Cookie Break," she would be writing her grocery list. She had to stop on the way home and purchase everything fresh to make dinner at home for Papa Frank ~ Mama always made sure Papa was treated in a very special way. Papa Frank was very proud of that and very grateful to Mama!

The Meal prepared each day by Mama and Salvino was like a "Present" wrapped for our Mama Lena's Guests ~ not to be touched until then. But, if one of Papa's favorites was the Dish of the Day, then an extra pan had to be made just for Papa and set aside for her to bring home to him that evening. Occasionally, Mama Lena and Papa Frank would dine at Mama Lena's Italian Kitchen and visit with the Guests! Everyone enjoyed that!

Mama's Extended Family happily includes the Most~Loved and Loving Sisters-In-Law and Brothers-In-Law, Cousins, Aunts and Uncles, Nieces and Nephews, and also some very Treasured Friends that Mama always considered Family, too! After her Childhood Family, These Special Ones were in Her Heart, next to Papa Frank and her Own Dear Children, Daughters~in~Law and Sons~In~Law, and All of her Precious Grandchildren, and her Great Grandchildren and Great~Great Grandchildren ~ Each One was Special to Mama!

Mama knew how we were trying to include all the loves of her life and relate every special story of her that we could. So, one day, she gently reminded us that we were supposed to be writing a Cookbook and a Story of Mama Lena's Italian Kitchen Restaurant, and not her entire personal life story. She just laughed and said, "You can write that book later!" This is how Our Cookbook became Our Story~Cookbook. We just could not resist sharing "some" of Mama's Personal Joys and the Joyful Times with you!

Mama did agree that time should be taken to remember Uncle Chico, who became a part of The Mama Lena's Family. He had been a professional tenor for many years and would come to the Restaurant late each afternoon, after Mama and Salvino finished the cooking. He loved coaching and vocalizing with Salvino, who also had a rich tenor voice. As the Evening began at Mama Lena's, Chico would then serenade Guests while Salvino and Brothers tended to the Dinner Service. As Dessert was served, Chico & Salvino sang together to the thrill of our Guests. Uncle Chico was a Mama Lena's Treasure, too!

Mama truly considered herself to be very blessed in her life ~ to have come from such a Happy and Loving Family as a Child and with such a Happy and Loving Family of Her Own Children. Everyone who had an opportunity to meet Mama, or had a chance to truly know her, or was fortunate enough to be loved by her ~ Everyone would tell you that the "Special Blessing" was actually Mama Lena herself!

This has been just a small glimpse at Mama Lena's Personal Life and Her Loving Family. We truly hope you have enjoyed getting to know Mama Lena, as she would have enjoyed getting to know you! Mama Lena was a very beautiful woman, known for many talents and attributes, especially for a Loving and Generous Heart, which she shared all her life. Always, the Love in Mama's Heart started with Her Loving Family ~ Her Real Treasure ~

~ *Mama Lena* ~

~ Photo Memories ~

~ Mama Lena ~
Age 15

~ Mama's Parents ~
Anna and Matteo Cardella

~ Grandpa Matteo ~
Age 80
"Dressed For The Feast"

~ Mama and Her Parents ~

~ Mama's Family ~
Mama, Brother Marty, Grandpa,
Brother Carl and Grandma

~ *Photo Memories* ~

~ *"Frankie, The Kid"* ~
Age 22

~ Papa Frank & His Sisters ~
Mary, Nannina, Giovannina,
Jennie and Angelina

~ Papa & Mama At A Party ~
Sisters Mary, Angelina & Jennie,
Steve ~ Angelina's Husband

~ Papa Frank's Parents ~
Antonio & Antonnina Madonna

~ *Photo Memories* ~

~ *Mama & Papa* ~
Golden Wedding Anniversary

~ *Mama & Papa's "Young Family"* ~
Tony, Annie & Jennie
Carl, Angelo & Marty
Bernice, Salvino & Frank, Jr.

~ *Mama & Papa's "Grown Family"* ~
Annie, Tony, Jennie, Angelo, Bernice, Marty, & Carl
Salvino, Papa Frank, Mama Lena & Frank, Jr.

33

~ Frankie, Salvino's Son ~
"In That Special Photo,
Over The Kitchen Entrance"

~ Sharing a Happy Time ~
Frankie, Margo & Salvino

~ "A Rare Moment" ~
Mama Lena, Sitting Down, To Enjoy a Meal
With Her Dear Friend, Catherine ~ Margo's Mother

~ Waiting for His Bride ~
Salvino and Mama

~ Photo Memories ~

~ Uncle Chico & Salvino ~
*Rehearsing an Opera
In Mama Lena's Dining Room*

~ Salvino & President Nixon ~
*After Appearing at the New York Hilton Hotel,
Salvino found a Surprise Guest in the Audience,
President Richard M. Nixon*

~ Salvino ~
On His Way to Hollywood

~ *Photo Memories* ~

~ *Backstage At The Empire Room* ~
*Salvino, Nibbling on Jimmy Durante's Ear,
While Uncle Chico, Mama & Papa Look On*

~ *Mama & Salvino* ~
*Salvino is Hamming It Up With
His Biggest Fan, Mama Lena*

~ *Salvino* ~
*Singing At Ben Pollack's Nightclub,
On The Sunset Strip,
Hollywood*

~ *Two Very Dear & Special Guests of Mama Lena's* ~
The Great Jimmy Durante, and Judge Abraham Lincoln Marovitz

Celebrity Guests & Stories

Mama Lena's Italian Kitchen was very fortunate and very honored in the over 14 years to have had some of the nicest people in the world pass through our doors and share the love and experience known as "Mama Lena's." We still bless "All" of those dear Guests daily in our prayers ~ they were answers to our hopes and dreams. They also were a very special part of what was The Mama Lena's Experience. We Shared with Them All The Best Treasures We Possessed ~ They Shared with Us Their Appreciation and Loyalty. Forever, We Will Be Truly Thankful to Them ~ God Bless Each and Every One of Them!

Our Wonderful Guest List included Many Celebrities from The Arts and The Entertainment and The Sports Fields. We were especially fortunate to have had so many come our way. These Wonderfully Talented and Artistic People do Lend a Special Sparkle to Our World ~ Here, We Highlight Some of Them and Relate Three Charming Stories for Your Enjoyment!

Story # **1** ~ "Remembering Jimmy Durante" ~

For Salvino personally, this most beloved entertainer, held a special place in his heart, touching his life at two different times. First, Salvino had worked as a Page in the Studios at NBC, Hollywood, for Jimmy's TV Show. There, he had the opportunity to meet and visit often with the great Durante. Then, Jimmy Durante came into Salvino's life a second time, when he dined at Mama Lena's Italian Kitchen, as the guest of the esteemed Judge Abraham Lincoln Marovitz. Judge Marovitz is a true Chicago treasure and long-time friend of Jimmy Durante and Mama Lena's! Jimmy was extremely generous of himself that happy evening, going from table to table, greeting each of our Guests personally. He was the same kind and giving man Salvino had met years before, who took every chance to visit with his Staff. It was a true delight to have had this lovable man at Mama Lena's!

Story # *2* ~ "A Dining Room of Sports' Greats" ~

One day Salvino received a call from an executive of Sears, Roebuck and Co. This fond friend of Mama Lena's asked a favor ~ Could he reserve the entire room for a Friday afternoon luncheon meeting he was planning? Luncheons were usually booked for Sundays at Mama Lena's as it was very difficult to add another seating to an already very full day, However, Salvino did not hesitate for this very fine and loyal Guest. The day of the luncheon arrived, and Salvino saw his friend's shadow in the curtained red door. As he opened the door to greet him, the man said, "Salvino, I would like you to meet Ted Williams, Gordie Howe, Sir Edmund Hillary, and another 25 of the most renowned athletes and Hall of Famers that Sears is fortunate to sponsor on their Sports' Lines." Surprised and thrilled, it was like a dream come true for Salvino to have a chance to meet and serve so many admired Sports' Greats at one time !

Story # *3* ~ "Remembering Joe Di Maggio" ~

This is Margo's favorite story ~ One evening, as Salvino seated the 6:00 Dinner Guests he noticed a gentleman entering the front door. Mama Lena's had been recommended to him as "the place" to dine with his special guests, waiting in his limousine. Salvino explained the 6:00 Seating was filled to capacity by reservation. However, we did have one table available for the 8:30 Seating. The man was grateful for the reservation, and said he would take his group to site-see Chicago and gladly return for our second seating!

With perfect timing, the four men arrived at 8:30 for Dinner. They brought their wine and big smiles. As Margo and I introduced ourselves, we learned this friendly man was the Mr. Coffee Vice President ~ and his guests~ two Mr. Coffee executives and a Very Special Guest ~ Mr. Joe Di Maggio! What a delight! Yes, in person, he had that same shy smile, soft words and gracious ways that everyone knew him by. Joe not only was a man of sport's greatness, but he was also a genuine person, a kind and accommodating man to all our Guests and very humble to any compliments. After dinner, he paid us the best compliment of visiting and "feeling at home" at Mama Lena's! Several times thereafter when Margo and I met Joe, he always remembered and was his gracious and sweet self.

Surprises such as the ones we related were not unusual, so our dear Mama Lena never did get to bed early ~ we were always calling her at the end of each seating to speak with a "special someone!" Papa Frank would always answer the phone, and as soon as he heard our voices, he would call out, "L" ~ "It's for you!" The affectionate name "L" was Papa Frank's way of always calling Mama, not for use by anyone else but him! And we happen to know, they both loved staying up late for those calls! They would sit and have Ice Cream together and wait for the phone to ring! Here are some of the very special Celebrity Guests that had late~night conversations with Mama Lena and Papa Frank ~

Entertainment Guests

Kaye Ballard
Lenny Barr
Candice Bergen
Peter Boyle
James Caen
Judy Canova
Buddy Charles
Chuck Connors
Pat Cooper
Sammy Davis, Jr.
Dennis Day
Jimmy Durante
Barbara Eden
James Farentino
Alana Hamilton
George Hamilton
Daryl Hannah
Werner Klempner
Michele Lee
Arthur & Lois Marx
Johnny Mercer
Audie Murphy
Bob & Ginny Newhart
Nehemiah Persoff
Faith Quabis
Maureen Stapleton
Claire Trevor
Haskell Wexler
Henny Youngman

Theater & Arts' Guests

Joan Sutherland

American Ballet Company
Chicago Symphony Orchestra
Joffrey Ballet Company
Lyric Opera Company
Second City Players

Sports Greats' Guests

Joe Di Maggio
Sir Edmund Hillary
Paul Horning
Gordie Howe
Jake La Motta
Brian & Joy Piccolo
Ron Santo
Virginia Wade
Ted Williams
Tony Zale

Special Thanks for the Special Memories to One and All Listed Above! Also, Our Very Special Thanks To All Our Treasured Mama Lena's Guests ~ You Are All Celebrities to Us! We Truly Cherish the Memories Shared with All of You ~ Our Sincere & Heartfelt Thanks !

Acknowledgments

This special section contains the very deep gratitude we wish to convey to the generous Ladies and Gentlemen of the Press, Radio and TV Media, who faithfully reviewed our Mama Lena's Italian Kitchen Restaurant for so many years. For the many thousands of wonderful words written, and for all the years of loyalty in following us, we very sincerely thank you from the bottom of our hearts!

We so often tried to treat you to a Dinner, but we always heard, "It's not necessary, as we are just doing our job ~ a job we enjoy doing at Mama Lena's." We truly appreciated all your compliments, your friendship and your being "at home" with us at Mama Lena's.

Some of you are still here with us, while others have passed on. To all of you here with us and to the families of the others, may we say each one of you is always in our prayers of thanksgiving. Your kindness meant so much to us! We carefully reviewed our scrapbook so not to overlook anyone. But, if, inadvertently, we did miss someone, please accept our most sincere apology and the same deep personal thanks we are expressing now.

~ Once again ~ Special Regards and Gratitude from Our Hearts, to Each One of You ~

Jon and Abra Anderson
Columnists, Chicago Sun-Times

Jerry G. Bishop
Talk Show Host, Radio & TV

Jay Bolino
Editor, Chicago Key Magazine

Rita Boyd, Editor & Columnist
Chicago Life Magazine &
Chicago Key Magazine

Meg McSherry Breslin
Staff Writer, Chicago Tribune

Edward Robert Brooks, Food Critic &
Columnist, Chicago Sun-Times

Gary Cummings, Columnist.
"Dining Out" ~ Chicago Today

Cynthia Dagnal
Columnist ~ "Dining Out"
Chicago Today

40

Maggie Daly
  Columnist
  Chicago Tribune

Mike Douglas
  Talk Show Host &
  TV Interviewer

Fletcher, Beth
  Feature Writer
  The Reader Paper of Chicago

Don Harris
  Feature Writer
  Chicago American

Terry Hunter
  Columnist ~ "Let's Eat Out"
  Chicago Sun-Times

Irv Kupcinet
  Columnist ~ "Kup's Column"
  Chicago Sun-Times and CBS-TV

Kay Loring
  Food Critic & Columnist
  Chicago Tribune

Frank Mathie
  Feature Reporter
  WLS-TV (ABC), Chicago

Wally Phillips
  Radio Talk Show Personality
  WGN-Radio, Chicago

Norman Ross
  TV Commentator
  WLS-TV (ABC), Chicago

Warner Saunders
  TV Talk Show Host ~ CBS-TV

Hal Tate, Columnist
  "Roaming Around"~ North Loop News

William Wells
  Columnist ~ "Dining Out"
  Chicago Sun-Times

Jerry C. Davis, Food Critic & Columnist
  "Wining and Dining"
  Chicago Sun-Times

John Rae Earl, Food Critic & Columnist
  "Wife's Night Out"
  Chicago American

Aaron Gold
  Columnist ~ "Tower Ticker"
  Chicago Tribune

Robert J. Herguth
  Columnist
  Chicago American

Allen and Carla Kelson,
  Editors and Columnists
  The Chicago Magazine

Roy Leonard
  Radio & TV Personality
  WGN Radio & TV, Chicago

Louis Martin
  Reviewer
  Chicago Defender Newspaper

Otto C. Neumann
  Reviewer ~ Chicago Chapter
  International Wine & Food Society

Ray and Ann Quisno
  Dean of Reporters
  Chicago Tribune

Kay Rutherford
  Columnist
  Chicago Sun-Times

Marian Smith
  Editor, Chicago Key Magazine

Sheldon and Judith Wax
  Editors ~ Playboy Magazine

Robert Wiedrich
  Columnist ~ "Tower Ticker"
  Chicago Tribune

41

~~~~~~

Section II

Our Cookbook Section

of

Treasured Recipes

~~~~~~

~ *Chapter One* ~
The Appetizers

Pages 45 ~ 57

~ *Opening The Evening* ~

At Mama Lena's Italian Kitchen, we loved to welcome our Guests by having a Treat waiting for them when they arrived.

Serving of the Antipastos ~ Italian Appetizers ~ actually prepares the taste buds for Dinner. It also allowed Guests time to visit a bit with their friends or dates, sip some wine and just relax and take in the ambiance and romantic atmosphere of Mama Lena's.

Always, our main intention was to allow the Guests to relax, let their cares drift away and thoroughly enjoy their evening out. It was our thrill to have these lovely Guests, so we presented our most loving efforts and best culinary treasures from the beginning to the end of each evening at Mama Lena's Italian Kitchen.

Eggplant ~ Caponata ~ ala Madonna

Caponata di Melanzane

There are so many very delicious dishes that originated in Sicily and with the people of Sicily. Therefore, it is very difficult to pick "Just One Favorite." However, we sincerely feel the Caponata di Melanzane could very well rate the honor! Mama Lena's Recipe of this time~honored dish was given to Mama by her Mother, Grandma Anna, and this special recipe is over two hundred years old. Our Treasured Recipe of this delectable Appetizer~Relish, which delighted Mama Lena's Italian Kitchen Guests for many years, is one we are very proud of. As we share this with you, we hope it will become a special favorite of yours, and a recipe you will hold in same high regard that we do! Enjoy!

Ingredients   **Serves 4~6**

The Eggplant Mixture	2	Lbs. of Eggplant (Cut into 1~1/2" Cubes)
	2	Pinches of Salt
	2	Pinches of Pepper
	1	Cup of Olive Oil (To Saute)
The Marsala Marinade	1/4	Cup of Marsala Wine (Sweet)
	3/4	Cup of Raisins
	1/2	Cup of Pine Nuts
The Vegetables	1	Large Sweet Onion (Finely Chopped)
	4	Large Stalks of Celery (Diced)
	1/2	Cup of Green Olives (Pitted & Slivered)
	3	Tablespoons of Capers (Whole) (Drain Off Liquid)
The Wine Vinegar	1/2	Cup of Red Wine Vinegar
	1/4	Cup of Sugar (Granulated)
The Tomato Sauce	1	Can (6 Oz.) of Tomato Paste (Mix with 3 Oz. of Hot Water)
	2	Pinches of Salt
	1	Pinch of Pepper
	1	Pinch of Red Pepper Flakes (Optional ~ If You Prefer It Hot)
The Italian Toasts	1	Recipe of Mama Lena's Miniature Italian Toasts (See Recipe ~ Chapter Ten)
The Garnish	1/8	Cup of Romano Cheese (Finely Grated)

Preparation ~ Eggplant ~ Caponata ~ ala Madonna

**The
Eggplants
~ Clean & Saute ~**

1. Wash The Eggplants, and Dry with Paper Towels.
   Trim Off The Stems and Any Damaged Skin.
2. Cut The Eggplants into Cubes, About 1~1/2" Each.
   Now, Season The Eggplant Cubes with
   2 Pinches of Salt and 2 Pinches of Pepper.
3. Place Just 1/2 Cup of The Olive Oil in a
   Large Skillet, and Heat The Oil to Medium.
4. Saute The Cubed Eggplant, Until
   Lightly Browned on All Sides, About 3~5 Minutes.
5. Place The Eggplant and The Oil in a Large Bowl.

**The
Tomato Sauce
~ Prepare ~**

1. In The Same Skillet, Mix 6 Oz. of The Tomato Paste
   and 3 Oz. of Hot Water, 2 Pinches of Salt
   and 1 Pinch of Pepper. (If You Prefer Spicy,
   Add The Optional Red Pepper Flakes Now).
2. Cook on Medium and Stir Constantly, Until
   The Mixture comes to a Boil. Remove from Heat.
3. Add The Cooked Tomato Sauce to The Eggplant, and
   Gently Mix Together. Set Aside To Cool & Marinate.

**The
Raisins & Nuts
~ Marinate ~**

1. In a Sauce Pan, Heat The Marsala Wine, Until Warm.
2. In a Medium Bowl, Place The Raisins, and
   Pour Warm Marsala Wine on Raisins to Soften.
3. Add The Pine Nuts to The Raisins and Marsala Wine.
   Gently, Mix Together.
4. Seal Airtight with Plastic. Set Aside To Cool & Marinate.

**The
Vegetables
~ Saute & Marinate ~**

1. Into Same Skillet, Pour Remaining 1/2 Cup of Oil.
   Heat The Olive Oil to Medium.
2. Saute The Onion and The Celery for About 3~4 Minutes.
   Add The Green Olive Slivers. Saute 2 Minutes More.
   Add The Capers. Saute for 1 Minute More.
3. Turn Heat Off, While You Prepare The Vinegar & Sugar.
4. In a Small Sauce Pan, Heat Red Wine Vinegar to a Boil.
   Add The Granulated Sugar. Stir Sugar Constantly,
   Until Completely Dissolved, About 1~2 Minutes.
5. Remove Pan from Heat. Transfer The Wine Vinegar and
   The Sugar to a Large Bowl. Add The Sauteed Onion,
   Celery, Green Olives & Capers. Mix In Well.
6. Seal Airtight with Plastic. Set Bowl Aside to Cool and
   Allow Marinate for 1 Hour. (Continue ~ Next Page)

Preparation ~ Eggplant ~ Caponata ~ ala Madonna

**The
Caponata
~ First Marinade ~**

1. **Marinate Separately for 1 Hour The Following 3 Bowls:**
   ~ Combined Eggplant, Olive Oil & Tomato Sauce
   ~ Combined Raisins, Wine & Pine Nuts, and
   ~ Combined Vegetables & Sweet Red Wine Vinegar.

**The
Caponata
~ Second Marinade ~**

1. **After 1 Hour of Marinating The Above, To Develop
   The Distinct Tastes of Each Special Ingredient ~
   Then, It is Time to Combine All 3 Bowls, and
   Marinate All Together for 1 Hour More.**

2. **Add Some Ingredients from Each Bowl to A Large Bowl,
   A Little At a Time, and Blend ~ Until All 3 Mixtures
   are Very Gently and Very Completely Blended.**

3. **You Now have A Caponata di Melanzane Mixture, and
   It's All Ready for The Final Marinade!**

4. **Seal Airtight with Plastic, and Refrigerate.
   Allow to Properly Marinate for 1 Hour More.**

**The
Italian Toasts**

1. **Prepare Mama Lena's Miniature Italian Toasts Recipe.
   (See Recipe ~ Chapter Ten)**

2. **Spoon 1 Teaspoon of The Caponata onto Each Toast.**

**The
Caponata
~ Ready to Serve ~**

1. **Place All Finished Toasts on a Decorative Platter.**
2. **Sprinkle Lightly with Romano Cheese to Nicely Garnish.
   The Caponata Is Wonderfully Ready to Serve!**

Serving Suggestions & Special Note

*This Delicious & Exciting Appetizer~Relish has many uses and is Always A Delight to Serve!
On a Buffet, we serve in a Crystal Dish with Italian Toasts in a Basket. Or, Serve Finished
on Italian Toasts on a Nice Platter to accent This Colorful & Appealing Treat. The Delightful
Caponata di Melanzane is also very delicious on our various Italian Breads and Focaccio.
This Special Recipe has Great Taste, Aroma and Color, and Great Versatility, too!*

*Our Caponata is such a Treasure to us that you will notice we have used This Special Recipe
in Many Other Dishes in Our Book. So, when you see that one of Our Other Recipes calls for
Caponata di Melanzane ala Madonna ~ Return Here ~ To Our Book's First Recipe! Enjoy!*

Ricotta Cheese Spread
Our Basic Spread

Mama Lena's Variety of Appetizer Spreads consists of ~ Five Delightfully Delicious Spreads! All Our Spreads are Easy To Prepare and Make an Appetizing Presentation! Start here with Our Basic Spread ~ which is simply delicious, as prepared and served as we suggest below, on our Miniature Italian Toasts. Try then The Variety, by making any of the other Spreads, using this Basic Recipe as Their Base. These Spreads are great to serve before dinner, for parties, or just to have with a nice wine. We always depended on these different and special treats to delight our Guests ~ We think you will, too! Enjoy!

Ingredients   Serves 4~6

The Ricotta Spread	1	Cup of Fresh Ricotta Cheese (Drain Liquid Before Using)
	1/4	Cup of Cooked Pasta Water (Saved from your Cooked Pasta)
	1/4	Cup of Parmesan Cheese (Coarsely Grated)
	1	Pinch of Salt
	2	Pinches of White Pepper
	1	Pinch of Parsley
The Italian Toasts	1	Recipe of Mama Lena's Miniature Italian Toasts (See Recipe ~ Chapter Ten)
The Garnish	1/8	Cup of Romano Cheese (Grated)
	1	Pinch of Mint ~ Mix into Romano Cheese

Preparation ~ Ricotta Cheese Spread ~ Our Basic Spread

The Ricotta Spread ~ Prepare ~

1. Drain The Ricotta Cheese of All Liquid. Discard The Liquid. Place Ricotta in a Bowl, and Break Apart with a Fork.
2. Add The Pasta Water, Salt, White Pepper and Parsley. Blend All Together Gently with a Large Spoon.
3. Add The 1/4 Cup of Parmesan Cheese. Blend In Gently.
4. Cover Bowl Airtight with Plastic, and Refrigerate for 30 Minutes to Properly Chill.

The Ricotta Spread ~ Serve ~

1. Prepare 1 Recipe of Mama Lena's Miniature Italian Toasts.
2. Ready To Serve ~ Take Chilled Spread From Refrigerator.
3. Drop 1 Teaspoon of Ricotta Spread on Each Small Toast.
4. Place All Finished Toasts on a Decorative Serving Platter.
5. Sprinkle Tops with Mixed Romano Cheese & Mint. Enjoy!

Anchovy, Dill & Capers Spread

Ingredients   Serves 4~6

The Anchovy Spread	1	Recipe of Our Basic Ricotta Cheese Spread
	1	Tablespoon of Anchovy Paste
	1	Tablespoon of Capers (Cut into Halves)
	2	Pinches of Dill
	2	Tablespoons of Butter (Unsalted)
	3	Tablespoons of Olive Oil
The Italian Toasts	1	Recipe of Mama Lena's Miniature Italian Toasts (See Recipe ~ Chapter Ten)
The Garnish	1/8	Cup of Romano Cheese (Grated)
	1	Pinch of Dill (Mix into Romano Cheese)

Preparation ~ Anchovy, Dill & Capers Spread

The Anchovy Spread

1. Make 1 Recipe of Our Basic Ricotta Cheese Spread.
   Cover with Plastic, and Refrigerate for 30 Minutes.
2. Then, in A Skillet, Heat The Butter on Medium to Melt.
   Add The Olive Oil.
3. Spread Anchovy Paste into Oil & Butter. Stir 1 Minute.
4. Add The Capers and Dill into the Heated Anchovy Paste,
   Butter and Oil.   Stir Well for 1 Minute.
5. Remove Skillet from The Heat.   Cover The Pan.
   Let It Stand Until Completely Cool, About 5 Minutes.
6. Take Chilled Basic Ricotta Spread from The Refrigerator.
   Add The Anchovy, Butter, Oil, Dill & Caper Mix to
   The Ricotta Cheese Mix.   Blend Together Gently.

Assemble & Garnish

1. Prepare 1 Recipe of our Miniature Italian Toasts.
   (See Recipe ~ Chapter Ten)
2. Spoon 1 Teaspoon of The Anchovy, Dill & Capers Spread
   onto Each Prepared Toast.
3. Place All The Finished Toasts on A Decorative Platter.
4. Sprinkle The Mixed Romano Cheese & Dill over
   The Tops for a Nice Garnish!   Enjoy!

Clam & Tarragon Spread

Ingredients   Serves 4~6

**The
Clam Spread**

1	Recipe of Our Basic Ricotta Cheese Spread
1	Small Can of Minced Clams (Drain Off Liquid)
2	Tablespoons of Butter (Sweet & Lightly Salted)
2	Tablespoons of Olive Oil
2	Pinches of Tarragon

**The
Italian Toasts**

1	Recipe of Mama Lena's Miniature Italian Toasts *(See Recipe ~ Chapter Ten)*

The Garnish

1/8	Cup of Romano Cheese (Grated)
1	Pinch of Parsley (Mix Into Romano Cheese)

Preparation ~ Clam & Tarragon Spread

**The
Clam Spread**

1. Make 1 Recipe of Our Basic Ricotta Cheese Spread.
   Cover with Plastic and Refrigerate for 30 Minutes.
2. Then, in A Skillet, Heat Butter to a Melt.   Add Olive Oil.
3. Drain The Clams of Juice.   Discard The Clam Juice.
4. Saute The Clams in The Butter and Olive Oil for 1 Minute.
5. Add The Tarragon. Stir Constantly for 1 Minute More.
6. Strain Clams of All Butter & Oil. Cool Clams Completely.
7. Take Chilled Basic Ricotta Spread from Refrigerator.
   Add The Sauteed Clams & Tarragon.   Blend Gently.
8. Seal Blended Mix with Plastic, and Refrigerate.
   Chill for 30 Minutes More.

**Assemble &
Garnish**

1. Prepare 1 Recipe of our Miniature Italian Toasts.
   (See Recipe ~ Chapter Ten)
2. Spoon on 1 Teaspoon of The Mixed Clam & Tarragon
   Spread on Each Prepared Toast.
3. Place All Finished Toasts on a Decorative Platter.
4. Sprinkle Mixed Romano Cheese & Parsley over
   The Tops for a Nice Garnish!   Enjoy!

Escargot, Garlic & Thyme Spread

Ingredients   Serves 4~6

**The
Escargot Spread**
- 1 Recipe of Our Basic Ricotta Cheese Spread
- 1 Small Can of Escargot (Snails) (Finely Chopped)
     (Drain Juice ~ Discard Juice)
- 2 Tablespoons of Butter (Sweet & Lightly Salted)
- 2 Tablespoons of Olive Oil
- 1 Clove of Garlic (Finely Minced)
- 1 Pinch of Thyme

**The
Italian Toasts**
- 1 Recipe of Mama Lena's Miniature Italian Toasts
     (See Recipe ~ Chapter Ten)

The Garnish
- 1/8 Cup of Romano Cheese (Grated)
- 1   Pinch of Chives (Mix Into Romano Cheese)

Preparation ~ Escargot, Garlic & Thyme Spread

**The
Escargot Spread**
1. Make 1 Recipe of Our Basic Ricotta Cheese Spread.
   Cover with Plastic and Refrigerate for 30 Minutes.
2. Then, in A Skillet, Heat The Butter to a Melt. Add Olive Oil.
3. Drain The Escargot of Juice. Discard The Escargot Juice.
4. Finely Chop Escargot. Saute Escargot in The Butter and
   Olive Oil for About 2 Minutes.
5. Add The Minced Garlic & Thyme. Saute 2~3 Minutes More.
6. Strain The Escargot, Garlic & Thyme. Set Aside to Cool.
7. Take Chilled Basic Ricotta Cheese Spread from Refrigerator.
   Add Cooled Escargot, Garlic & Thyme. Blend Gently.
8. Seal The Blended Mix with Plastic, and Refrigerate.
   Chill The Spread for 30 Minutes More.

**Assemble &
Garnish**
1. Prepare 1 Recipe of our Miniature Italian Toasts.
2. Spoon on 1 Teaspoon of The Escargot, Garlic & Thyme
   Spread on Each Prepared Toast.
3. Place All The Finished Toasts on A Decorative Platter.
4. Sprinkle The Mixed Romano Cheese & Chives over
   The Tops for a Nice Garnish!   Enjoy!

Pimento & Parmesan Cheese Spread

Ingredients

Serves 4~6

The Pimento Spread

1	Recipe of Our Basic Ricotta Cheese Spread
1	Small Jar of Diced Pimentos (Finely Chopped) (Drain Off Liquid) (Do Not Use Liquid)
1	Tablespoon of Mayonnaise
1	Pinch of Celery Salt
1	Pinch of White Pepper
2	Pinches of Chives
2	Tablespoons of Parmesan Cheese (Coarsely Grated)

The Italian Toasts

1	Recipe of Mama Lena's Miniature Italian Toasts (See Recipe ~ Chapter Ten)

The Garnish

1/8	Cup of Romano Cheese (Grated)
1	Pinch of Chives (Mix Into Romano Cheese)

Preparation ~ Pimento & Parmesan Cheese Spread

The Pimento Spread

1. Make 1 Recipe of Our Basic Ricotta Cheese Spread. Cover with Plastic and Refrigerate for 30 Minutes.
2. Drain off The Liquid from The Diced Pimentos, and Chop Pimentos Finely. (Do Not Use The Liquid).
3. Take Ricotta Cheese Spread from Refrigerator, and. Add Chopped Pimentos, Mayonnaise, Celery Salt, White Pepper, 2 Pinches of Chives, and Parmesan Cheese. Blend All Together Gently.
4. Seal The Mixed Spread with Plastic, and Refrigerate. Chill The Spread for 30 Minutes More.

Assemble & Garnish

1. Prepare 1 Recipe of our Miniature Italian Toasts.
2. Spoon 1 Teaspoon of The Pimento & Parmesan Cheese Spread on Each Prepared Toast.
3. Place All Finished Toasts on A Decorative Platter.
4. Sprinkle The Mixed Romano Cheese & Chives on The Tops for a Nice Garnish!   Enjoy!

Eggplant, Prosciutto & Mozzarella Rolls

Melanzane, Prosciutto & Mozzarella Panino

This Delightfully Rich, yet Delicate, Appetizer is Such a Fabulous Opener for any occasion! Mama Lena's Guests could not resist This Very Delicious Treat! This Very Special Creation is Just Unique and an Absolute Delight to Serve! Try This Salvino Specialty! Enjoy!

Ingredients   Serves 4~6

The Eggplant	2	Lbs. of Eggplant (Cut Lengthwise ~ 1/2" Thick Slices)
	1	Cup of Olive Oil (To Saute)
	1	Clove of Garlic (Cut into 4 Slices)
	2	Pinches of Salt
	2	Pinches of Red Pepper Flakes
	1	Box of Toothpicks
The Prosciutto	1/2	Lb. of Prosciutto (Italian Ham) (Have Cut into Very Thin Slices ~ Almost Shaved)
The Cheese Sauce	1/2	Lb. of Mozzarella Cheese (Sliced Thin)
	1	Cup of Mama Lena's Basic Tomato Sauce (See Recipe ~ Chapter Five)
The Garnish	1/8	Cup of Parmesan Cheese (Grated)
	1/4	Bunch of Fresh Parsley

Preparation ~ Eggplant, Prosciutto & Mozzarella Rolls

1. **Wash The Eggplant and Dry with Paper Towels. Trim Off Stems and Any Damaged Skin. Slice, as Indicated Above.**
2. **In an Extra~Large Skillet, Heat The Olive Oil to Medium. Saute The Garlic, Until Light Brown. Remove Garlic & Discard.**
3. **Add Eggplant Slices to Hot Olive Oil. Saute 2~3 Minutes Each Side. Take Eggplant from Oil with a Slotted Spoon. Set on a Flat Plate.**
4. **Sprinkle The Eggplant Lightly with Salt and Red Pepper Flakes. Place a Slice of Prosciutto Ham Across Each Eggplant, and Roll Them Up, Binding with 2~3 Toothpicks.**
5. **Place The Eggplant & Prosciutto Rolls into a Shallow Baking Pan. Bake in a Preheated 350 Degree Oven for 10 Minutes.**
6. **Take Pan from Oven. Place a Slice of Mozzarella Cheese over Each Eggplant & Prosciutto Roll. Spoon 1 Tablespoon of Mama Lena's Basic Tomato Sauce Over The Cheese.**
7. **Return The Baking Dish to The Oven. Change The Oven Setting from Bake to Broil. Broil, Until The Cheese Melts and The Tomato Sauce Bubbles and Looks Light Brown, About 1 Minute.**
8. **Remove Pan from Oven Immediately. Place on a Decorative Platter. Remove All Toothpicks. Sprinkle with Parmesan Cheese, and Place Parsley Sprigs on Platter for a Nice Garnish! Enjoy!**

Antipasto Variety Platter

Antipasto Varieto Piatto

Our Mama Lena's Antipasto Variety Platter includes a plentiful array of Fresh and Delicious Selections and also makes a beautiful Presentation! Every Antipasto Cold Platter, no matter how many selections it offers, must have a Star to be a Center Attraction! At Mama Lena's, our Star Attraction always was our Eggplant Appetizer~Relish ~ The Caponata di Melanzane. We took care to make our Presentation very appealing to Guests ~ Mama always said, "People eat first with their eyes before any food reaches their mouths to taste." Follow closely and you will find it easy and fun to prepare Mama Lena's Antipasto Variety Platter! Enjoy!

Ingredients   Serves 6~10

The Center	2	Cups of Caponata di Melanzane ala Madonna (See First Recipe ~ Chapter One)
The Cheeses	1/2	Lb. of Provolone Cheese (Cut into Triangles)
	1/2	Lb. of Fontinella Cheese (Cut into Small Chunks)
The Meats	1/4	Lb. of Cappicolla (Sliced Thin at Market)
	1/4	Lb. of Prosciutto (Italian Ham) (Sliced Thin at Market)
	1/4	Lb. of Genoa Salami (Sliced Thin at Market)
	1/4	Lb. of Pepperoni (Thinly Sliced, By Hand)
The Vegetables	1	Pint of Cherry Tomatoes (Whole)
	1	Small Jar of Artichoke Hearts (Cut into Halves)
	1	Medium Fennel (Cut Bulb to 4" Strips) (Use Fennel Stalks & Leaves for the Centerpiece)
	1	Medium Bunch of Hearts of Celery (Cut into 4" Strips)
	3	Medium Peppers (Cut into 4" Strips) (1 Red, 1 Green & 1 Yellow)
	2	Large Carrots (Cut into 4" Strips)
	1	Cup of Radishes (Whole)
	1	Small Bunch of Scallions (Whole)
	1	Cup of Mixed Olives (Marinate in 2 Tablespoons of Oil) (Half Large Green & Half Italian Black Olives)
The Dressing	1	Recipe of Mama Lena's Italian Dressing Supreme (See Recipe ~ Chapter Three)
The Italian Toasts	1	Recipe of Mama Lena's Miniature Italian Toasts (See Recipe ~ Chapter Ten)
The Garnish	1	Lb. of Romaine Lettuce (Whole Leaves)
	1/4	Cup of Parmesan Cheese (Finely Grated)
	1	Small Can of Anchovies (Whole)

Preparation ~ Antipasto Variety Platter

The Vegetables
~ Prepare ~

1. *Fennel ~ Cut The Bulb from The Stalks & The Leaves.*
   ~ Bulb will be Sliced into Thin Strips, and
   ~ Fennel Stalks & Leaves will make a Centerpiece.
   ~ Separate The Bulb Sections from Each Other.
   ~ Trim The Core Ends & The Stalk Tops.
2. *Celery ~ Separate All The Stalks from Each Other.*
   ~ Trim The Core Ends & The Stalk Tops.
3. *Lettuce ~ Separate The Leaves from Each Other.*
   ~ Trim Core Ends & Any Damaged Part of Leaves.
4. *Peppers ~ Core The Center, and Discard The Seeds.*
5. *Carrots ~ Peel Off Other Skin, and Discard It.*
6. *Radishes ~ Trim The Ends and Any Damaged Skin.*
7. *Scallions ~ Trim The Ends and The Stems Tops.*
8. *Cherry Tomatoes ~ Trim Off Stems and Any Damaged Skin.*
9. *All Above Vegetables ~ Wash Well and Dry on Paper Towels.*
10. *Cut The Vegetables to The Sizes Stated on The Ingredients.*
    ~ Cover with Plastic & Refrigerate, Until Ready to Use.
11. *Artichoke Hearts ~ Keep Refrigerated, Until Ready to Use.*
    ~ Drain & Discard The Liquid. Cut Hearts into Halves.
12. *Green & Black Olives ~ Combine Both Style Olives in ~*
    ~ 2 Tablespoons of Extra Virgin Olive Oil, and
    ~ Cover with Plastic and Marinate for 1 Hour.

The Cheeses
~ Prepare ~

1. *Provolone Cheese ~ Cut into Nice 1/2" Thick Triangles.*
2. *Fontinella Cheese ~ Cut into Small Chunks about 1/2" Thick.*
   ~ Cover Separately with Plastic. Set in Refrigerator.

The Meats
~ Prepare ~

1. *The Cappicolla, The Prosciutto & The Salami Meats ~*
   ~ Have Thinly Sliced at Market. Evenly Roll Each Piece.
   ~ Cover with Plastic. Set in Refrigerator.
2. *The Pepperoni Stick ~ Slice on an Angle to make Long,*
   Thin Oval Pieces. Cover with Plastic & Refrigerate.

The
Caponata

1. *Prepare 1 Recipe of The Caponata di Melanzane.*
   ~ (See First Recipe ~ Chapter One)
   ~ Refrigerate, Until Ready to Assemble The Platter.

The
Italian Toasts

1. *Prepare 1 Recipe of Mama Lena's Miniature Italian Toasts.*
   ~ (See Recipe ~ Chapter Ten)
   ~ Wrap in Cloth Napkin in a Basket, Until Ready to Use.

The
Italian Dressing

1. *Prepare 1 Recipe of Mama Lena's Italian Dressing Supreme*
   ~ (See Recipe ~ Chapter Three)
   ~ Seal with Plastic. Refrigerate, Until Ready to Serve.

Preparation ~ Antipasto Variety Platter

The
Finished Platter
~ Assemble ~

1. *Trays ~ A Heavy Gauge 24" Round Tray with Edge for Support,*
   ~ Or a Rectangle Tray 18" Wide x 24" Long.
2. *Lettuce ~ Start at Edges, Placing Lettuce Leaves All Around Tray.*
   ~ Layer Lettuce Leaves into The Center of Tray.
3. *Bowls ~ Place A Medium~Size Glass Bowl in Center to hold The*
   Caponata di Melanzane ~ Place 2 Small Glass Bowls on Sides
   of The Caponata Bowl to hold The Mama Lena's Italian Dressing.
4. *Fennel Bulb, Celery, Peppers & Carrots ~*
   ~ These Vegetables have been Cut into 4" Slices.
   ~ Stack Them, Alternating The Colors, Around The Bowls.
5. *Cappicolla, Prosciutto & Genoa Salami Rolls ~*
   ~ Gradually Come Out from The Above Vegetables, and
   ~ Attractively Stack The Rolled Meats Around The Vegetables.
6. *Provolone Cheese & Pepperoni Slices ~*
   ~ Place Around The Edges of The Platter Attractively,
   ~ Alternating The Cheese & Pepperoni to Make a Nice Border.
7. *Fontinella Cheese ~ Place Chunks of Cheese All Around Rolled Meats.*
8. *Green & Black Olives ~*
   ~ Place The Olives in between The Chunks of Cheese on The Meats.
9. *Cherry Tomatoes ~*
   ~ Set with The Olives & Fontinella Cheese, Over The Rolled Meats.
10. *Artichoke Hearts ~ Place The Artichoke Hearts on Top of Rolled Meats.*
    ~ Alternate with Olives, Cherry Tomatoes & Fontinella Cheese.
11. *Radishes & Scallions ~ On Each End of The Dressing Bowls ~*
    ~ Place The Scallions, Standing Up in a Bunch At Each End, and
    ~ Surround Scallions with Stacked Radishes to Support Scallions.
12. *Caponata di Melanzane ~ Fill Center "Star" Bowl with The Caponata.*
13. *Italian Dressing Supreme ~ Fill The Two Glass Bowls on Each Side*
    of The Caponata Bowl with The Italian Supreme Dressing.
14. *Anchovies ~ Open The Canned Anchovies and Drain off The Liquid.*
    ~ Roll Anchovies & Tuck In Around Edge of Each Serving Bowl.
15. *Fennel Stalks & Leaves ~ Wedge Stalks In Toward The Bottom of*
    The Center Bowl of Caponata. Stacked Vegetables will hold up
    The White Fennel Stalks with Their Graceful Leaves, and
    Create a Very Lovely Effect for A Great Presentation.
16. *Parmesan Cheese ~ Sprinkle Finely Grated Parmesan Cheese Over*
    The Caponata and The Dressing, and Very Lightly Over The Tray.
17. *Italian Toasts ~ Set in A Basket, with A Nice Decorative Napkin.*
    ~ Sprinkle The Toasts & Over Tray Very, Very Lightly with
    The Finely Grated Parmesan Cheese for a Nice Effect!

Mama Lena's Antipasto Variety Platter is Beautifully Ready to Serve! Enjoy!

~ *Chapter Two* ~
Soups & Broths

Pages 59 ~ 71

Amaretto Sausage Soup

Amaretto Salicce Zuppa

Amaretto Sausage Soup is wonderfully simple to prepare ~ yet delightful beyond words. Mama and Salvino both knew just how delightful the effects of the Amaretto Liqueur are in any cooking. Most Italians admire the smooth taste of the Amaretto. At Mama Lena's, this delicious Soup disappeared so fast, we were sure Guests had just inhaled it rather than actually eating it! Once, you try this very unique recipe, we think you will love it, too. The next time you make it, we are sure you will want to make a double recipe! Enjoy!

Ingredients   Serves 4~6

The Italian Sausage	1	Lb. of Italian Sausage (Sweet, Mild, Or Hot)
To Saute	2	Tablespoons of Butter (Sweet & Lightly Salted)
	2	Tablespoons of Olive Oil
The Amaretto Marinade	4	Oz. of Amaretto Liqueur (To Marinate The Italian Sausage)
The Meat Broth	2	Quarts of Meat Broth (See Recipe ~ Chapter Two) ~ <u>OR</u> ~
	2	Beef Bouillon Cubes in 2 Quarts of Water (Alternate Choice for Soup Base)
	2	Pinches of Salt
	2	Pinches of Pepper
	1	Pinch of Basil
	1	Pinch of Mint
The Pasta	3	Tablespoons of Pastina (Soup Pasta) (Add Pastina to Soup, Uncooked)
The Garnish	1/4	Cup of Romano Cheese (Coarsely Grated)
	1/4	Bunch of Fresh Parsley

Preparation ~ Amaretto Sausage Soup

**The
Italian Sausage
~ Prepare ~**

1. *Take Italian Sausage, and Cut Open The Casing.
   Remove Loose Sausage Meat to Saute. Discard Casing.*
2. *In a Large Skillet, Heat Butter on Medium to a Melt.
   Add The Olive Oil, and Blend in With Butter.*

**The
Italian Sausage
~ Saute ~**

1. *In the Hot Butter and Olive, Saute The Sausage Meat,
   Until Browned, About 4~5 Minutes.*
2. *In a Strainer, Drain The Sausage of The Oil and Butter.
   Allow The Sausage to Drain Completely,
   About 2~3 Minutes. Discard The Butter and Oil.*

**The
Italian Sausage
~ Marinate ~**

1. *In a Large Bowl, Combine The Browned Sausage
   With All The Amaretto Liqueur.*
2. *Cover Bowl Tightly with Plastic. Set Aside to Marinate.*

**The Soup Broth
~ Cook ~**

1. *In a 6 Qt. Pan, Add 2 Qts. of The Meat Broth, ~ OR ~*
2. *If you are Choosing The "Quick" Alternate Way,
   Combine 2 Qts. of Water with 2 Bouillon Cubes.
   Bring to a Boil Until Cubes are Dissolved.*
3. *Then, Combine The Liquid with The Salt, Pepper,
   Basil and Mint. Bring to a Boil Again.*
4. *Cover Pan. Reduce The Heat. Simmer Broth for 1 Hour.*

**The
Meat & Broth
~ Combine & Cook ~**

1. *Add Marinated Amaretto Sausage to The Broth Mixture.
   Stir Well. Cover Pan. Simmer 30 Minutes More.*
2. *Now, Add Uncooked Pastina to The Soup. Cover Pan.
   Simmer Entire Soup for a Final 10~15 Minutes.
   (The Pastina Will Cook Itself During This Simmer).*

Serving Suggestion

*Serve This Delightful Amaretto Sausage Soup in a Warm Soup Tureen with Serving Ladle.
Sprinkle The Soup Top Lightly with Grated Romano Cheese. Then, Place Parsley Sprigs
Lightly on Top of The Soup, and also around Soup Tureen Platter for a Nice Presentation.
Serve with Mama Lena's Italian Bread and Breadsticks. Our Ricotta Cheese Spread
Appetizer before The Soup is a Compliment! Select a Soft Red Wine to further compliment!
Now you have a Lovely Light Dinner, as this Delightful Soup is a Dinner in itself! Enjoy!*

Escarole & White Bean Soup

Scarola Bianco Fagaioli Zuppa

Mama would make her Escarole & Bean Soup for us when we were children, believing it could cure whatever was ailing us! It must have worked ~ because it did make us feel better and happier each time we had it. At our Mama Lena's Italian Kitchen, we also noticed our Guests always seemed satisfied and content, too, after they enjoyed a Bowl of This Lovely Soup! So, once you try Mama Lena's Delicious Soup, perhaps you will find yourself feeling better and happier after having it, too! We hope so! Enjoy!

Ingredients   **Serves 4~6**

The Escarole Leaves	1~1/2	**Lbs. of Escarole (Nice, Fresh & Dark Leaves)**
	2	**Pinches of Salt (Add to Simmering Broth)**
To Saute	2	**Tablespoons of Butter (Sweet & Lightly Salted)**
	2	**Tablespoons of Olive Oil**
	1	**Clove of Garlic (Minced)**
	1	**Tablespoon of Lemon Rind**
	1	**Pinch of Red Pepper Flakes**
	3	**Tablespoons of Cream Sherry**
The Vegetable Broth	2	**Quarts of Vegetable Broth (See Recipe ~ Chapter Two) ~ OR ~**
	2	**Vegetable Bouillon Cubes in 2 Quarts of Water (Alternate Choice for Soup Base)**
The Beans	1	**Can of Cannellini Beans (White Italian Kidney Beans)**
The Pine Nuts	1/4	**Cup of Pine Nuts (Add Last)**
The Garnish	1/4	**Cup of Romano Cheese (Coarsely Grated)**
	1/4	**Bunch of Fresh Parsley**

62

Preparation ~ Escarole & White Bean Soup

The
Escarole Leaves
~ Prepare ~

1. **Separate The Leaves of The Escarole.**
   Trim off The Core Ends and Any Damaged Parts.
   Rinse Well with Cool Water. Dry with Paper Towels.
2. **Break The Escarole Leaves into Halves. Set Aside.**

The
Saute Mixture

1. **In a Large Stock Pot, Melt The Butter on Medium.**
   Add The Olive Oil.
2. **Add The Garlic, and Saute for About 1 Minute.**
3. **Add The Lemon Rind and The Red Pepper Flakes.**
   Saute Together for 1 Minute More.
4. **Add The Cream Sherry. Stir All Together Well.**
   Cook for About 1~2 Minutes.

The
Vegetable Broth
~ Prepare ~

1. **Add The Vegetable Broth, and Bring to a Boil. ~ OR ~**
2. **For The "Quick" Alternate Way, Combine**
   2 Qts. of Water & 2 Vegetable Bouillon Cubes.
   Bring to a Boil, Until Cubes are Dissolved.
3. **Add The Cream Sherry and The Garlic, Oil & Butter,**
   Lemon Rind & Red Pepper Flakes. Stir Together.
4. **Raise Heat. Bring The Mixture to a Boil.**
   Then, Lower Heat. Simmer for 30 Minutes.

The Soup
~ Combine & Cook ~

1. **Add The Escarole and Salt to the Simmering Broth.**
   Stir In. Cover Pan. Reduce Heat to Medium.
   Slow Boil for 15 Minutes, Stirring Often.
2. **Add Italian White Beans to The Broth and Escarole.**
   Cover Pan. Cook on Medium for 5 Minutes More.
3. **Add The Pine Nuts. Cover The Pan. Remove from Heat.**
   Allow to Sit at Least 5 Minutes More.

Serving Suggestion

Serve Mama's Escarole & White Bean Soup in a Warm Soup Tureen with Serving Ladle. Sprinkle Soup Top Lightly with Grated Romano Cheese. Place Parsley Sprigs on Soup and around Soup Tureen Platter to Garnish.. Serve This Delight with warm Italian Bread and Crispy Breadsticks. A Soft Rose or Soft White Wine would be a Nice Compliment! Expect to "Feel Good" after This Delicious Soup ~ Mama would want you to! Enjoy!

Mama's Minestrone Soup

Minestrone Minestra

Mama's Minestrone Soup warmed the hearts of Mama Lena's Guests for years when they would literally be blown into our Restaurant by the Chicago Wind at their backs! We were very happy to have our Minestrone Soup waiting for them as they flew in our door. It was Mama's winter favorite, too! We all had enjoyed this so much since our childhood days when all of us kids would return home from school, and see the Big Stock Pot bubbling on the stove! This Recipe is a Larger Recipe of This Treasure. We always found that just one helping of Mama's Minestrone only makes you want to have More!   Enjoy!

Ingredients   Serves 8~10

The Meats	1	Lb. of Italian Sausage *(Sweet, Mild or Hot, As You Prefer)* *(Remove Casing ~ Cook Loose Meat)*
	1	Lb. of Pork Shoulder *(Boneless)* *(Cut into Small Pieces)*
To Saute	1/4	Cup of Olive Oil
	1	Clove of Garlic *(Finely Chopped)*
	1	Large Onion *(Finely Chopped)*
Meat Broth	3~1/2	Quarts of Meat Stock *(See Recipe ~ Chapter Two)* ~ <u>OR</u> ~
	3	Meat Bouillon Cubes in 3~1/2 Quarts of Water *(Alternate Choice for Soup Base)*
The Seasonings	2	Pinches of Salt
	2	Pinches of Pepper
	3	Pinches of Basil
	2	Pinches of Rosemary *(Ground)*
	2	Pinches of Thyme
	2	Pinches of Sugar *(Granulated)*
	3	Pinches of Parsley
	1	Bay Leaf *(Whole)* *(Discard Leaf at End of Cooking)*
Tomatoes & Beans	1	Medium Can (15 Oz.) Plum Tomatoes, Crushed in Puree
	1	Can of Lima Beans
	1	Can of Kidney Beans
The Vegetables	4	Large Potatoes *(Cut into Cubes)*
	4	Large Carrots *(Cut into Thin Slices)*
	4	Stalks of Celery & Leaves *(Cut into 1/2" Pieces)*
	1	Leek *(Small Slices)* *(Separate Leaves & Wash Well)*
The Wine	1/2	Cup of Cream Sherry
The Macaroni	1	Lb. of Small Elbow Macaroni *(Cooked Firm ~ Al Dente)*
The Garnish	1/2	Cup of Parmesan Cheese *(Coarsely Grated)*

Preparation ~ Mama's Minestrone Soup

**The
Saute Mixture**
1. In a Large Stock Pot, Heat The Olive Oil on Medium.
2. Add The Chopped Onions, and Saute for 2~3 Minutes.
3. Add The Garlic. Saute Together for 1 Minute More.
4. Add The Loose Sausage Meat & The Pork Shoulder Pieces.
Brown The Meat Well, for About 3~4 Minutes..

**The Broth &
The Seasonings**
1. Add All The Meat Stock to The Pot. Stir Well. ~ <u>OR</u> ~
2. For The "Quick" Alternate Way, Combine
3~1/2 Quarts of Water with 3 Meat Bouillon Cubes.
Bring to Boil, Until The Cubes are Dissolved.
3. Add All The Seasonings. Stir Well. Bring Mixture to a Boil.
4. Cover Pot. Reduce Heat. Simmer for 1 Hour.
Stir Often. Skim Top Grease & Discard It.

**The
Vegetables,
Tomatoes & Beans**
1. Clean & Cut All The Vegetables, as Indicated on Ingredients.
Add The Vegetables to The Meat & Broth.
Cover Pot. Simmer 30 Minutes.
2. After 30 Minutes, Remove One~Half of The Vegetables.
Mash Vegetables. Return Them to Broth to Flavor Broth.
3. Add ~ The Crushed Tomatoes and Liquid, and
~ Lima Beans and Lima Bean Juice, and
~ Kidney Beans and Kidney Bean Juice.
Stir All Into Mixture Very Gently.
4. Simmer Again for 30 Minutes More. Stir Often.
Occasionally, Skim off The Top Grease and Discard It.

**The
Sherry Wine**
1. Add The Cream Sherry Wine to The Soup. Stir In Well.
2. Simmer Uncovered for 20 Minutes to Thicken Soup.

**The Macaroni
~ Add Last ~**
1. Add The Small Elbow Macaroni (Cooked Al Dente).
Stir In Well. Keep The Pot Uncovered.
2. Skim Top Grease & Discard. Remove The Pot from Heat.
Cover Pot. Let It Stand for 10 Minutes.

Serving Suggestion

This Most Delightful Soup should be served in a Warm Soup Tureen with Serving Ladle. Sprinkle Top Lightly with Coarsely Grated Parmesan Cheese. This Very Flavorful Soup ~ Mama's Minestrone ~ is very satisfying, so you can serve only with a favorite Dry Red Wine and our Italian Bread and Breadsticks. You will love this one, as much as Mama! Enjoy!

Shrimp & Sherry Wine Soup

Gamberetti Shere' Minestra

Our Mama Lena's Shrimp and Sherry Wine Soup is our classic soup treat, especially for Seafood Lovers. It's a wonderfully flavorful Soup, which presents a delight with every spoonful! It's very attractive in its presentation and aroma, as well ~ This is so very important when serving food to your guests. Our Guests' eyes would just light up when they saw this lovely Soup arrive at their tables! We know your guests will react the same way. We're happy to share such a special Mama Lena's Treasure with you! Enjoy!

Ingredients   Serves 4~6

The Bay Shrimp	1	Lb. of Bay Shrimp (Small Pink Shrimp) (Frozen)
The Cream Sherry Wine	1	Cup of Cream Sherry Wine
To Saute	2	Tablespoons of Butter (Sweet & Lightly Salted)
	3	Tablespoons of Olive Oil
	1	Clove of Garlic (Minced)
	1	Tablespoon of Lemon Rind
The Fish Broth	2	Quarts of Fish Broth (See Recipe ~ Chapter Two) ~ **OR** ~
	1	Can of Clam Juice in 2 Quarts of Hot Water
The Seasonings	2	Pinches of Basil
	2	Pinches of Rosemary (Ground)
	2	Pinches of Tarragon
	2	Pinches of Red Pepper Flakes
The Pasta	1	Cup of Maruzzelle Pasta (Tiny Sea~Shell Pasta) (Cooked Firm ~ Al Dente)
The Garnish	1/4	Cup of Asiago Cheese (Coarsely Grated)
	1/4	Bunch of Fresh Parsley

Preparation ~ Shrimp & Sherry Wine Soup

**The
Shrimp & Sherry
~ Marinate ~**

1. Wash The Frozen Shrimp in Cool Water, and
    Drain Well in a Colander for About 2~3 Minutes.
2. Pour The Cream Sherry Wine into a Large Bowl.
3. Add The Shrimp to The Cream Sherry. Mix Well.
4. Cover Bowl with Plastic. Refrigerate for 30 Minutes,
    Allowing Shrimp & Sherry to Marinate Well.

**Garlic & Lemon
~ Saute ~**

1. In a Large Stock Pot, Melt Butter on Medium.
    Add The Olive Oil.
2. Add The Garlic. Saute Garlic for 1 Minute,
    Until Just Light Brown.
3. Add The Lemon Rind. Saute 1 Minute More.
4. In a Strainer, Drain off The Butter and Olive Oil.
    Discard The Butter and The Olive Oil.
    Return The Garlic & Lemon Rind to The Pot.

**The
Fish Broth
~ Prepare ~**

1. Add The Fish Broth to The Garlic & Lemon Rind. ~ **OR** ~
2. Mix 1 Can of Clam Juice and 2 Quarts of Warm Water
    to The Garlic & Lemon Rind.
3. Then, Add The Basil, Rosemary, Tarragon, and
    Red Pepper Flakes. Stir In Well. Bring to a Boil.
4. Cover Pot. Reduce Heat. Simmer for 30 Minutes.

**Shrimp & Sherry Soup
~ Combine & Cook ~**

1. Add The Shrimp & Cream Sherry Wine to The Broth.
2. Now, Add The Cooked Maruzzelle Pasta to The Broth.
    Stir in All Very Well.
3. Uncover Pan. Simmer for 15 Minutes. Stir Often.
4. Remove from Heat. Cover Pan. Let Stand for 5 Minutes.

Serving Suggestion

Serve This Lovely Shrimp and Sherry Wine Soup in a Decorative Warm Soup Tureen with Serving Ladle & Cover. Sprinkle The Top Lightly with Coarsely Grated Asiago Cheese and Garnish with Parsley Sprigs. Also, Place Parsley Sprigs around The Tureen Platter for a Nice Touch! Accompany This Delicious Soup with our Hot Cheese Bread and a Nice Dry White Wine. Try It Just This Way ~ It Makes A Delightful Treat!   Enjoy!

Chicken Broth

Pollastro Brodo

Mama Lena's Broths are Delicious Soup Bases, as well as Great Liquids for other dishes. They are Very Flavorful Additions to a soup or any dish! Our Broths are made from fresh ingredients and create wonderful Cooking Bases that you can freeze. Use a Broth Base, as needed, to prepare Soups or other dishes. The Chicken, Fish, Meat and Vegetables used in making The Broths can also be used in many other dishes ~ Nothing Is Wasted! It's great to have one or two of These Delightful Broth Bases in your freezer. Try one and you'll never want to be without it! It's easy ~ Start now with our Chicken Broth! Enjoy!

Ingredients   Makes 2 Quarts

3	Lbs. of Stewing Chicken (Rinsed & Cut into Pieces)
3	Pinches of Salt (To Salt Rinsed & Cut Chicken)
2	Tablespoons of Butter (Sweet & Lightly Salted)
3	Tablespoons of Olive Oil
1	Large Onion (Sliced Very Thin)
1	Large Scallion (Minced, Including Green Parts)
3	Quarts of Water (Cool)
5	Stalks of Celery (Chopped)
4	Large Carrots (1/2" Slices)
2	Large Fresh Plum Tomatoes (Cut into Small Pieces) ~ <u>OR</u> ~
1	Medium Can (15 Oz.) of Plum Tomatoes, Crushed in Puree
1/2	Bunch of Fresh Parsley (Chopped)

Preparation ~ Chicken Broth

1. **In a Large Stock Pot, Melt Butter on Medium Heat. Add The Olive Oil.**
2. **Saute The Sliced Onions and The Minced Scallions, About 2 Minutes.**
3. **Add The Chicken Pieces (Rinsed, Cut & Salted).**
   Saute The Chicken, Until Lightly Browned, About 4~5 Minutes.
4. **Add 2 Cups of Water. Cook on Medium, Until The Water Evaporates.**
5. **Add In The Remaining 2~1/2 Quarts of Water, and also**
   The Celery, Carrots, Tomatoes and Parsley. Stir All In Well.
6. **Cover Pan. Cook 1~1/2 Hours on Medium. Skim Top of Broth.**
7. **After 1~1/2 Hours of Cooking, Remove The Chicken.**
   Store Chicken Separately to Use Later for Your Other Recipes.
8. **Uncover The Pan. Boil The Mixture on Medium High for 1 Hour.**
9. **Skim Foam from Top of Broth Again. Let Stand & Cool. Refrigerate**
   Overnight. Then, Remove and Discard Fat from The Top of Broth.
10. **Strain The Broth. Store Broth in Four Separate 2~Cup Containers.**
    Use Broth Immediately, or Freeze It for Up to 3 Months.
11. **Check Through The Strained Vegetables for Any Chicken Bones.**
    Mash The Strained Vegetables. Add 1 Pinch Salt, 1 Pinch Pepper,
    1 Tablespoon of Butter and 1 Tablespoon of Grated Cheese.
    Now, you have a Great Vegetable Side Dish! Enjoy!

Fish Broth

Pesce Brodo

Mama Lena's Fish Broth is Filled with Many Exciting Flavors! It's a Wonderful Base for Soups and Other Dishes! It's a True Delight in our Shrimp & Sherry Wine Soup!   Enjoy!

Ingredients   Makes 1 Quart

4	Small Lobster Tails (Rinsed in Lemon Water)
1	Quart of Cold Water
1	Tablespoon of Lemon Juice
2	Tablespoons of Butter (Sweet & Lightly Salted)
3	Tablespoons of Olive Oil
1	Large Onion (Sliced Very Thin)
1	Large Scallion (Minced, Including Green Stems)
2	Quarts of Water (Hot)
2	Pinches of Salt <u>and</u> 2 Pinches of Chives
1/2	Bunch of Fresh Parsley
1	Tablespoon of Anchovy Paste
2	Large Carrots (Cut into 1/2" Pieces)
3	Stalks of Celery (Chopped)
2	Large Fresh Tomatoes (Cut into Small Pieces) ~ <u>OR</u> ~
1	Medium Can (15 Oz.) of Plum Tomatoes, Crushed in Puree
1	Small Can of Clam Juice

Preparation ~ Fish Broth

1. Mix 2 Quarts of Cold Water with 1 Tablespoon of Lemon.
   Take The Lobster Tails with Shells & Rinse Well with Cold Water.
   Add The Rinsed Lobster Tails with Shells. Soak for 30 Minutes.
   Drain Lobster Tails with Shells. Set Aside. Discard Lemon Water.
2. In a Large Stock Pot, Melt Butter on Medium. Add Olive Oil, and Blend.
3. Saute The Sliced Onions and The Minced Scallions for 2 Minutes.
4. Add 2 Quarts of Hot Water, and Bring All to a Boil.
5. Add The Salt, Chives and Parsley to Boiling Water. Stir In. Reduce Heat.
6. Add Lobster Tails with Shells. Cover The Pan. Simmer for 15 Minutes.
7. Take Lobster Tails with Shells Out. Set Them Aside to Cool.
8. Add The Anchovy Paste, Carrots, Celery, Tomatoes and The Clam Juice.
   Stir In Well. Cover The Pan. Cook on Medium for 1 Hour.
9. Meanwhile, Cut Shells from The Lobster Tails with a Kitchen Scissors.
   Properly Store Lobster Tails for Later Use for Other Recipes.
10. Return Empty Shells to Stock Pot. Stir In. Now, On Medium~High Heat
    Cook The Shells with The Vegetables, The Seasonings and Liquid,
    Uncovered, for 1 Hour More. (1/3 of Broth will Evaporate Now).
11. Turn Off Heat. Let The Broth Stand and Cool. Refrigerate Overnight.
12. In Morning, Remove and Discard Fat from The Top of The Broth.
13. Remove The Four Lobster Shells from The Broth. Discard The Shells.
14. Strain The Broth. Store The Broth in Two 2~Cup Containers
    Use Immediately, or Freeze for Up to 3 Months.   Enjoy!

Meat Broth

Carne Brodo

Mama Lena's Meat Broth is made Our Traditional Way, with Both Beef and Veal Shanks. The Most Versatile of All Our Broths and A Perfect Base for Mama's Minestrone Soup! You will just love the Hearty Taste of This Very Delicious Broth! Let's get started! Enjoy!

Ingredients   Makes 2 Quarts

1	Lb. of Veal Shank (Cut into Half and Salted)
1	Lb. of Beef Shank (Cut into Half and Salted)
1/2	Lb. of Soup Bones (Cut Up) (Purchase at Meat Market)
3	Pinches of Salt (To Salt The Cut Shanks)
2	Tablespoons of Butter (Sweet & Lightly Salted)
3	Tablespoons of Olive Oil
1	Large Onion (Sliced Very Thin)
1	Large Scallion (Minced, Including Green Stems)
3	Quarts of Water (Hot)
4	Large Carrots (Cut into 1/2" Slices)
5	Stalks of Celery (Chopped)
2	Large Fresh Plum Tomatoes (Cut into Small Pieces) ~**OR**~
1	Medium Can (15 Oz.) of Plum Tomatoes, Crushed in Puree
1/2	Bunch of Fresh Parsley (Chopped)

Preparation ~ Meat Broth

1. In a Large Stock Pot, Melt Butter on Medium Heat. Add The Olive Oil.
2. Saute The Sliced Onions and The Minced Scallions for About 2 Minutes.
3. Add The "Salted" Veal Shanks and Beef Shanks.
    Brown The Meat Evenly on All Sides, for About 5 Minutes.
4. Add The Bones. Stir In with The Browned Shanks for 2 Minutes More.
5. Add 2 Cups of Water. Cook on Medium, Until The Water Evaporates.
6. Add Final 2~1/2 Quarts Hot Water, Carrots, Celery, Tomatoes, & Parsley.
7. Cover Pan. Cook 1~1/2 Hours on Medium. Occasionally,
    Skim The Foam from The Top. Discard The Foam.
8. After 1~1/2 Hours of Cooking Time, Remove The Bones. Discard Them.
    Remove Tendered Meat. Store Properly for Use in Other Recipes.
9. Uncover The Pan. Now, Boil for 1 Hour on Medium~High Heat.
10. Skim The Foam Again. Let Stand and Cool. Once The Broth has Cooled,
    Refrigerate Overnight to Allow The Great Flavors to Settle In.
11. In The Morning, Remove and Discard The Fat from The Top of Broth.
12. Strain The Meat Broth. Store in Four 2~Cup Containers.
    Use Immediately, or Freeze for Up to 3 Months. Enjoy!

Vegetable Broth

Verdura Brodo

Mama Lena's Vegetable Broth is A Delicious Base that Pleasantly Blends In with Many Soups and Other Dishes! This Special Broth is a Delightful Base that you can always depend on to simply enhance and compliment the true flavors of any dish! It's a Recipe that Grandma made for Grandpa. You will find many uses for This Lovely Broth!   Enjoy!

Ingredients   *Makes 2 Quarts*

3	**Tablespoons of Butter (Sweet & Lightly Salted)**
3	**Tablespoons of Olive Oil**
2	**Large Onions (Sliced Very Thin)**
2	**Large Scallions (Minced, Including Green Stems)**
12	**Large Green Pimento Olives (Cut into Halves)**
4	**Large Carrots (1/2" Slices)**
6	**Stalks of Celery (Chopped)**
1	**Leek (Use Bulb Only ~ Rinse Well ~ Chop into Small Pieces)**
1/2	**Bunch of Fresh Parsley (Chopped)**
2	**Large Fresh Plum Tomatoes (Cut into Small Pieces) ~ OR ~**
1	**Medium Can (15 Oz.) of Plum Tomatoes, Crushed in Puree**
3	**Large Pinches of Salt**
3	**Quarts of Hot Water**

Preparation ~ Vegetable Broth

1. **In a Large Stock Pot, Melt The Butter on Medium Heat.**
   Add The Olive Oil, and Blend The Oil into The Butter.
2. **Add The Onions and The Scallions. Saute for About 3~4 Minutes.**
3. **Add The Green Pimento Olives. Saute for 2 Minutes More.**
4. **Add 2 Cups of Hot Water and 1/4 of The Chopped Celery,**
   The Sliced Carrots and Chopped Leek. Mix Well.
   Cook All Together, Until The Water Evaporates.
5. **Now, Add The Remaining 2~1/2 Quarts of Hot Water, and**
   The Salt, The Remaining Carrots and Celery and Leek.
   Also, Add All The Plum Tomatoes and The Parsley. Mix Well.
6. **Cover Pan. Cook 2 Hours on Medium. Skim Off Any Top Foam.**
7. **Uncover The Pan. Cook 1/2 Hour on Medium High Heat,**
   (Some Liquid will Evaporate Now). Skim The Top Again.
8. **Remove from The Heat. Let Stand and Cool. Refrigerate Overnight.**
9. **In The Morning, Skim The Top of Any Foam, and Discard It.**
   Strain The Broth. Store in Four 2~Cup Containers.
   Use Immediately, or Freeze for Up to 3 Months.   Enjoy!

~ *Chapter Three* ~
Salads & Dressings

Pages 73 ~ 89

Artichoke Hearts & Bibb Lettuce Salad

Insalata Carciofini Bibbe

Mama Lena's Artichoke Hearts & Bibb Lettuce Salad is one of our Most Delicate Salads, especially when served with our Sweet & Sour Herb Dressing! That's the way we served it to our Guests, and it always delighted them. Once you have prepared it this way, you will also be delighted with the contrasting, yet delicate, tastes! Enjoy!

Ingredients   Serves 4~6

The Artichoke Salad	1	**Small Jar of Artichoke Hearts**
	1/2	**Lb. of Asparagus Spears**
	1	**Small Fennel Bulb**
	2	**Lbs. of Bibb Lettuce**
The Herb Dressing	1	**Recipe of Sweet & Sour Herb Dressing** (See Recipe ~ Chapter Three)
The Garnish	1/2	**Cup of Romano Cheese (Grated)**

Preparation ~ Artichoke Hearts & Bibb Lettuce Salad

The Bibb Lettuce

1. **Separate Lettuce Leaves. Rinse Well in Cool Water. Drain on Paper Towels.**
2. **Trim Lettuce Leaves of All Core Ends and Any Damaged Edges.**
3. **Break the Trimmed Lettuce into Small Pieces.**
4. **Place Paper Towels across Bottom of Mixing Bowl. Set Lettuce on Towels to Absorb Excess Water.**
5. **Cover Top of Lettuce with Paper Towels to Protect.**
6. **Refrigerate Covered Lettuce, Until Ready to Use.**

Preparation ~ Artichoke Hearts & Bibb Lettuce Salad

**The
Artichoke Hearts**

1. Rinse Artichoke Hearts in Cool Water. Cut into Halves.
2. Place The Artichoke Hearts in a Bowl, and
      Spoon on our Sweet & Sour Herb Dressing, covering
      The Artichokes. Mix Well, Until Well Coated.
3. Cover with Plastic and Marinate The Artichokes for at
      Least 30 Minutes, Or Until Ready to Serve.

**The
Asparagus**

1. Rinse The Asparagus Well with Cool Water.
2. Trim Off Bottom 1/3 of The Asparagus, and Discard It.
3. Slice The Tips and The Stems into Even Pieces for Salad.
4. Place in a Bowl, and Drizzle on A Little Dressing to Cover.
5. Seal in Plastic. Marinate The Asparagus for 30 Minutes,
      Or Until Ready to Serve.

**The
Fennel Bulb**

1. Trim The Fennel Stalks away from The Fennel Bulb.
2. Separate The Pieces of The Fennel Bulb.
3. Rinse Well in Cool Water and Drain on Paper Towels.
4. Trim Off the Core Ends and Any Damaged Edges.
5. Slice Fennel Bulb Pieces into Narrow Strips.
6. Place in a Bowl, and Drizzle on A Little Dressing to Coat.
7. Seal in Plastic. Marinate The Fennel for 30 Minutes,
      Or Until Ready to Serve.

**The Salad
~ Combine & Serve ~**

1. Remove Paper Towels from The Chilled Bibb Lettuce.
2. Add One~Third of The Dressing to The Bibb Lettuce, and
      Very Gently Toss with Dressing to Lightly Coat.
3. Arrange The Lettuce on a Chilled Decorative Platter.
4. Place The Artichoke Hearts as a Center on
      Top of The Dressed Bibb Lettuce.
5. Alternate Asparagus and Fennel Bulb Pieces
      Nicely Around The Rest of The Lettuce.
6. Drizzle Lightly The Extra Dressing Across
      The Artichokes, The Asparagus and The Fennel.

Serving Suggestion

Sprinkle Top of Salad Lightly with Grated Romano Cheese. Serve some extra Grated Romano Cheese and extra Sweet & Sour Dressing in Serving Dishes on the Side. Accompany with our Herbs & Spices Bread and a White Wine ~ This Lovely Salad is Wonderful with just The Bread & Wine, but it's a True Delight when served with Any of our Mama Lena's Entrees. This Delicate Salad is a compliment to Every Meal.   Enjoy!

Mama Lena's
Italian & Antipasto Salad Supreme

Insalata Antipasto Suprema

Our Mama Lena's Italian & Antipasto Salad Supreme was named such as it was our Restaurant's Most Favored Salad. Guests loved our Italian & Antipasto Salad so much, they sent back plates so clean, it appeared they had never been used! At Mama Lena's, we always served this Salad dressed with our Mama Lena's Italian Dressing Supreme. This Combination was so very delicious, and soon became known as one of our "Special" Specialties! It also was Mama's Favorite Salad ~ she loved it just the way Salvino prepared it, and so did all our Guests! You can be sure that all Mama Lena's Guests, Mama, Papa and The Family would want to join you for this Honored Salad! Enjoy!

Ingredients   Serves 4~6

The Lettuce	1	**Large Iceberg Lettuce (1~1/2 Lbs.)**
		(Break Lettuce into Bite~Size Pieces, by Hand)
The Tomatoes	1/2	**Lb. of Cherry Tomatoes (Cut into Halves) ~ <u>OR</u> ~**
	3	**Large Fresh Plum Tomatoes (Cut into Quarters)**
The Anchovies	4	**Anchovy Fillets (Cut into 4 Pieces per Fillet)**
The Vegetables	1/8	**Lb. of Italian Black Olives (Whole)**
	1/8	**Lb. of Italian Green Olives (Whole)**
	1	**Small Jar of Artichoke Hearts (Drain Off Liquid)**
		(Cut Into Halves)
	1	**Very Small Onion (Chopped)**
	1	**Small Red Pimento Pepper (Chopped)**
	2	**Stalks of Celery (Chopped)**
	1	**Small Can of Garbanzo Beans**
		(Drain Off Liquid)
The Cheese & Salami	1/2	**Lb. of Cheese (Cut into 1/2" Thick Small Triangles)**
		(Use Fontinella or Provolone Cheese)
	1/2	**Lb. Mild Salami (Cut on an Angle into Thin Slices)**
		(For Spicier Taste ~ Use Hot Salami or Pepperoni)
The Garnish	1/8	**Cup of Fennel Leaves (Finely Chopped)**
	1/4	**Cup of Pine Nuts**
The Dressing Supreme	1	**Recipe of Mama Lena's Italian Dressing Supreme**
		(See Recipe ~ Chapter Three)

Preparation ~ Italian & Antipasto Salad Supreme

**The
Iceberg Lettuce
~ Prepare ~**

1. **Rinse The Lettuce under Cool Water.
Place on Paper Towels to Drain of Excess Water.**
2. **Trim Core Ends and Damaged Edges from Lettuce.
Break The Lettuce into Small Pieces.**
3. **Place Paper Towels on Bottom of Mixing Bowl to
Absorb Excess Water. Cover Top of Lettuce with
Paper Towels to Protect. Refrigerate To Chill.**

**The
Tomatoes & Dressing
~ Prepare ~**

1. **Add The Cherry Tomatoes to One~Half of
The Mama Lena's Italian Dressing Supreme.
Gently Mix, Just Until The Tomatoes are
Well Coated with The Dressing.**
2. **Remove The Tomatoes with a Slotted Spoon.
Cover with Plastic. Refrigerate To Chill.**

**The
Vegetable & Dressing
~ Prepare ~**

1. **Now, Add the Following to The Dressing Supreme,
The Anchovies, Black Olives, Green Olives,
Artichoke Hearts, Onion, Red Pimento Pepper,
Celery, and Garbanzo Beans.**
2. **Gently Mix Well, Until All The Vegetables are
Well Coated with The Italian Dressing.
Cover The Bowl with Plastic Wrap, and
Refrigerate To Chill for At Least 30 Minutes.**

**The
Lettuce & Dressing
~ Prepare ~**

1. **After Chilling, Make a Small Opening in The Plastic
on The Vegetables. Drizzle Marinated Dressing
onto Top of The Chilled Lettuce. Toss Well.
Save Extra Dressing for a Serving Bowl.**

Serving Suggestion

*Serve The Italian & Antipasto Salad Supreme on a Nice Large "Chilled" Decorative Platter.
Arrange The Platter, as follows ~ The Dressed Letttuce across The Platter ~ The Tomatoes
in The Center of The Lettuce ~ The Dressed Vegetables Placed around The Tomatoes ~
Place The Cheese Triangles & The Salami Slices Attractively around The Edge of Platter ~
Sprinkle Top of The Salad Supreme with Finely Chopped Fennel Leaves and Pine Nuts!
This Special Salad is So Delicious and Delightful, that is Great to have just alone with our
Delicious Mama Lena's Tomato Cheese Bread ~ Another All~Time Mama Lena's Favorite!
Select a Nice Wine to Accompany. Serve Salad with extra Supreme Dressing on The Side.
Now you are ready to experience the True Taste of Mama Lena's Italian Kitchen! Enjoy!*

Lettuce & Tomato ~ Basic Salads

Lettuga Pomodoro Insalata

At Mama Lena's our choices of Lettuce & Tomato Salads always depended on the Market and what was in Season for the Best Taste and Quality. The Market now offers such a nice variety of Lettuces and Tomatoes throughout the year, so you can always come up with a great Basic Lettuce & Tomato Salad. Our Key to a Great Basic Salad is the same as Success for All Our Recipes ~ "Careful Preparation is Always the Key, Even to the Most Simple Dish!" We chose Anchovy & Capers Dressing here, but you can choose any of our Dressings. Enjoy!

Ingredients   Serves 4~6

The Lettuce	1	**Large Lettuce of Choice (1~1/2 Lb. Size)**
		(Fields of Green, Iceberg, Leaf or Romaine)
The Tomatoes	1	**Lb. of Tomatoes of Your Choice**
		(Cherry, Plum or Large Vine~Style)
The Dressing	1	**Recipe of Mama Lena's Anchovy & Capers Dressing**
		(See This Recipe or Other Dressings ~ Chapter Three)

Preparation ~ Lettuce & Tomato ~ Basic Salads

The Lettuce

1. **It's Best to Never Use a Knife to Cut The Lettuce, as the Leaves get Damaged and Tend to Rust, Once Cut by Knife.**
2. **Remove All The Leaves by Hand. Wash under Cool Water.**
3. **Drain The Lettuce on Paper Towels for Excess Water.**
4. **Trim off Core Ends & Damaged Parts. Break to Desired Sizes.**
5. **Line Bottom of Bowl with Paper Towels to Absorb Excess Water.**
6. **Cover Lettuce with Paper Towels. Refrigerate, Until Ready to Use.**

The Dressing

1. **Prepare 1 Recipe of Mama Lena's Anchovy & Capers Dressing.**

The Tomatoes

1. **Rinse The Tomatoes Well in Cool Water. Dry on Paper Towels.**
2. **Trim off Cores & Damaged Parts, carefully with a Medium Knife.**
3. **Cut ~ Cherry Tomatoes to Halves ~ Plum Tomatoes to Quarters ~ ~ Large Vine~Style Tomato into 8 Pieces Each ~**
4. **Place The Tomatoes in The Dressing, and Blend Gently.**
5. **Remove Tomatoes with a Slotted Spoon. Seal in Separate Bowls, The Tomatoes & Dressing. Refrigerate, Until Ready to Use.**

The Basic Salad ~ Combine ~

1. **Combine Salad, Just Prior to Serving, so It's Chilled & Crisp!**
2. **Uncover a Small Area in The Plastic on The Dressing. Drizzle The Chilled Dressing Evenly over the Lettuce. (Dressing now has Natural Juice of Tomatoes for Flavor).**
3. **Drizzle "Half" of The Dressing on Lettuce. Gently Toss to Coat.**
4. **Place Tomatoes in Center of Lettuce to Serve a Great Salad!**
5. **Serve Remaining Dressing in a Side Serving Dish. Enjoy!**

Tomato, Scallion & Red Onion Salad

Insalata Pomodoro Cipolla

Mama Lena's Tomato, Scallion & Red Onion Salad was the favorite salad of Papa Frank. This reminded him of a Salad that his Mother, Grandma Antonnina, used to make when he was a small boy in Sicily. He told how delicious it was with the Tomatoes, Scallions & Red Onions right from the hillside gardens. Papa enjoyed This Delicious Salad the best with our Asiago Cheese Dressing. We asked our Guests at Mama Lena's and they agreed with Papa Frank and preferred it just the same way. This Delightful and Tasty Salad is a great salad to accompany any Mama Lena Entree! Papa would tell you so! Enjoy!

Ingredients   Serves 4~6

The Tomatoes	1	**Lb. of Cherry Tomatoes (Cut into Halves) ~ OR ~**
	6	**Large Fresh Plum Tomatoes (Cut into Quarters)**
The Scallions	4	**Scallions (Finely Chopped, Including Green Stems)**
The Red Onions	1	**Medium Red Onion (Thinly Sliced)**
The Dressing	1	**Recipe of Mama Lena's Asiago Cheese Dressing (See Recipe ~ Chapter Three)**
The Garnish	1/4	**Cup of Asiago Cheese (Finely Grated)**

Preparation ~ Tomato, Scallion & Red Onion Salad

1. **Rinse Tomatoes and Scallions. Trim and Cut The Tomatoes, as Indicated. Finely Chop Scallions, with Green Stems.**
2. **Peel The Red Onion, and Trim Off The Core Ends. Rinse Well with Cold Water, and Cut into Thin Slices.**
3. **In a Large Wooden Bowl, Place The Scallions and Onions, and Mix with One~Half of The Asiago Cheese Dressing.**
4. **Add The Tomatoes to The Scallions, Onions & Dressing, and Gently Mix so Tomatoes are Coated with Dressing, too.**
5. **Serve Remaining Half of The Dressing in a Nice Serving Dish.**

Serving Suggestion

Serve on a Lovely Decorative Salad Platter. Sprinkle Salad Lightly with Asiago Cheese. Papa Frank made a Fine Feast of This Salad. He loved to have This Delicious Salad with our Garlic & Sweet Onion Bread and Red Wine. Try Papa's Way ~ It's Delightful! Enjoy!

Vegetable Salad

Verdura Fresco Insalata

Our Mama Lena's Fresh Vegetable Salad was a Salad that originated with Mama's Mother, Grandma Anna, who always prepared special dishes featuring Grandpa's Fresh Vegetables. We served This Salad proudly, knowing that it originated from Grandma and Grandpa. Our White Wine Vinaigrette is just the perfect compliment to match This Delicious Vegetable Salad. This Combination is truly superb with the fantastic medley of fresh textures and fresh tastes. This Salad is Delicious and Interesting, too!   Grandpa would be smiling!   Enjoy !

Ingredients   Serves 4~6

The Vegetables		
~Marinate ~	1/4	Cup of Asparagus (Cut into 1" Pieces)
	1/4	Cup of Broccoli (Dark Green ~ Flowers Only)
	1/4	Cup of Carrots (Coarsely Grated)
	1/4	Cup of Cauliflower (Small Clusters ~ Flowers Only)
	1/4	Cup of Celery (Diced)
	1	Small Cucumber (Slice 1" Thick, then Quartered)
	1/4	Cup of Fennel Bulb (Diced)
	1	Small Red Pimento Pepper (Cut into 1/2" Strips)
	1	Small Yellow Pepper (Cut into 1/2" Strips)
	5	Radishes (Cut into Thin Slices)
	1/2	Lb. of Cherry Tomatoes (Cut into Halves) ~ <u>OR</u> ~
	1/2	Lb. of Plum Tomatoes (Cut into Quarters)
	2	Small Zucchini (Slice 1" Pieces, then Cut Them in Half)

The Vegetables		
~Add Last~	1/2	Cup of Fresh Mushrooms (Cut into Thin Slices)
	1	Small Sweet Red Onion (Slice into Thin Slices)
	2	Scallions (Cut Bulbs & Stems into 1/2" Pieces)
	1	Fresh Lemon (For Juice over The Mushrooms)

The Fresh Spinach		
	1	Lb. of Fresh Spinach (Washed & Drained on Paper Towels)

The Dressing	1	Recipe of White Wine Vinaigrette Dressing (See Recipe ~ Chapter Three)

The Garnish	1/4	Cup of Romano Cheese (Grated)
	1/2	Cup of Fennel Leaves (Chopped Finely)

Preparation ~ Vegetable Salad

The "Vegetables To Marinate"

1. *Wash Well All The " Vegetables to Marinate."*
   Dry All Vegetables on Paper Towels.
2. *Cut The Vegetables to Sizes Indicated in The Ingredients.*
3. *Prepare 1 Recipe of "White Wine Vinaigrette Dressing."*
4. *In an Extra~Large Bowl, Combine Dressing & Vegetables.*
   Mix In Gently, Coating Vegetables Well.
5. *Cover Bowl Airtight with Plastic Wrap, and Refrigerate.*
   Allow Vegetables to Marinate in Dressing for 1 Hour.

~ While The Cut "Vegetables to Marinate" are Marinating in
The Vinaigrette Dressing, Prepare The Spinach and
The "Vegetables to Add Last" for The Salad ~

The Fresh Spinach

1. *Separate The Spinach Leaves, and*
   Wash Very Well under Cool Water.
2. *Trim Core Ends and Any Damaged Ends.*
3. *Leave the Spinach Leaves Whole ~ Do Not Break Spinach.*
4. *Place on Paper Towels to Drain of Excess Water.*

The "Vegetables To Add Last"

1. *First, Wash and Dry The Red Onion and Scallions.*
   Trim and Cut to Sizes Indicated in The Ingredients.
2. *Lastly, Clean Mushrooms with a Damp Paper Towel.*
   Cut The Fresh Mushrooms, and
   Drizzle Fresh Lemon Juice over Them.

Separate Marinade Dressing & Vegetables

1. *After 1 Hour of Marinating, Remove from Refrigerator,*
   The "Vegetables To Marinate," which have
   marinated well in The Vinaigrette Dressing.
2. *Make a Small Opening in The Plastic Cover on The Top.*
   Drain All Dressing from The "Vegetables to Marinate."
   (Drain Dressing directly into a Serving Bowl for Table).
3. *Use Both "Vegetables to Marinate" & "Vegetables to Add Last"*
   Arrange in Salad, as Follows:

Serving Suggestion

On a Large Chilled Platter, Arrange The Spinach Leaves (Whole). Place The Marinated Vegetables across The Spinach Leaves. Drop Red Onion Slices and Scallions all across the Vegetables. Then, Arrange The Mushroom Slices on Top. Evenly Spoon on our Dressing of White Wine Vinaigrette across entire Salad and Vegetables. Sprinkle Lightly with Grated Romano Cheese. Sprinkle Fennel Leaves across the Romano Cheese for a Nice Garnish! Looks Lovely and Tastes Lovely, too! Serve with a Pasta with Red Cream Sauce and Herbs & Spices Bread. A Dry White Wine will compliment Grandpa's Special Salad. Enjoy!

Caesar Superb Salad & Dressing

Caesare Superba Salsa Insalata

Our Mama Lena's Caesar Superb Salad & Dressing is a Unique and Delicious Combination, and one in which we use only "Cooked Eggs." Salvino really does deserve Applause for This Very Special Recipe, and he did receive them from our Guests who loved his rendition of Caesar Salad and Dressing! Salvino even made his own Homemade Caesar Garlic Croutons to really finish his Very Special Recipe in Style! We know you will receive applause when you serve our Caesar Superb Salad & Dressing for your family and guests! Enjoy!

Ingredients   Serves 4~6

The		
Caesar Dressing	3	Anchovy Fillets (Cut into Small Pieces)
		(Use Canned Anchovies, Packed in Oil)
	2	Tablespoons of Cream Sherry
	1	Large Clove of Garlic (Leave Whole to Rub Bowl)
		(Later, Sliver for Croutons)
	1	Cup of Extra Virgin Olive Oil
	2	Tablespoons of White Wine Vinegar
	2	Tablespoons of Lemon Juice (From Half of Fresh Lemon)
		(Use Other Half Lemon for Garnish)*
	3	Pinches of Salt
	2	Pinches of Black Pepper (Coarsely Ground)
	1/2	Teaspoon of Worcestershire Sauce
	1/2	Teaspoon of Dijon Mustard
	2	Hard~Boiled Eggs (Use Only Chopped Yolks)
	2	Cloves of Garlic (Finely Chopped)
	1/4	Cup of Parmesan Cheese (Grated)
	1/4	Cup of Romano Cheese (Grated)
The		
Romaine Lettuce	1~1/2	Lbs. of Romaine Lettuce (Crisp, Light Romaine)
The	5	Slices of Italian Bread for Garlic Croutons
Garlic Croutons		(See Recipe ~ Next Page) ~ <u>OR</u> ~
	3	Dozen Large Seasoned Commercial Croutons
	2	Tablespoons of Butter (Sweet & Lightly Salted)
	3	Tablespoons of Olive Oil
The Garnish	1/4	Cup of Parmesan Cheese (Grated)
	1/2	Lemon* (Thinly Sliced)

Preparation ~ Caesar Superb Salad & Dressing

The
Caesar Dressing
~ Prepare ~

1. *In a Small Bowl, Place The Chopped Anchovy Fillets into The Cream Sherry. Cover Bowl with Plastic, and Marinate in Refrigerator, while Preparing Dressing.*
2. *In a Large Wooden Bowl, Rub One Whole Garlic Clove Around Bowl, Until The Bowl is Well Flavored. Refrigerate The Bowl, Until Ready to Use. (Sliver Garlic Clove. Save Garlic for The Croutons)*
3. *In a Blender, Combine The Olive Oil, White Wine Vinegar, Lemon Juice, Salt, Pepper, Worcestershire Sauce, and Dijon Mustard. Blend for 2 Minutes.*
4. *Add Egg Yolks, Chopped Garlic, 1/4 Cup of Parmesan Cheese & 1/4 Cup of Romano Cheese. Blend Again for 1 Minute More. Set Blender & Mix in Refrigerator.*

The
Romaine Lettuce
~ Prepare ~

1. *Separate The Romaine Lettuce Leaves. Rinse Them Well. Drain Leaves Thoroughly on Paper Towels.*
2. *Trim Each Lettuce Leaf. Break in Small Pieces by Hand.*
3. *Place Finished Lettuce in the Chilled Wooden Bowl. Cover Again in Plastic and Refrigerate.*

The
Homemade Croutons
~ Prepare ~

1. *Take 5 Slices of Italian Bread, about 1/2" Thick. Toast The Bread Lightly in Toaster.*
2. *Slice Toasted Bread into 12 Equal Cuts Per Slice ~ Five Slices of Bread will Yield 60 Croutons.*
3. *Heat a Large Skillet to Medium Heat, and Melt Butter. Add Olive Oil and "Slivered" Garlic, saved above. Saute The Slivered Garlic for About 1 Minute.*
4. *Add The Croutons to The Butter, Oil and Slivered Garlic. Saute, Until Croutons are Browned on All Sides.*
5. *Remove with a Slotted Spoon. Drain on Paper Towels.*

The Caesar Salad
~ Assemble & Serve ~

1. *Remove from Refrigerator ~ Marinated Sherry Anchovies, The Chilled Romaine in the "Garlic" Wooden Bowl, and The Blender Top with The Dressing Mixture.*
2. *Uncover The Romaine Lettuce in the Wooden Bowl. Add Marinated Sherry Anchovies. Toss Gently.*
3. *Place Blender Top, Filled with Mixture, on Blender Base. Blend Chilled Mixture for 1~2 Minutes More.*
4. *Gently, Add The Blended Mixture of Oil & Seasonings to The Romaine & Anchovies. Toss Well Again.*
5. *Then, Add Homemade Garlic Toasted Croutons on Top.*
6. *Lastly, Sprinkle Lightly with Parmesan Cheese. Place Thin Lemon Slices on Edges of Bowl. Enjoy!*

Anchovies & Capers Dressing

Alici Capperi Salsa

Mama Lena's Anchovies and Capers Dressing was a Dressing that Mama truly loved to have on her Iceberg Lettuce Salads ~ She really favored Anchovies. This Special Dressing with the Anchovies, Capers & Fennel presents a Delightfully Different Combination of Flavors. This is a Dressing that Mama's Mother and Father enjoyed also. The Anchovies are a favorite of most Italians, especially Sicilians, and those born and raised near the Sea, as Mama's Family was. Once you try this recipe, you will see that This Very Delicious Dressing is an Excellent Topping to any Salad! A True Tribute to Sicily! Enjoy!

Ingredients   Serves 4~6

The Oil & Garlic	1	**Cup of Extra Virgin Olive Oil**
	2	**Cloves of Garlic (Chopped Extra Fine)**
The Anchovies	3	**Anchovy Fillets from the Jar (Chopped) ~ OR ~**
	2	**Tablespoons of Anchovy Paste**
The Capers & Fennel	3	**Pinches of Fennel (Fresh & Lacy Leaves)**
	1	**Teaspoon of Capers (Finely Chopped)**
The Garnish	2	**Teaspoons of Capers (Leave Whole)**
	1	**Tablespoon of Pine Nuts**

Preparation ~ Anchovies & Capers Dressing

1. **In a Large Skillet, Heat The Olive Oil to Medium, and Lightly Saute The Chopped Garlic.**
2. **Add The Chopped Anchovies to The Olive Oil & Garlic, and Saute Together for 2 Minutes More.   ~ OR ~**
3. **Add Anchovy Paste to The Olive Oil & Garlic, and Saute Until Paste is Smoothly Blended.**
4. **Now, Stir The Fennel and The Chopped Capers into The Oil, Garlic and Fresh Anchovies, Or Anchovy Paste. Saute All Together Now for 1~2 Minutes More.**
5. **Remove from The Heat. Place in a Bowl and Allow to Cool.**
6. **Once Cooled, Add The Pine Nuts & Whole Capers.   Mix Gently.**
7. **Cover Bowl Airtight with Plastic Wrap.   Refrigerate for At Least 1 Hour, or Until Ready to Serve.   Enjoy!**

Asiago Cheese Dressing

Asiago Formaggi Salsa

Our Mama Lena's Asiago Cheese Dressing is a Rich, Delightful Dressing, made with the finest Asiago Cheese and Extra Virgin Olive Oil. We often matched This Very Smooth and Very Special Dressing to our wonderfully tasty Salad of Tomato, Scallion & Red Onion ~ That's how Papa Frank preferred it! This Lovely Dressing is Delicious not only on Salads, but is Excellent on Chicken, Fish and Seafood. And, it makes a Very Delicious Dip for Salvino's Parsley Cheese Potatoes! Also, you will see that we use This Special Dressing in an Appetizer Spread. This Delectable Dressing is Very Versatile, too!   Enjoy!

Ingredients   Serves 4~6

The	1	**Cup of Extra Virgin Olive Oil**
Oil & Wine Vinegar	1/3	**Cup of White Wine Vinegar**
The		
Asiago Cheese	1/4	**Cup of Asiago Cheese (Grated)**
The		
Lemon & Lemon Rind	1	**Tablespoon of Lemon Juice**
		(Juice from 1 Fresh Lemon)
	1	**Tablespoon of Lemon Rind**
The Sugar	3	**Pinches of Sugar (Granulated)**
The Fennel Leaves	3	**Pinches of Fennel (Fresh Lacy Leaves)**

Preparation ~ Asiago Cheese Dressing

1. **Combine The Olive Oil and The White Wine Vinegar. Mix Together Well.**
2. **Add The Grated Asiago Cheese to The Olive Oil and The White Wine Vinegar. Blend Slowly, Until The Mixture is Very Smooth.**
3. **Gently, Stir In The Lemon Juice and The Lemon Rind, Keeping a Nice, Smooth Texture.**
4. **Add The Sugar, and Again Blend for a Smooth Texture.**
5. **Lastly, Gently Blend in The Fennel Leaves for a Unique Taste and Color to The Dressing.**
6. **Cover Bowl Airtight with Plastic Wrap, and Refrigerate. Allow Dressing to Marinate for At Least 1 Hour, or Until Ready to Serve.   Enjoy!**

Mama Lena's
Italian Dressing Supreme

Italiano Salsa Suprema

Mama Lena's Italian Dressing Supreme is a Simply, Delicious Blend of Very Fine Olive Oil, Italian Red Wine Vinegar, Freshest Herbs & Spices! Our Guests always cleaned their dishes when we served This Dressing Supreme! What really makes our seemingly simple dressing "So Delicious" is using The Very Best Ingredients ~ Real Extra Virgin Olive Oil ~ Light or Dark Styles ~ A Clear Italian Red Wine Vinegar ~ Your Freshest Herbs & Spices. Next ~ Marinate The Dressing ~&~ Properly Add The Dressing to The Salad. Just Follow The Way Salvino Mixes Salad ~ You'll enjoy your Dressings and Salads like never before! Start with This Special All~Time Favorite Dressing of our Mama Lena's Guests! Enjoy!

Ingredients   Serves 4~6

The		
Oil & Vinegar	1	Cup of Extra Virgin Olive Oil
	1/3	Cup of Italian Red Wine Vinegar
Garlic	1	Clove of Garlic (Press Out Juice Only)
Seasonings	3	Pinches of Salt
	2	Pinches of Pepper
	2	Pinches of Oregano
	1	Pinch of Basil
	1	Pinch of Mint
The Sugar	2	Pinches of Sugar (Granulated)

Preparation ~ Mama Lena's Italian Dressing Supreme

1. **Combine The Extra Virgin Olive Oil and The Red Wine Vinegar. Mix Together Very Well.**
2. **Using a Garlic Press, Press The Juice of One Garlic Clove into The Olive Oil and Red Wine Vinegar. Mix Well Again.**
3. **Stir In The Salt, Pepper, Oregano, Basil and Mint.**
4. **Add The Sugar. Mix In Very Well for 1~2 Minutes.**
5. **Cover Bowl Airtight with Plastic Wrap, and Refrigerate. Allow Dressing to Marinate At Least 1 Hour, or Until Ready to Serve.**

~ Special Note ~ Notice in Each of Our "Salad" Recipes ~
~ The Details on How to Mix In The Dressings ~
~ For a Successful Tasting Salad ~
Enjoy!

Sweet & Sour Herb Dressing

Dolce Acido Erbe Salsa

At Mama Lena's, Sweet & Sour Herb Dressing, a deliciously tasty dressing, was reserved for our Lovely Artichoke & Bibb Lettuce Salad. This Dressing is so Lightly Flavored with Spices, that it has just the right amount of sharpness and sweetness to make it a perfect compliment to any Salad of choice, especially the Delicate Artichoke & Bibb Lettuce Salad. We also used This Spicy Dressing as a lovely compliment to many of our Chicken, Fish & Seafood Dishes. Mama Lena's Guests loved This Dressing ~ You will, too! Enjoy!

Ingredients   Serves 4~6

The Oil & Vinegar	1	Cup of Extra Virgin Olive Oil
	1/3	Cup of White Wine Vinegar
The Sugar & Spices	1/4	Cup of Sugar
	1	Pinch of Onion Powder
	1	Pinch of Garlic Powder
	2	Pinches of Basil
	2	Pinches of Oregano
	2	Pinches of Parsley
	2	Pinches of Tarragon
	2	Pinches of Mint

Preparation ~ Sweet & Sour Herb Dressing

1. In a Large Skillet, Heat The White Wine Vinegar with The Sugar, The Onion Powder and The Garlic Powder. Bring The Mixture to a Boil, While Stirring It Constantly.
2. Stir In The Basil, Oregano, Parsley, Tarragon, and Mint.
3. Reduce Heat. Cover Pan. Simmer The Mixture for 2 Minutes.
4. Blend Olive Oil into Cooked Mixture. Stir Well. Cover Pan, and Simmer for 2 Minutes More.
5. Remove Pan from Heat to Cool. Cool About 10 Minutes.
6. Pour Sweet & Sour Dressing into a Bowl, and Seal it Airtight with Plastic Wrap. Refrigerate for At Least 1 Hour, or Until Ready to Serve.

Serving Suggestion

Serve as we did at Mama Lena's Italian Kitchen ~ Make 1 Recipe of our Artichoke & Bibb Lettuce Salad. Serve with a Vermicelli Pasta with Red Cream Sauce, Hot Cheese Bread, and a Soft Red Wine. This Very Special Dressing makes every Salad Delicious! Enjoy!

White Wine Vinaigrette Dressing

Bianco Vino Aceto Salsa

Mama Lena's White Wine Vinaigrette Dressing was the Dressing we selected for our Vegetable Salad. This sharper~blended dressing was the perfect compliment for the Freshness of the Vegetables. Our Guests really loved the Combination when we served it! We served our lovely White Wine Vinaigrette an Alternate Way ~ On a Leaf Lettuce Salad, with some Fresh Berries, Marinated in White Wine, spooned across the Top of the Lettuce which is tossed in White Wine Vinaigrette, too! Our Guests loved the Fresh Berries Combination also. We present both ways for your own preference and pleasure ! Enjoy!

Ingredients   Serves 4~6

The White Wine Dressing		
	1	Cup of Extra Virgin Olive Oil
	1/3	Cup of White Wine Vinegar
	3	Tablespoons of Lemon Juice (From 1 Fresh Lemon)
	1	Tablespoon of Fresh Lemon Rind
	3	Pinches of Salt
	2	Pinches of Pepper
	2	Pinches of Parsley
	1	Pinch of Red Pepper Flakes *(Optional)*
	3	Tablespoons of Green Pimento Olives (Finely Chopped)
	2	Scallions (Onion & Stems) (Trim Ends & Finely Chop)
	4	Tablespoons of Freshly Chopped Egg Yolks (Add Last) (Hard~Boil 2 Large Eggs, Cool, & Finely Chop Yolks)

The Vegetable Salad		
	1	Recipe of Mama Lena's Vegetable Salad (See Recipe ~ Chapter Three)

The ~ Alternate Way ~ Berries & Leaf Lettuce		
	1	Recipe of Simple Leaf Lettuce Salad (Your Choice) (See Recipe ~ Chapter Three)
	1	Cup of Fresh Berries (Raspberries or Blackberries)
	1/4	Cup of White Wine (A Light, Fruity White Wine)
	1/4	Cup of Sugar (Granulated)

Preparation ~ White Wine Vinaigrette Dressing

The
White Wine Dressing
~ For Vegetable Salad ~

1. **Combine The Olive Oil, White Wine Vinegar, The Lemon Juice and The Lemon Rind. Blend All Together Well.**

2. **Add The Salt, The Pepper and The Parsley. If using The Red Pepper Flakes, Add in Now. Stir All Together Well.**

3. **Add The Chopped Green Pimento Olives and The Chopped Scallions. Stir In Well.**

4. **Add The Chopped Egg Yolks, and Blend Carefully.**

5. **Seal your Bowl Airtight with Plastic Wrap. Refrigerate 1 Hour, or Until Ready To Serve.**

6. **Prepare The Vegetable Salad Recipe, as White Wine Vinaigrette Dressing is Marinating. (See Salad Recipe ~ Chapter Three)**

The
Alternate Way
On Berries & Leaf Lettuce

1. **Combine The Fresh Berries, The White Wine, and The Sugar in a Bowl. Seal Bowl Airtight. Refrigerate for at Least 1 Hour.**

2. **Follow Steps # 1 Through # 5 Above to Prepare The White Wine Vinaigrette Dressing.**

3. **Prepare The Leaf Lettuce Salad Recipe as White Wine Vinaigrette Dressing Marinates. (See Recipe ~ Chapter Three)**

4. **To Serve, Gently Toss Leaf Lettuce with The Dressing, Spoon Marinated Berries over The Top of The Tossed Salad. Great Looking & Tasting!**

Serving Suggestion

At Mama Lena's we served our White Wine Vinaigrette Dressing and Vegetable Salad with our Lamb and Pork Entrees, as well as many Pasta Dishes with our various Sauces. The Sharp White Wine Vinaigrette Dressing & Crisp Vegetables compliments those dishes. We served our White Wine Vinaigrette Dressing the Alternate Way with Leaf Lettuce and Fresh Berries for our lighter dishes. The Alternate Way was a perfect compliment to our Chicken, Fish and Veal Entrees ~ sharp, yet sweet from the fruit and lighter with delicate leaf lettuce. Mama Lena's White Wine Vinaigrette makes a nice Marinade, too! Enjoy!

~ Chapter Four ~
The Pastas

Pages 91 ~ 105

Pasta Dough
for
Seven Homemade Pastas

Casa Prepari Pasta ala Madonna

Mama Lena's Homemade Pasta Dough originated with Mama's Mother, Grandma Anna. When we were children, Mama and her Mother would make the Pasta Dough together. After Shaping and Cutting the Pasta, they would Dry the Pasta over the wooden clothing stand in the kitchen. It was a Special Treat to have the Homemade Pasta freshly made. Sometimes, we were "double treated," when they made a Filling the same day and stuffed a pasta ~ a treat usually reserved for special occasions! At our Restaurant, we were small in space, so we made our Homemade Pasta only on Sundays for our Guest's private parties when they would reserve the entire restaurant. We made Seven Different Pastas with This Great Dough! Try This Wonderful Dough to make A Pasta and treat your family and guests, too!   Enjoy!

Ingredients   Serves 10~12

6	Cups of Flour (Semolina Flour) (First Choice)
	(Purchase At An Italian Store) ~ <u>OR</u> ~
6	Cups of All Purpose Flour (Sifted)
	(Second Best Choice)

5	Large Eggs (Lightly Beaten)
1	Cup of Water (Cool) (1/2 Cup First ~ Add Rest, As Needed)
4	Pinches of Salt
2	Tablespoons of Olive Oil

Preparation ~ Homemade Pasta Dough

The Dough
~ Prepare ~

1. Wash and Thoroughly Dry The Kitchen Table or Counter.
2. Place About 5~1/2 Cups of Flour on The Table.
    Make a Well in Center of The Flour.
3. Sprinkle 4 Pinches of Salt Evenly Over The Flour.
4. Set The Lightly Beaten Eggs into The Center of the Well, and
    Add 1/2 Cup of Water and 2 Tablespoons of Oil to The Eggs.

The Dough
~ Mixing ~

1. Gradually, Blend The Flour into The Eggs, Water & Olive Oil,
    Until The Dough is Ready to Handle.
2. If The Dough is Too Firm, Add Cool Water, A Little At A Time,
    Until you have a Soft Dough. Flour The Table.
3. Knead The Dough for 10 Minutes, Until The Dough is
    Very Smooth Outside and Very Elastic To The Touch.
4. Shape in a Ball. Cover with Bowl. Let It Rest for 30 Minutes.

Preparation ~ Pasta Dough for Seven Homemade Pastas

The Dough   1.   **Wash and Dry Work Surface Again. Then Lightly Flour.**
~ Rolling ~   2.   **Divide The Dough into 3 Even Dough Balls.**
                            Then, Roll Out Each Dough Ball into a Thin
                            Flat Square Sheet, About 12" x 12 x 1/8" Thickness.

The Dough   1.   **Take Three Large Baking Racks or Shelves, and**
~ Drying ~   **Cover with Them with Thin White Tea Towels.**
            2.   **Hang The 3 Flat Sheets of Dough over Covered Racks.**
                            Allow Pasta to Air Dry About 10 Minutes on One Side.
            3.   **Then, Turn The Flat Sheets of Dough Over, and**
                            Let Dough Dry on Other Side, for 10 Minutes More.

The Dough
~ Shaping ~   1.   **When The Sheets of Dough are Air~Dried on Both Sides,**
                            Place Them on a Dry, Clean Table or Counter.
            2.   **Shape & Cut Your Preferred Shapes Immediately.**
                            Before The Dough can get "Dried Out."
            3.   **"Shape & Cut" Instructions for 7 Pastas Are As Follows ~**

Thin Ribbon Noodles

Fettucine   <u>Shape</u>   ~ *Bend Over One End of Each Sheet of Dough*
Linguine   *about 3 times to a 3" Wide Flat Roll.*
Vermicelli   *(Like a folded newspaper, but even flatter)*
               <u>Cut</u>   ~ *Using a Very Sharp Flat~Blade Knife, Cut Strips*
                          Across Flat Rolls of Dough. The Sizes Are:
                            ~ Fettucine ~ Cut into 1/4" Wide ~ Ribbons
                            ~ Linguine ~ Cut into 1/3" Wide ~ Ribbons
                            ~ Vermicelli ~ Cut into 1/8" Wide ~ Ribbons

Pastas to Be Filled

Cannelloni   <u>Shape</u>   ~ *Place Flat Rolled Dough Sheets on Table to be*
Manicotti   *Cut into Different~sized Pieces, To Prepare*
Ravioli   *Cannelloni & Manicotti, or Ravioli Forms.*
               <u>Cut</u>   ~ *With a Fluted Pastry Wheel (Like a Pizza Cutter),*
                            Cut The Dough Sheets. The Pasta Sizes Are:
                            ~ Cannelloni ~ 8" x 6" ~ Rectangle Pieces
                            ~ Manicotti ~ 8" x 6" ~ Rectangle Pieces
                            ~ Ravioli ~ 10" x 2" ~ Dough Strips to Cut

Wide Pasta Noodles

Lasagna   <u>Shape</u>   ~ *Place The Flat Rolled Sheets on Clean Table*
               <u>Cut</u>   ~ *With a Fluted Pastry Wheel, Cut The Dough*
                            Sheets to ~ 8" Long x 2" Wide ~ Ribbons.

Preparation ~ Pasta Dough for Seven Homemade Pastas

**The
Homemade Pastas
~ Cooking ~**

1. In a Large Pan, Boil 6 Quarts of Water.
   Once Water Boils, Add 2 Pinches of Salt and
   2 Tablespoons of Olive Oil to Water.
2. Add Pasta to Boiling Water, and Cook 6~7 Minutes.
   Gently Stir The Pasta with a Wooden Spoon.
   Stir The Homemade Pasta Very Gently, as
   The Fresh Pasta is Much More Delicate.
3. Check The Pasta Cooking at 5~6 Minutes, as
   The Fresh Pasta Cooks More Quickly, too.
   Commercial Pasta takes Almost Double The Time.
4. When Pasta is Ready to Your Taste, Drain Pasta in a
   Large Colander. Do Not Rinse Pasta with Water.

**The
Thin Ribbon Noodles
~ Serving ~**

1. Heat a Large Serving Platter in The Oven.
   Turn Oven to 200 and Set Platter in The Oven.
   After 3~5 Minutes, Turn Off Heat.
2. Serving The Thin Ribbon Noodles ~
   Fettucine ~ Linguine ~ Vermicelli ~
   Serve Immediately, After Draining in Colander.
3. Spoon 1 Cup of Sauce Across The Heated Platter, and
   Set The Pasta on Top of The Sauce. Then, Pour
   2 More Cups of Sauce Over Pasta. Toss Gently.
4. Sprinkle Pasta Lightly with 1/4 Cup of Freshly Grated
   Parmesan Cheese, and Garnish with Parsley.
5. Serve with an Appetizer Spread, our Italian Salad,
   warm Italian Bread and an Appropriate Wine for
   The Sauce You Choose. You will be Delighted!

**The
Wide Ribbon Noodles, Or
Pastas To Be Filled**

1. Follow Filling, Baking & Serving Suggestions in ~
   " Pasta Tips ~ Cooking, Filling & Serving."
   That's The Section Immediately Following This.
   Enjoy!

Pasta Tips
Cooking, Filling & Serving

Chapter Four has The Pasta Dough Recipe & How to Shape & Cut Seven Homemade Pastas, and Two Recipes for The Pasta Fillings ~ Meat & Spinach and Ricotta Cheese & Spinach. This Tips Section has the Best Ways ~ To Cook Pastas ~ To Fill Pastas ~ To Serve Pastas ~ We also suggest The Sauces from Chapter Five that are most complimentary to each Pasta. Here you bring all your great efforts together for a Beautiful Finish! We know you'll do Great! Mama Lena & Grandma Anna would be proud of you!   Enjoy!

Thin Ribbon Noodles
Fettucine
Linguine
Vermicelli

1. **Shape & Cut Noodles as in Homemade Pasta Dough Recipe.**
   Fettucine ~1/4" ~ Linguine~1/3" ~ Vermicelli~1/8"
2. **As Instructed in The Homemade Pasta Dough Recipe ~**
   ~ Cook The Homemade Pasta for   ~ 6 ~ 7 Minutes.
   ~ Cook The Commercial Pasta for ~ 10 ~ 12 Minutes.
3, **Serve Any of These Three Thin~Ribbon Noodles with**
   Any of our Sauces in Chapter Five.

Wide Pasta Noodles
Lasagna
~Baked~

1. **Shape & Cut The Lasagna Noodles as in**
   Homemade Dough Recipe ~ Size ~ 8" Long x 2" Wide.
2. **Cook These Homemade Wide Noodles for About 8 Minutes.**
   Commercial Noodles Cook for About 10~12 Minutes.
   Drain Pasta Before Assembling It. Do Not Rinse.
3. **Heat 6 Cups of Mama Lena's Basic Tomato Sauce.**
   This Quantity Includes Extra Sauce for Serving Dish.
   Heat on Medium~Low Heat.
4. **Assemble The Lasagna Dish in an Oblong Pan, As Follows:**
   ~ Pour 1 Cup of Warmed Sauce Across Bottom of Pan
   ~ Place First Layer of Wide Noodles
   ~ Spread 1 Cup of The Cheese Filling or The Meat Filling
   ~ Pour 1/2 Cup of Warmed Sauce Across The Filling
   ~ Repeat Above Sequence One More Time.
   ~ Top with a Layer of Wide Noodles.
   ~ Cover Noodle Top Completely with Sauce.
   ~ Lastly, Sprinkle Parmesan Cheese over Top of Sauce
5. **Seal Top of Pan Airtight with Foil.**
6. **Bake in a Preheated 350 Degree Oven for 30 Minutes.**
7. **At 30 Minutes, Remove The Foil and Continue Baking.**
   Bake Uncovered for 10 Minutes More.
8. **After 10 Minutes, Leave The Pan in The Oven, and**
   Switch The Oven Heat to Broil for 3~5 Minutes.
9. **When Lasagna Top is Golden Brown, Remove from The Oven.**
   Cool The Lasagna for 15 Minutes Before Cutting.
   Cut into 4" Squares, and Serve The Lasagna
   with Extra Sauce in a Serving Dish on The Side.
   (Pasta Tips Section Continues ~ Next Pages)

Pasta Tips ~ Cooking, Filling & Serving

The Cannelloni

1. Cannelloni can be Filled with Either One of Our Fillings ~ Ricotta Cheese & Spinach ~<u>OR</u>~ The Meat & Spinach.
2. The Sauce for The Cannelloni is Usually a White Sauce. Use 1 Recipe of White Cream Sauce Supreme. *(See Recipe ~ Chapter Five)*

The Manicotti

1. Manicotti can be Filled with either of Our Fillings ~ Ricotta Cheese & Spinach ~<u>OR</u>~ The Meat & Spinach.
2. The Sauce for The Manicotti is Usually a Red Sauce. Use 1 Recipe of Red Cream Sauce Supreme. *(See Recipe ~ Chapter Five)*

The Homemade Pasta Cannelloni Manicotti

1. Shape & Cut Dough, as in Homemade Pasta Dough Recipe.
   Cannelloni ~ 8" x 6" ~ Rectangle Pieces
   Manicotti ~ 8" x 6" ~ Rectangle Pieces
2. Cook The Pasta Dough Pieces Until Tender, About 6 Minutes. Remove Carefully from Water with a Flat Slotted Spoon. Drain on a Clean Flat Cotton Towel.
3. Lay Out The Cooked and Drained Dough Pieces on a Long Sheet of Wax Paper.
4. Spoon 2 Tablespoons of Filling onto each Dough Piece.
5. Take the Two Sides and Pinch Together like a Pie Crust. Once Edges are Sealed, Pinch Ends The Same Way. Pinching is an Attractive and Great Way to Seal.
6. In a Deep Baking Dish, Pour 1 Cup of Warm Sauce. Arrange The Filled & Sealed Pasta in The Sauce. (Line Up Carefully, So Each Pasta Does Not Touch). Pour More Warm Sauce Across The Top to Cover Well.
7. Sprinkle Top of The Sauce with Grated Parmesan Cheese.
8. Seal The Pan Airtight with Foil.
9. Bake in a Preheated 325 Degree Oven for 15~20 Minutes. Remove The Foil, Just Prior to Serving.

The Commercial Pasta Cannelloni Manicotti Conchiglie

1. If you do not have time to prepare The Homemade Pastas To Be Filled ~ Then The Commercial Cannelloni, Manicotti, and Conchiglie (Large Pasta Shells) are Just Right to use. Follow Package Cooking Time, and Drain Them of Cooking Water, but Do Not Rinse.
2. Fill Each Commercial Cannelloni and Manicotti with 2 Heaping Tablespoons of the Filling and Each Conchiglie (Large Shell) with 1 Heaping Tablespoon of Filling ~ The Ricotta Cheese & Spinach Filling, Or ~ The Meat & Spinach Filling.
3. Also, Use The Sauce of your Choice ~ We suggest either White Cream Sauce or Red Cream Sauce Supreme.
4. Follow Steps # 6 through # 9 Above to Bake. Now, you can "Quickly" have a Sensational Pasta Dish! Enjoy!

Pasta Tips ~ Cooking, Filling & Serving

**The
Mama Lena's
Golden Ravioli**

Mama Lena's Golden Ravioli Recipe is a Very Different and Delightful Recipe. The Ravioli are Pan~Fried to a Light Golden Brown, and called The Golden Ravioli!

1. *For a Lighter Fare, Fill with The Ricotta Cheese Filling. Serve with Mama Lena's Basic Tomato Sauce*
2. *For a Bolder Fare, Fill with The Meat & Spinach Filling. Serve with Mama Lena's Tomato & Meat Sauce.*

**Golden Ravioli
~ Shape & Cut ~**

1. *Shape & Cut The Ravioli. as in Homemade Pasta Dough Recipe ~ To ~ 10" Long x 2" Wide Dough Strips.*
2. *Lay The Dough Strips Side by Side on a Floured Counter. Starting About 1" from The End Edge, Evenly Place 1 Teaspoon of Filling, About 1" Apart, and That should Yield 4 Teaspoons Per Strip.*
3. *Place a Fresh Dough Strip Over Each Strip With Filling, and Cut into Even Squares, About 2" Each.*
4. *Press Each Square Edge Together Gently, Sealing Evenly with a Fork.*
5. *Repeat, Until All Filling & Strips have been made into The Filled & Sealed Ravioli.*
6. *If there is Any Excess Dough, Roll Out Again, and Use It to make More Ravioli.*

**Golden Ravioli
~ Cook & Fry ~**

1. *Bring a Large Pan of Water to a Boil. Add 2 Pinches of Salt. Cook The Ravioli for About 7 Minutes. Drain The Ravioli for 3 Minutes, But Do Not Rinse. (When using Frozen Ravioli, Defrost Before Boiling).*
2. *In a Large Skillet, Heat 1 Cup of Olive Oil to Medium. (Add Extra Oil, As Needed)*
3. *Fry 4~5 Ravioli At A Time. Turn Each Ravioli Once, Until The Ravioli are a Light Golden Brown, for About 2~3 Minutes. Repeat, Until All The Ravioli have been Fried a Light Golden Brown.*
4. *Remove Carefully with a Slotted Spoon. Drain The Golden Ravioli on Paper Towels.*

Serving Suggestion ~ Golden Ravioli

On a Large Heated Decorative Platter, Pour 1 Cup of The Warm Sauce across The Platter. Place The Ravioli over The Sauce. Then, Pour 1~2 Cups of Sauce across The Top of Ravioli. Sprinkle The Ravioli Lightly with Grated Parmesan Cheese, and Garnish with Parsley Sprigs. Serve with our Mama Lena's Italian & Antipasto Supreme Salad & Dressing and some of our Mama Lena's Tomato Cheese Bread. A Lambrusco Wine compliments This Very Delightful Mama Lena's Dish. Mama & Grandma Anna would love to join you for this Delight! Enjoy!

Meat & Spinach Filling for Pastas

Carne Spinaci Stuffato Pastas

Our Meat and Spinach Filling for The Pastas is a Flavorful Blend of Meats, Cheeses, Herbs, Nuts and Wine. Mama and Salvino worked together to enhance Grandma's Basic Recipe for Mama Lena's Guests. This Unique Filling is the result of their loving efforts, and was so very appreciated by our Guests any time we served This Delightfully Tasty Filling in a Pasta Dish! Follow our Easy Instructions on Preparing This Delicious Meat & Spinach Filling and refer to "The Pasta Tips ~ Cooking, Filling & Serving" Section in This Chapter ~ For Pastas & Sauces to use with your Filling. Your family and guests will love this, as our Guests did! Enjoy!

Ingredients   Serves 4~6

The Mixed Meats
1/2 Lb. of Beef (Finely Ground)
1/4 Lb. of Pork (Finely Ground)
1/4 Lb. of Veal (Finely Ground)

The Seasonings
1/4 Cup of Olive Oil
1 Medium Onion (Finely Chopped)
1 Clove of Garlic (Finely Minced)
2 Pinches of Salt
2 Pinches of Pepper
3 Pinches of Parsley
2 Tablespoons of Capers
   (Rinse in Cool Water & Drain)
1/2 Cup of Cream Sherry

The Spinach & Cheese Mixture
2 Cups (1 Lb.) of Fresh Spinach (Finely Chopped)
1 Pinch of Salt
2 Large Eggs (Lightly Beaten)
1/2 Teaspoon of Lemon Peel (Grated)
1 Pinch of Nutmeg
1/4 Cup of Parmesan Cheese (Grated)
1/4 Cup of Romano Cheese (Grated)
1/4 Cup of Pine Nuts

1/2 Cup of Mama Lena's Bread Crumbs
   (Italian Seasoned) (Add A Little At Time)
   (See Recipe ~ Chapter Ten)

98

Preparation ~ Meat & Spinach Filling

**The
Mixed Meats &
Seasonings**

1. *In a Large Skillet, Heat The Olive Oil on Medium.
    Saute Onions for 3 Minutes, Until Transparent.
    Add The Garlic, and Saute for 1 Minute More.*
2. *Add The Ground Meat Mix to The Onions and Garlic.
    Cook Meat, Until Evenly Browned, About 3~4 Minutes.*
3. *Pour The Browned Meat, Onion & Garlic into a Strainer,
    and Drain Off The Olive Oil. Discard The Oil.*
4. *Wipe Empty Skillet of Excess Oil with Paper Towels.
    (Do Not Wash The Skillet).*
5. *Return The Same Skillet to Medium Heat, and
    Add The Drained Meat, Onion and Garlic.
    Season with Salt, Pepper, Parsley, Capers, and
    The Cream Sherry. Stir Together Well.*
6. *Cover Skillet. Simmer Meat & Seasonings for 10 Minutes.*
7. *Remove The Skillet from Heat. Set Aside.*

**The
Spinach & Cheese
Mixture**

1. *Fill a Large Pot (8 Qt.) to One~Half with Water.
    Bring Water and 1 Pinch of Salt to a Boil.
    Add, The Cleaned Spinach Leaves to Boiling Water.*
2. *Cover The Pot. Reduce Heat to Medium, and
    Cook The Spinach for 5 Minutes.*
3. *Drain Spinach in Colander and Cool. Finely Chop Spinach.*
4. *In Large Bowl, Place The Chopped Spinach, and
    Add Lightly Beaten Eggs. Mix Together.*
5. *Sprinkle Lemon Peel, Nutmeg, Parmesan and Romano
    Cheese and Pine Nuts Across Spinach & Eggs Mixture.
    Mix All Together Very Well.*

**The
Meat & Spinach Fillings
~ Combine ~**

1. *Again, Drain Off Any Liquid from The Meat Mixture in
    a Colander or Large Strainer.*
2. *Add Meat & Seasonings Mix ~To~ Spinach & Cheese Mix.
    Start to Blend Together Gently with a Wooden Spoon.*
3. *Add The Bread Crumbs to The Entire Mixture,
    A Little At A Time. Blend, Until Mixture is Just Firm.
    (You May Not Need To Use All The Bread Crumbs).*

Serving Suggestion

*Serve This Delicious Meat & Spinach Filling with your Favorite Pasta. (The Pastas & Sauces
are outlined in Pasta Tips Section). Accompany your Pasta with the Meat & Spinach Filling
with our Italian & Antipasto Salad & Dressing Supreme, warm Hot Cheese Bread and a Nice
Red Wine. Serve as an Entree or Side Dish to a Mama Lena's Entree ~ Delicious Both Ways!
Sweetly Finish with Mama's Biscotti and Coffee. You will be Very Delighted! Enjoy!*

Ricotta Cheese & Spinach Filling for Pastas

Rekota Spinaci Stuffato Pastas

Our Ricotta Cheese & Spinach Filling is our Lighter~Textured, Lightly Rich and Lovely, Filling for Cannelloni, Manicotti, Lasagna, Ravioli & Shells. It makes a Very Light and Lovely Entree for any Dinner Party. Many Guests favored This Light Filling with our Mama Lena's Homemade Pasta, just because of that Lightness of the Dish. This Filling is so Light, that it also makes it perfect to serve your Filled Pasta as a Side Dish and still have a Main Entree with your Dinner for your guests. Our Guests loved This Filling any way and any time we served it. Anyway you serve it, it will be a Special Treat!   Enjoy!

Ingredients   Serves 4~6

The Ricotta Cheese Mixture	2	**Cups (1 Lb.) of Fresh Ricotta Cheese** (Purchase Fresh Ricotta at The Deli Counter)
	2	**Pinches of Salt**
	2	**Pinches of Pepper**
	3	**Pinches of Parsley**
	1	**Pinch of Mint**
	2	**Eggs (Large) (Lightly Beaten with The Sugar)**
	3	**Pinches of Sugar (Granulated)**
	1/2	**Cup of Parmesan Cheese (Grated)**
	1/2	**Cup of Romano Cheese (Grated)**
	1/4	**Cup of Pine Nuts**
The Fresh Spinach	2	**Cups (1 Lb.) of Fresh Spinach (Finely Chopped)**
	1	**Pinch of Salt**
The Bread Crumbs	1/2	**Cup of Mama Lena's Bread Crumbs** (Italian Seasoned) (See Recipe ~ Chapter Ten) (Add a Little at a Time)

Preparation ~ Ricotta Cheese & Spinach Filling

The
Fresh Spinach
~ Prepare ~

1. **Fill a Large Pan (8 Qt.) to One~Half with Water, and**
   Bring Water and 1 Pinch of Salt to a Boil.

2. **Add The Washed & Cleaned Spinach Leaves (Whole)**
   to the Boiling Water.

3. **Cover Pan. Reduce The Heat to Medium, and**
   Cook Spinach for 5 Minutes.

4. **Drain The Spinach in a Colander, and Let It Cool.**

5. **Finely Chop The Cooled Spinach.**

The
Cheese Mixture
~ Prepare ~

1. **Drain Excess Liquid from The Ricotta Cheese before Use.**

2. **In a Large Bowl and with a Wooden Spoon,**
   Add The Ricotta Cheese, The Salt, Pepper,
   Parsley and Mint. Mix, Until Well Blended.

3. **In a Small Bowl, Place 2 Eggs and 3 Pinches of Sugar.**
   Lightly Beat The Eggs and The Sugar Together.
   Then, Gently Blend Into The Ricotta and The Spices.

4. **Add The Parmesan Cheese and The Romano Cheese to**
   The Mixture. Blend In Very Well.

5. **Then, Add The Pine Nuts. Gently Blend Into The Mixture.**

The Filling
~ Combine ~

1. **Now, Add The Chopped Spinach to The**
   Prepared Cheese Mixture. Blend Together Well.

2. **Start Adding Bread Crumbs , A Little At A Time.**
   Blend Them In, Until Mixture Becomes Just Firm.
   (You May Not Need To Use All The Bread Crumbs).

Serving Suggestion

The Ricotta Cheese and Spinach Filling is now Lightly Firm and Ready to be used to either Stuff or Layer The Homemade, or The Commercial Pasta, as you prefer. Serve your Filled Pasta as a Side Dish or as an Entree. Accompany your Lightly Filled Pasta with our Appetizer ~ Eggplant, Prosciutto & Mozzarella Rolls ~ and a Lettuce & Tomato Salad with Anchovy & Capers Dressing and Herbs & Spices Bread. A Lovely White or Rose Wine will perfectly compliment. Finish Sweetly with Mama's Cookies & Coffee! Enjoy!

Pasta Con Sarde
Original "Old~Fashioned" Recipe
Finnocchio Sarde Pasta

Mama, and her Mother before her, prepared The Pasta Con Sarde Pasta only once a year, for the Feast of St.Joseph, March 19th, which is a very honored event for Italian people. At the Restaurant, we initially served this as a Side~Dish. However, our Guests loved the dish so much, that we changed it to an Entree, and prepared it at least once a month for over 14 years. In sharing Grandma Anna's unique recipe, which is well over 200 years old, we do hope it becomes very special to you and yours for many years, too! We present Two Ways to prepare Finnochio Sarde ~ "Old~Fashioned" or "Quick" Styles. Both Recipes produce Excellent Results. Serve over our Homemade Vermicelli Pasta, or serve it on the "Traditional" St. Joseph Pasta, Bucatini. You are going to love this Recipe! Enjoy!

Ingredients   Serves 4~6

The Fresh Fennel	1	Lb. of Fresh Fennel Bulb (Chop into Pieces)
	1	Pinch of Salt
The Marinade	1/2	Cup of Raisins (White and Seedless)
	2	Tablespoons of Capers (Whole) (Rinse in Cool Water in a Strainer)
	1/4	Cup of Cream Sherry
The Sardines & Tomatoes	1	Large Onion (Finely Chopped)
	1/2	Cup of Olive Oil
	2	Cups (1 Lb.) of Fresh Sardines (Chop into Pieces) (Purchase Fresh, Trimmed and De~boned) ~ **OR** ~
	2	Cans of Sardines (3~1/2 Oz. Each)
	6	Ripe Tomatoes (Medium~Size) (Peeled, Seeded and Diced)
	2	Pinches of Salt
	2	Pinches of Pepper
	3	Pinches of Basil (Fresh, Finely Chopped)
	4	Pinches of Sugar (Granulated)
The Toasted Topping	1/4	Lb. of Butter (Sweet & Unsalted)
	1/2	Cup of Pine Nuts
	1/4	Cup of Romano Cheese (Grated)
	1/4	Cup of Mama Lena's Bread Crumbs (Italian Seasoned) (See Recipe ~ Chapter Ten) (Serve Toasted)
The Pasta	1	Lb. of Mama Lena's Homemade Vermicelli (See Recipe ~ Chapter Four) ~ **OR** ~
	1	Lb. of Bucatini # 6 Style ~ The "Traditional" (A Commercial Pasta ~ Purchase at Italian Store)
	2	Pinches of Salt
	2	Tablespoons of Olive Oil

Preparation ~ Pasta Con Sarde ~ Original "Old~Fashioned" Recipe

The Fresh Fennel
~ Prepare ~

1. Peel and Discard The Outer Part of The Bulb, Getting to The Heart of Bulb. Peel The Heart Leaves Apart.
2. Fill a Large Saucepan (8 Qt.) with 6 Qt. of Water and 1 Pinch of Salt, and Bring to a Boil.
3. Add The Fennel Leaves to The Boiling Water. Reduce Heat to Medium. Cover Pan. Cook 15 Minutes.
4. Drain in Colander. *(Save The Fennel Water to use with The Tomatoes, and To Cook The Pasta Later).
5. Chop The Cooked and Cooled Fennel Leaves into Very Small Pieces. Place in a Bowl and Set Aside.

The
Sherry Marinade

1. Mix The White Raisins, Capers & Cream Sherry in a Bowl.
2. Cover Bowl with Plastic. Marinate for 30 Minutes.

The
Sardines & Tomatoes
~ Prepare ~

1. In a Large Skillet, Heat The Olive Oil to Medium, and Saute The Onions for About 3 Minutes.
2. Add The Sardines to The Onions. Saute for 4 Minutes.
3. Add The Tomatoes, Salt, Pepper, Basil and Sugar, and 1 Cup of Fennel Water (Saved)* Stir Well. Cover Pan. Cook 25 Minutes on Medium. Stir Often.
4. Add The Chopped Fennel and The Marinade of Cream Sherry, Capers and White Raisins. Reduce Heat. Cover Pan and Cook for 15 Minutes. Stir Often.
5. Remove Pan from Heat. Keep Covered. Let Mixture Settle.

The
Toasted Topping
~ Prepare ~

1. In a Large Skillet, Melt The Butter on Medium Heat.
2. Add The Bread Crumbs and The Pine Nuts To The Butter. Quickly Stir Bread Crumbs with a Wooden Spoon To Toast Well, but Not Burn ~ About 2 to 3 Minutes.
3. Turn Off Heat. Immediately Remove Pan from Heat. Cool The Toasted Bread Crumbs & Pine Nuts.

The
Fennel~Water Pasta
~ Cooking ~

4. Once Cooled, Add The Romano Cheese. Blend Well.

1. Bring The Fennel Water, you saved, to a Boil. Add 2 Tablespoons of Olive Oil & 2 Pinches of Salt. Cook The Homemade Pasta ~ 8 Minutes. Cook The Bucatini #6 Pasta ~ 12 Minutes.
2. Drain The Pasta, But Do Not Rinse with Water.

Serving Suggestion

Heat a Large Oval Serving Dish. Pour 1 Cup of Warm Sauce. Place The Pasta and 1 Cup More of Warm Sauce. Toss Gently. Sprinkle The Toasted Bread Crumb Mixture Evenly Across The Top of The Pasta and Sauce. Pasta Con Sarde is Ready to Serve! Accompany Pasta with our Italian & Antipasto Supreme Salad & Dressing and Italian Bread. Chianti Wine compliments! Sweetly Finish with Mama Lena's Sweet Cream Cannoli for A True Feast Day Dinner! Enjoy!

Pasta Con Sarde
New "Quick" Recipe

Finnochio Sarde Pasta

Perhaps, you do not have the time to prepare this Superb Dish the " Traditional" Way, as in the Original "Old~Fashioned" Recipe. But, we really do want you to experience this Family Treasure so we have prepared this New "Quick" Recipe for you which allows you~ To Prepare This Dish "Quickly," and still have The Exquisite Effects of The Original Recipe! We hope This Choice is Helpful to You! We are so thrilled with This Feast Day Dish from Grandma Anna's Day, that we had to make it possible for You to try it, too!   Enjoy!

Ingredients   Serves 4~6

The		
Marinade	1/4	Cup of Raisins (White and Seedless)
	2	Tablespoons of Capers (Whole)
		(Rinse in Strainer in Cool Water)
	1/4	Cup of Cream Sherry
The		
Tomato Sauce	6	Cups of Mama Lena's Basic Tomato Sauce
		(Double The "Quick" Recipe)
		(See Recipe ~ Chapter Five)
Canned,	1	Can of Finocchio Con Sarde Condiment (8~1/2 Oz.)
Imported Sardines		
In Fennel		(Purchase this at an Italian Store ~ It will have
		Fennel, Sardines, and Seasonings all Condensed.
		But you will still need Extra Capers and Raisins
		to Marinate, and also The Pine Nuts, as Listed)
The		
Toasted Topping	1/4	Lb. of Butter (Sweet & Unsalted)
	1/4	Cup of Pine Nuts (Whole)
	1/4	Cup of Romano Cheese (Grated)
	3/4	Cup of Mama Lena's Bread Crumbs (Italian Seasoned)
		(See Recipe ~ Chapter Ten) (For Pan Toasting)
The Pasta	1	Lb. of Mama Lena's Homemade Vermicelli
		(See Recipe ~ Chapter Four) ~ <u>OR</u> ~
	1	Lb. of The "Traditional" St. Joseph Pasta,
		Bucatini # 6 ~ Commercial Pasta
	2	Pinches of Salt
	2	Tablespoons of Olive Oil

Preparation ~ Pasta Con Sarde ~ New "Quick" Recipe

The
Sherry Marinade

1. In a Medium Bowl, Mix The White Raisins, The Capers and The Cream Sherry.
2. Cover with Plastic. Allow To Marinate for 30 Minutes.

The Fennel,
Sardines, Tomatoes
& Seasonings

1. Prepare Mama Lena's "Quick" Basic Tomato Sauce. (You Must Double Recipe ~ So Use an 8 Qt. Pan)
2. Place The Contents of The Canned Finocchio Sarde into a Bowl. Mash The Contents with a Fork.
3. Add The Mashed Finocchio Sarde to The Tomato Sauce. Stir In Well. Cover Pan. Stir Often, and Continue to Cook on Medium for 10 Minutes More.
4. Add The Marinade of Cream Sherry, The White Raisins and The Capers, and Stir In Well. Cover Pan. Reduce Heat. Simmer for 15 Minutes, Stirring Often.
5. Turn Heat Off and Remove Pan. Keep Pan Covered, Allowing The Mixture time for The Texture to Settle.

The
Toasted Topping

1. In a Large Skillet, Melt The Butter on Medium Heat.
2. Add The Bread Crumbs and The Pine Nuts. With a Wooden Spoon, Keep Moving Them Quickly, Toasting Nicely, But Not Burning, for 2~3 Minutes.
3. Turn Off Heat, Remove Pan, and Cool The Toasted Bread Crumbs and Pine Nuts.
4. Once Cooled, Add The Romano Cheese, and Blend Well.

The
Pasta Cooking

1. Fill an 8 Qt. Pan with 6 Qt. of Water & 2 Pinches of Salt. Bring Water to a Boil. Add 2 Tablespoons of Olive Oil.
2. Pasta Cooking for Homemade Vermicelli ~ 8 Minutes, Or Cook Commercial Bucatini # 6 Pasta ~ 12 Minutes.
3. Drain The Pasta, But Do Not Rinse.

Serving Suggestion

Heat a Large Oval Pasta Bowl. Pour 1 Cup of Warm Sauce first, then The Pasta and then 1 Cup More of Sauce. Toss Gently Together. Now, Sprinkle The Top with The Toasted Bread Crumbs, Pine Nuts & Cheese Mixture. Place Extra Sauce in a Hot Gravy Bowl. Serve with our Italian & Antipasto Salad Supreme, and our warm Italian Bread. The Pasta Mama personally preferred was her own Homemade Vermicelli, but at the Restaurant we served our Guests the "Traditional" Bucatini #6 Pasta like they always serve at the St. Joseph's Feast. Whichever Pasta you use ~ Vermicelli or Bucatini ~ and whichever Recipe you use, the Old Fashioned or the Quick Style, we know you will feel like you're at The Feast enjoying the St. Joseph's Table with Mama and Family! Enjoy!

~ Chapter Five ~
The Sauces

Pages 107 ~ 127

"Large" Basic ~ Tomato Sauce

Grande Salsa Pomodoro ala Madonna

This is our "Large" Recipe of Mama Lena's Basic Tomato Sauce. The Best Use of This Quantity is for Large Dinners and for Parties of 30 Guests. And, the Other Best Use is to Freeze Sauce in Separate Containers to be used for Small or Medium Dinner Parties at a Later Date. We prefer to make This Large Recipe, Freeze It, and Have It Available Any Time we may need Tomato Sauce for a Recipe. At Mama Lena's, we very often used our Basic Tomato Sauce in Appetizers, Pastas, or Baked in Chicken, Fish and Meat Entrees. This Sauce is also used for our very special Mama Lena's Tomato Cheese Bread Recipe! You will find many uses for Mama Lena's Delicious Basic Sauce, too!   Enjoy!

Ingredients   **Serves a Party of 30, or
                                                        Freeze for Smaller Uses**

**The
Tomatoes**   5   Lbs. of Fresh Ripe Tomatoes
                    (Seeded and Finely Crushed)   ~ <u>OR</u> ~

                3   Cans of Plum Tomatoes, Crushed in Puree
                    (Large Cans ~ 28 Oz. Size Each Can)

**The
Sauce Mixture** 1   Medium Can (12 Oz.) of Tomato Paste
                 3   Medium Cans of Hot Water
                     (12 Oz. Each Can ~ 36 Oz. Total)

                1/4 Cup of Olive Oil
                 1   Lb. of White Onions (Finely Chopped)
                 2   Cloves of Garlic (Sliced Thin)

**The
Seasonings**   1   Tablespoon of Salt
                 1   Teaspoon of Pepper

                 3   Tablespoons of Parsley
                 2   Tablespoons of Basil
                 3   Tablespoons of Oregano
                 2   Tablespoons of Sugar (Granulated)

                 1   Bay Leaf (Dried) For Flavor Only
                     (Cook The Bay Leaf with The Sauce, and Then
                     Discard Leaf Immediately after Sauce is Cooked).

Preparation ~ "Large" Basic ~ Tomato Sauce

Garlic & Onions
~ Saute ~

1. *In a Large Skillet, Heat The Olive Oil to Medium.*
   Saute Garlic for 1~2 Minutes, Until Light Brown.
   Remove Garlic from Olive Oil. Discard The Garlic.
2. *Place The Chopped Onions into The Olive Oil, and*
   Saute Until Transparent, About 4~5 Minutes.
   Turn Oil Off.
3. *Pour The Garlic~flavored Olive Oil and Onions into a*
   Large Strainer. Save Oil to Later Make Garlic Bread.
   Save The Onions to Use in The Sauce.

The Tomato Sauce
~ Mixing ~

1. *In a Large Pot, Place The Fresh Ripe Tomatoes ~ OR ~*
   Place 3 Cans of Plum Tomatoes, Crushed in Puree.
2. *Add 1 Can of Tomato Paste and 3 Cans of Hot Water*
   to your Fresh, Or Canned Tomatoes. Mix Well.
3. *Stir In The Salt, Pepper, Parsley, Basil, Oregano*
   and Sugar. Mix In Well.
4. *Add The Sauteed Onions, and Stir In Very Well.*
5. *Lastly, Add The Bay Leaf to The Top of The Sauce.*

The Tomato Sauce
~ Cooking ~

1. **Stir Frequently.* It's Very Important to Stir Sauce Often!*
   Stir During The Entire Cooking, To Be Certain
   That The Sauce Does Not Settle or Burn.
2. *Cover The Pot of Sauce Mixture. Heat on Medium~High.*
   Bring The Sauce to a Full Boil.
3. *Once Sauce has reached a Full Boil, About 10~15 Minutes,*
   Stir The Sauce Very Well Again, and
   Lower Heat to Medium~Low. Cover Pan Again.
4. *Sauce should be Cooking with a Gentle Rolling Action*
   Across The Top of The Sauce. Cover Pan Again.
   Cook This Way for 50 Minutes. * Stir Frequently.*
5. *After 50 Minutes, Uncover The Pan. Cook Sauce Uncovered*
   for 30 Minutes More, so Sauce will Thicken Properly.
   * Stir Frequently ~ During This Entire Time *
6. *Turn Off Heat. Let Sauce Cool Completely, About 1 Hour.*
   Remove and Discard The Bay Leaf.
7. *Once The Sauce has Cooled Properly, Scoop The Sauce*
   Out and Into Storage Containers for Future Use.
8. **It's Always Best to Cook The Large Basic Sauce Recipe*
   a Day or So Ahead of Time, for Two Reasons ~
   The Sauce Tastes Better, As It Settles, And
   It's Ready When You Are Ready To Use It! * Enjoy!

"Quick" Basic ~ Tomato Sauce

Presto Salsa Pomodoro ala Madonna

"Quick" Basic Tomato Sauce is Mama Lena's Delightfully Delicious Basic Tomato Sauce, but in a Recipe for 4~6 Servings for Regular Dinners. For Larger Parties, use our "Large" Basic Recipe ~ See the previous pages. We also use the "Quick" Sauce on our Pasta, Chicken, Fish & Meat Entrees, depending on the Quantity we need. And, of course, Mama Lena's Tomato Cheese Bread Recipe, one of our Restaurant's most special favorites, is made with This Sauce, too! You will use This Delightful Recipe often! Enjoy!

Ingredients   Serves 4~6

The Tomatoes

2	Lbs. of Fresh Ripe Tomatoes (Finely Crushed and Seeded) ~ <u>OR</u> ~
1	Can of Plum Tomatoes, Crushed in Puree (Large Can ~ 28 Oz. Size Can)
2	Tablespoons of Tomato Paste

The Seasonings

1	Clove of Garlic (Minced)
1	Medium Onion (Finely Chopped)
1/4	Cup of Olive Oil
3	Pinches of Salt
2	Pinches of Pepper
3	Pinches of Parsley
3	Pinches of Basil
3	Pinches of Oregano
3	Pinches of Sugar (Granulated)

Preparation ~ "Quick" Basic ~ Tomato Sauce

1. In a Large Pan (6 Qt.), Heat The Olive Oil to Medium Heat.
2. Add The Onion to The Oil. Saute Onion for 3 Minutes, Until Light Brown.
3. Add Garlic to Pan. Saute The Garlic with Onion for 1 Minute More.
4. Pour Oil, Onion & Garlic into a Strainer. Save Oil to make Garlic Bread.
5. Place The Onion & The Garlic Back into The Pan.
6   Add The Fresh, Crushed and Seeded Tomatoes   ~ OR ~
    Canned Plum Tomatoes. Stir Well. Heat on Medium for 3 Minutes.
7. Add 2 Tablespoons of Tomato Paste. Stir Well, Until Very Smooth.
8. Add The Salt, Pepper, Parsley, Basil, Oregano & Sugar. Stir In Well.
9. Cook Sauce on Medium~High Heat, Until Sauce Comes to a Full Boil.
10. Cover Pan. Lower Heat to Medium. Simmer The Sauce for 20 Minutes.
    (Stir Sauce Often ~ Cover Pan Each Time Until Finished)
11. The "Quick" Sauce Is Ready, When You Are Ready To Use It! Enjoy!

"Meat Style" Basic ~ Tomato Sauce

Salsa Pomodoro Carne

"Meat~Style" Basic Tomato Sauce is Mama Lena's Real Tasty Delicious Sauce ~ A Very Special Sauce that is used to top so many Pasta Dishes! But, It really is Best and Most Especially Delightful the true "Old~Fashioned Way"~ Served on Old~Fashioned Spaghetti! This Sauce was so loved by one of the Chicago Restaurant Writers, she had some Artwork done with Mama dishing up a Large Bowl of Old Fashioned Spaghetti with her Delicious Meat Sauce! We really loved that ~ as Mama really loved That Old~Fashioned Dish! Enjoy!

Ingredients   Serves 4~6

The Meat	1	Lb. of Ground Chuck (Finely Ground) (85% Lean)
	2	Pinches of Salt
	1	Pinch of Pepper
The Tomatoes	1	Lb. of Ripe Tomatoes (Seeded & Finely Crushed) ~ <u>OR</u> ~
	1	Medium Can (15 Oz.) of Plum Tomatoes, Crushed in Puree
	2	Tablespoons of Tomato Paste
	1	Medium Can (15 Oz.) of Water (Hot)
The Seasonings	1	Clove of Garlic (Minced)
	1	Large Onion (Finely Chopped)
	1/4	Cup of Olive Oil
	3	Pinches of Salt
	2	Pinches of Pepper *and* 3 Pinches of Parsley
	3	Pinches of Basil *and* 2 Pinches of Sugar
	3	Pinches of Oregano (Granulated)

Preparation ~ "Meat Style" Basic ~ Tomato Sauce

1. **In an Extra~Large Skillet, Heat The Olive Oil to Medium. and Saute Onions for 3 Minutes. Add Garlic, and Saute for 1 Minute More.**
2. **Season Ground Chuck with Salt & Pepper. Separate Meat with a Fork. Add The Meat to Onions & Garlic. Brown Meat for About 5 Minutes.**
3. **Strain The Meat, Onions and Garlic into a Large Strainer, and Let The Oil drain off. Discard The Oil. Set The Meat Mixture Aside.**
4. **Wipe The Oil from Skillet with a Paper Towel. (Do Not Wash Skillet).**
5. **Pour The Tomatoes (Fresh ~<u>OR</u>~ Canned), Hot Water, Tomato Paste, Salt, Pepper, Parsley, Basil, Oregano, and Sugar into The Skillet. Mix Well. Cover Pan. Cook Sauce on Medium~High for 30 Minutes, Until The Sauce reaches a Full Boil. Stir The Sauce Often.**
6. **Then, Add Sauteed Ground Meat, Onions & Garlic to Sauce. Uncover Pan.**
7. **Cook The Meat Sauce on Medium~Low for 15 Minutes More. Stir Often.**
8. **Turn Off Heat. Let The Sauce Stand and Settle for 10 Minutes. Enjoy!**

Marinara Sauce ~ ala Madonna

Salsa Marinara ala Madonna

Mama Lena's Marinara Sauce is Thick and Tasty. It's a Simply Delightful Sauce to have with any type of Pasta. You will always be satisfied with this little Treasure! Our Guests really loved our Marinara Sauce whenever it was served. At Mama Lena's, we always served an extra helping of one of our Italian Breads, as Guests just could not leave any of This Delicious Sauce after the Pasta was finished! It's a Very Special Treat! Enjoy!

Ingredients   Serves 4~6

**The
Tomatoes**

2	Lbs. of Fresh Ripe Tomatoes (Seeded & Finely Chopped) ~ OR ~
1	Can of Plum Tomatoes, Crushed in Puree (Large Size ~ 28 Oz.) (Drained of All Juice)
2	Tablespoons of Tomato Paste

**The
Seasonings**

1/4	Cup of Olive Oil
1	Large White Onion (Finely Chopped)
2	Cloves of Garlic (Cut into Quarters)
2	Tablespoons of Anchovy Paste
3	Pinches of Salt
2	Pinches of Pepper
2	Pinches of Oregano
2	Pinches of Parsley
2	Pinches of Sugar
1	Pinch of Mint

Preparation ~ Marinara Sauce ala Madonna

1. **In a Large Skillet, Heat The Olive Oil to Medium.
   Saute The Garlic to Light Brown, About 1~2 Minutes.
   Remove Garlic from The Oil, and Discard The Garlic.**
2. **Add The Chopped Onions to The Oil. Saute, Until Transparent,
   About 3~4 Minutes. Drain Onions in a Strainer. Discard Oil.**
3. **To The Skillet, Add The Anchovy Paste. Stir In Well, Until Smooth.**
4. **Now, Add in The Fresh ~ OR ~ Canned Tomatoes, and The Onions.
   Cook on Medium~High, Until Sauce Boils, About 15 Minutes.**
5. **Add The Salt, Pepper, Oregano, Parsley, Sugar, and Mint.
   Stir The Seasonings into Tomatoes, Onions & Anchovy Paste.**
6. **Lower Heat and Cover Pan. Simmer The Sauce for 15 Minutes More.
   Stir Often. Serve With 1 Lb. of Your Favorite Pasta! Enjoy!**

A Tribute to The Tomato

Pomodoro Honore

Mama Lena's Italian Kitchen cooked with Fresh Tomatoes for over 14 Years. But with the Seasons changing and the Market always changing, too, we turned to the Best Friend any restaurant could have ~ Stanislaus Food Products and The Dino Cortopassi Family. They were there for us on our first day of business and their wonderful products helped us through over 14 years of our restaurant business. They continued to help us for many years after in our catering business to put out our great food with their Fine Tomato Line.

Our Family grew Tomatoes in Sicily for hundreds of years ever since the Tomato arrived in Sicily. We have a great respect for the Tomato and all the wonderful dishes that come from this delicious item. As Children, we would eat a Tomato the way most children eat an Apple! And in Sicily, we were told by Grandma, the Tomato is called "Golden Apple" ~ It receives Praise & Respect!

Grandma Anna, Mama Lena and Salvino just could not do without the Versatile Tomato! This Gem ~ The Tomato ~ Is responsible for many of Our Very Delectable Pasta Sauces, Our Salad Recipes, Our Entree Gravies, and Our Delicious Breads.

Our Tribute is not only to The Tomato, but it's also to Dino Cortopassi & Family for the Fine, Superior Products that have helped us maintain Excellence and Consistency and a Level of Unique Tastes in Our Treasured Recipes for so many years.

We favor these products ~ "Full~Red ®," "Tomato Magic ®, " and, of course, "7/11 ®" ~ for Our Sauces, but the Stanislaus Food Products line is very comprehensive, so you may wish to explore their other Great Tomato Products. We most gratefully acknowledge this Very Fine Company ~ Stanislaus Food Products ~ owned and run by a Very Fine Family ~ for their Quality, Consistency and Integrity all these Years ~ You are a True Tribute to the Restaurant Profession and to The Grand Tomato! We Thank You Very Much, Dino ~ Keep Up The Great Work!

"Velvet Cloud" ~ *Tomato Sauce*

Velluto Nuvola Pomodoro

This Mama Lena's Treasure ~ Our Velvet Cloud Tomato Sauce ~ is well worth preparing! It was created by Salvino to honor Margo as his Bride! Salvino liked to serve This Very Special Sauce on Farfalle Butterfly Pasta, a delicious and pretty pasta ~ Margo's favorite! At the Restaurant, we always prepared This Beautiful Sauce for Special Dates, such as Valentines and Sweetest Days! It's our Tribute to Love, but very lovingly Margo says that This Special Treasure is truly A Tribute to Salvino's Smooth, Velvety~Textured Sauces! This is a True Romantic Treasure!   Enjoy!

Ingredients   Serves 6~8

The Tomatoes	3	Lbs. of Fresh Ripe Tomatoes (Seeded & Finely Chopped) ~ **OR** ~
	2	Cans of Plum Tomatoes, Crushed in Puree (Large Cans ~ 28 Oz. ~ Each)
	2	Tomato Paste (Medium Cans ~ 12 Oz. ~ Each)
	2	Cans of Hot Water (Medium Cans ~ 12 Oz. ~ Each)
The Seasonings	1/4	Cup of Olive Oil
	1	Large White Onion (Finely Chopped)
	1	Clove of Fresh Garlic (Minced)
	3	Pinches of Salt
	2	Pinches of Pepper
	3	Pinches of Sugar (Granulated)
	3	Pinches of Parsley
	3	Pinches of Oregano
	3	Pinches of Basil
	1	Bay Leaf (For Flavor ~ Discard After Cooking Sauce)
	1	Can of Garbanzo Beans (12 Oz. Can) (Add Last)
The " Velvet Cloud " Mixture	1	Lb. of Fresh Ricotta Cheese
	2	Large Eggs (Lightly Beaten)
	1	Pinch of Sugar (Granulated)
	1	Pinch of Salt
	1	Pinch of Pepper
	1	Pinch of Mint
The Farfalle Pasta	1	Lb. of Farfalle Butterfly Pasta (Medium~Size Farfalle) (Follow Cooking Instructions on the Package)
The Garnish	1/4	Bunch of Fresh Parsley
	1/4	Cup of Romano Cheese (Grated)

Preparation ~ "Velvet Cloud" ~ Tomato Sauce

The
Tomato Sauce

1. *In a Large Pan (8 Qt.), Heat The Olive Oil to Medium.*
   Saute Onions, Until Transparent, 3~4 Minutes.
2. *Add The Garlic. Saute Onions & Garlic for 1 Minute More.*
3. *Pour The Oil, Onions & Garlic into a Large Strainer.*
   Save The Oil to later make your Garlic Bread.
   Put The Onions and The Garlic Back into The Pan.
4. *Add The Fresh Tomatoes ~OR~ The Canned Tomatoes,*
   The Tomato Paste and Hot Water. Mix Together Well.
5. *Add The Salt, Pepper, Sugar, Parsley, Oregano, Basil,*
   and The Bay Leaf. Stir In Well.
6. *Cover Pan. On Medium~High for About 15 Minutes.*
   Cook Sauce, Bringing to a Full Boil. Stir Frequently.
7. *Now, Reduce Heat to Medium. Now, Uncover The Pan.*
   Let Sauce Cook with a Gentle, Rolling Action
   Across Top of Sauce for 35 Minutes. Stir Often.
8. *Reduce Heat Again to Medium~Low. Simmer The Sauce,*
   Cook, Uncovered, for 25 Minutes More. Stir Often.

The
"Velvet Cloud"
Mixture

1. *In a Large Bowl, Combine The Fresh Ricotta Cheese,*
   2 Large & Lightly Beaten Eggs, and The Sugar,
   Salt, Pepper, and Mint. Blend Together Well.
2. *Slowly, Add Mixture to The Tomato Sauce. Stir In Well.*
3. *Cook The Sauce on Medium~High Again, About 5 Minutes.*
   (Sauce should come to a Full Boil Again).
4. *Keep Pan Uncovered. Cook 20 Minutes More on Medium.*
5. *Turn Off Sauce. Remove The Bay Leaf and Discard It.*
6. *Drain The Garbanzo Beans. Stir Beans into The Sauce.*
7. *Cover The Pan. Let The Sauce Settle for 10 Minutes.*

The
Farfalle Pasta

1. *Cook The Farfalle Pasta, by The Package Instruction.*
   (Cook This Pasta to a Softer Texture, Not Al Dente).
2. *Strain The Cooked Pasta in a Large Colander,*
   But Do Not Rinse The Pasta.

Serving Suggestions

Warm a Deep Decorative Platter. Pour 1 Cup of Velvet Cloud Sauce Across The Platter. Then, Place Farfalle Butterfly Pasta on Top of The Sauce. Pour 1 Cup More of The Sauce over Top of Pasta. Toss Gently. Lightly Sprinkle Romano Cheese over Top of The Pasta. Garnish around The Platter with Parsley Sprigs. Serve with our Tomato Cheese Bread, our Artichoke & Bibb Lettuce Salad and a Chilled Bottle of White or Rose' Dinner Wine, to compliment This Very Delicate Sauce! For a Very Sweet Finish to a Sweet Meal, serve our Sweet Cannoli and Cappuccino! A Sweet Dinner ~ just the way Salvino & Margo love it ! May This Very Special Sauce bring Romance to Your Table, too!   Enjoy!

White Clam Sauce, Mushrooms & Pine Nuts

Bianco Vongole Pinola Salsa

Mama Lena and Papa Frank had both been raised having fresh seafood so they always used Fresh Clams in this recipe. At our Restaurant, we always used Fresh Clams also. But, it's very acceptable to use the Canned Clams. We are very proud of This Sauce and know it will taste great whether you are using the Fresh Clams or the Canned Clams. This Mama Lena's Treasure was one highly regarded by our Guests. Also, it was one of Mama's most favorite dishes! She really looked forward to this and you will, too! Enjoy!

Ingredients   Serves 4~6

The Clams **Fresh or Canned**	2	**Lbs. of Fresh Cherrystone Clams** **(In their Shells) ~ OR ~**
	2	**Cans of Whole Baby Clams in Juice (8 Oz. Each)**
The **White Clam Sauce**	1/2	**Cup of Olive Oil**
	1	**Large White Onion (Finely Chopped)**
	3	**Cloves of Garlic (Minced)**
	1/2	**Cup of Dry White Wine**
	1/2	**Cup of Water**
	1/2	**Cup of Clam Juice from Canned Clams ~OR ~** **(When Using The Fresh Clams, Buy a** **Small Can (4 Oz.) of Plain Clam Juice)**
	1	**Pinch of Salt**
	1	**Pinch of White Pepper**
	1	**Pinch of Cayenne Pepper**
	2	**Pinches of Parsley**
	2	**Pinches of Oregano**
	1	**Lb. of Mushrooms (Medium~Size Slices)**
	1/4	**Lb. of Large Green Olives (Pitted and Slivered)**
	1/8	**Cup of Olive Oil**
	1	**Tablespoon of Butter**
	1/2	**Cup of Pine Nuts (Add Last)**
The **Linguine Pasta**	1	**Lb. of Linguine Pasta (Cooked Firm ~ Al Dente)** **(Follow Cooking Instructions on the Package)**
The Garnish	1/4	**Bunch of Fresh Parsley**
	1/4	**Cup of Romano Cheese (Grated)**

Preparation ~ White Clam Sauce, Mushrooms & Pine Nuts

The Clams
~ Fresh or Canned ~

1. Soak The Fresh Clams Submerged in Cold Water,
   For About 1 Hour to Completely Remove Grit.
2. Scrub Clam Shells with a Stiff Brush under Cold
   Running Water, Until Shells are Clean and Shiny.
3. Open The Clam Shells. Save Clam Juice to Add to Sauce.
4. Chop The Clams. Set Aside to Later Add to The Sauce.
5. If Using The Canned Clams, Strain The Clam Juice.
   Use The "Clam Juice" in The Sauce Later.
   And, Add "Clams" to The Sauce in The Final Simmer.

The White Clam
Sauce

1. In Extra~Large Skillet, Heat Olive Oil on Medium Heat.
2. Saute The Onions, Until Transparent, About 3 Minutes.
3. Add Garlic. Saute Onions & Garlic for 1 Minute More.
4. Add The White Wine, Water, and Clam Juice. Stir In.
5. Add Salt, White Pepper, Cayenne Pepper, Parsley,
   and Oregano. Mix All Well, and Bring to a Boil.
6. Reduce Heat. Cover Pan. Simmer The Sauce 5 Minutes.

Saute Olives &
Mushrooms

1. In a Separate Skillet, Heat 1/8 Cup of Olive Oil
   and 1 Tablespoon of Butter to Medium Heat.
2. Saute The Green Olives and Mushrooms for 3~4 Minutes.
3. Cover The Pan, and Simmer All Again for 5 Minutes More.
4. Then, Add The Green Olives, Mushrooms, Oil & Butter
   To The Clam Sauce Mixture.

Clams & Pine Nuts
~ Add Last ~

1. Add The Fresh Clams and The Pine Nuts to The Sauce.
   Cover Pan. Simmer for 3~5 Minutes.   ~ OR ~
2. If Using Canned Clams, Add Them to The Sauce with
   Pine Nuts. Cover Pan. Simmer for 3~5 Minutes.
3. Serve The Clams Immediately after The Simmering,
   So The Clams will be Served Tender.

Serving Suggestion

On a Deep Heated Platter, Spoon on Half of The Sauce. Place Linguine on Top of Sauce, and Toss Lightly. When using The Fresh Clams, Arrange Clam Shells around The Pasta. With a Slotted Spoon, Place some Clams back into Empty Shells for a Nice Presentation. Then, Spoon on Other Half of The Sauce with Clams over The Pasta. Sprinkle The Dish Lightly with Grated Romano Cheese. Place Parsley Sprigs Nicely around The Clam Shells. ~ OR ~ When using Canned Clams, First Arrange Pasta. Spoon on The Sauce & Clams Over The Pasta. Toss Gently. Garnish Nicely with Romano Cheese & Parsley Sprigs. Accompany with Mama Lena's Caesar Salad Superb and Garlic & Sweet Onion Bread. White Wine will compliment! Try Mama Lena's Sweet Cream Cannoli & Coffee for Dessert! This will now be Your Favorite Pasta & Seafood ~ Just like Mama Lena!   Enjoy!*

Red Clam Sauce, Mushrooms & Pine Nuts

Pomodoro Vongole Pinola Salsa

Our Mama Lena's Red Clam Sauce is a rich tasting sauce, with a thick, smooth texture. The Red Clam Sauce was Grandma and Grandpa's favorite, so we honored them when we would make this one! Now, Try Grandma Anna & Grandpa Matteo's special favorite! See which Clam Sauce is your favorite ~ Or, maybe you'll be like our Guests, who loved "Both"~ our Red Clam Sauce ~ and ~ our White Clam Sauce! We hope so! Enjoy!

Ingredients   Serves 4~6

The Clams **Fresh or Canned**	2	Lbs. of Fresh Cherrystone Clams (In Their Shells) ~ **OR** ~
	2	Cans of Whole Baby Clams in Juice (8 Oz. Each)
The **Red Clam Sauce**	1/2	Cup of Olive Oil
	2	Large White Onions (Finely Chopped)
	4	Cloves of Garlic (Minced)
	1	Can of Plum Tomatoes, Crushed in Puree (Large Can ~ Size 28 Oz.)
	1/2	Cup of Hot Water
	1/2	Cup of Dry Red Wine
	1/2	Cup of Clam Juice from Canned Clams ~ **OR** ~ (When Using Fresh Clams, Purchase a Small Can (4 Oz.) of Plain Clam Juice)
	2	Pinches of Salt
	2	Pinches of White Pepper
	1	Pinch of Cayenne Pepper
	3	Pinches of Parsley
	3	Pinches of Oregano
	1	Lb. of Mushrooms (Medium~Size Slices)
	1/4	Lb. of Large Green Olives (Pitted & Slivered)
	1/8	Cup of Olive Oil
	1	Tablespoon of Butter (Sweet & Lightly Salted)
	1/2	Cup of Pine Nuts
The **Linguine Pasta**	1	Lb. of Linguine Pasta (Cooked Firm ~ Al Dente) (Follow Cooking Instructions on the Package)
The Garnish	1/4	Bunch of Fresh Parsley
	1/4	Cup of Romano Cheese (Grated)

Preparation ~ Red Clam Sauce, Mushrooms & Pine Nuts

The Clams
~ Fresh or Canned ~

1. Soak Fresh Baby Clams Submerged in Cold Water
    for 1 Hour, to Completely Remove The Grit.
2. Scrub Clam Shells with a Stiff Brush under Cold
    Running Water, Until Shells are Clean and Shiny.
3. Open The Clam Shells. Save Clam Juice to Add to Sauce.
4. Chop The Clams. Set Aside to Later Add to The Sauce.
5. If Using Canned Clams, Strain The Clam Juice.
    Use The "Clam Juice" in The Sauce Later.
    And, Add "Clams" to The Sauce in The Final Simmer.

The Red Clam
Sauce

1. In a Large Pan (8 Qt.), Heat The Olive Oil on Medium.
2. Saute The Onions, Until Transparent, About 4 Minutes.
3. Add Garlic. Saute Onions & Garlic for 2 Minutes More.
4. Pour The Onions, Garlic & Oil through a Strainer.
    Discard Oil. Put The Onions & Garlic back into Pan.
5. Add Can of Plum Tomatoes, The Water, The Clam Juice,
    and The Dry Red Wine. Mix Together Well.
6. Add Salt, White Pepper, Cayenne Pepper, Parsley
    and Oregano. Mix Well and Bring to a Boil.
7. Reduce Heat. Cover Pan. Simmer 30 Minutes. Stir Often.

Saute Olives &
Mushrooms

1. Separately ~ In a Large Skillet, Heat 1/8 Cup of
    Olive Oil and 1 Tablespoon of Butter to Medium.
2. Saute The Green Olives and Mushrooms for 3~4 Minutes.
3. Cover Pan. Simmer for 5 Minutes More. Then Strain.
4. Add The Olives & Mushrooms to Sauce. Discard Oil & Butter.

Clams & Pine Nuts
~ Add Last ~

1. Add The Fresh Clams and The Pine Nuts to The Sauce.
    Cover Pan. Simmer for 3~5 Minutes. ~ <u>OR</u> ~
2. If Using Canned Clams, Add Them & Pine Nuts to The Sauce.
    Cover Pan. Simmer for 3~5 Minutes.
3. Serve The Clams Immediately after The Simmering,
    So The Clams will be Served Tender.

Serving Suggestion

On a Deep Heated Platter, Spoon on Half of The Sauce. Place Linguine on Top of Sauce and Toss Together Lightly. When using The Fresh Clams, Arrange Clam Shells around Pasta. With a Slotted Spoon, Place some Clams back into Their Empty Shells for a Nice Presentation. Then, Spoon on The Other Half of The Sauce with Clams over The Pasta. Sprinkle The Dish Lightly with Grated Romano Cheese. Place The Parsley Sprigs Nicely around The Clam Shells. * ~ OR ~ When using Canned Clams, First Arrange Pasta. Spoon on The Sauce and Clams Over The Pasta. Toss Gently. Garnish Nicely with Grated Romano Cheese & Parsley Sprigs.* Serve The Red Clam Sauce Dish with our Antipasto & Italian Supreme Salad & Dressing, Hot Cheese Bread and Soft Red Wine. Anisette & Vanilla Biscotti and Coffee for a Sweet Dessert. Just like Grandma Anna & Grandpa Matteo, you will love This Dish! Enjoy!

Butter, Parsley, Oil & Garlic Sauce

Burro Prezzemolo Con Aglio Salsa

Salvino created This Sauce for a Richer, Smoother Sauce, using Butter and Oil as a Base. Butter Parsley Sauce is perfect on The Farfalle and Rotini Pastas, or as a Topping Sauce on Fish or Veal. This is an Easy Sauce to prepare, but has a great texture and fine flavor! You will find that This Special Sauce is ~ Always a Pleasure to Serve!   Enjoy!

Ingredients   Serves 4~6

The		
Butter & Oil	1/4	Cup of Olive Oil
Sauce	2	Cloves of Garlic (Finely Chopped)
	1/2	Lb. of Butter (Sweet & Lightly Salted)
	1	Pinch of White Pepper
	1	Pinch of Cayenne Pepper
		(Optional ~ If You Prefer Spicy Hot)
	3	Pinches of Dry Parsley ~ <u>OR</u> ~
		(1/4 Cup of Fresh Parsley, Chopped)
	2	Pinches of Dry Mint ~ <u>OR</u> ~
		(1/8 Cup of Fresh Mint, Chopped)
The Pasta	1	Lb. of Farfalle Pasta (Cooked Firm ~ Al Dente)
		(Medium~Size Butterfly Pasta)
		(Follow Cooking Instructions on the Package)
The Garnish	1/4	Bunch of Fresh Parsley
	1/4	Cup of Romano Cheese (Grated)

Preparation ~ Butter, Parsley, Oil & Garlic Sauce

1. **In a Large Skillet, Heat The Olive Oil to Medium.**
   Add The Garlic. Saute Garlic, Until Light Brown, About 1 Minute.
   With a Slotted Spoon, Remove Garlic from Oil.   Discard Garlic.
2. **Add The Butter, White Pepper and Red Pepper, if you prefer it Hot.**
   Mix Into The Garlic~flavored Olive Oil, and
   Cook on Medium Heat, Until The Butter Melts.
3. **Add The Parsley and Mint. Stir In Well. Cook All for 2 Minutes More.**
   Serve This Sauce Immediately, While It is Hot!

Serving Suggestion

Arrange Pasta on a Heated Decorative Platter. Spoon Sauce Across The Top of The Pasta. Toss Very Gently. Sprinkle Lightly with Grated Romano Cheese and Garnish with Parsley Sprigs. Serve with our Artichoke & Bibb Lettuce Salad and Herbs & Spices Bread. A Nice Dry White Wine would be a perfect compliment to This Simply Delightful Sauce!   Enjoy!

Butter & Almond Caper Sauce

Burro al Madorie Capperi Salsa

Mama and Salvino created This Exquisite Sauce especially for Mama Lena's Italian Kitchen, and our Guests just loved it.! This Sauce is a Unique Combination of Flavors and Tastes that makes any Pasta Dinner an Elegant One! This Special Sauce has a Romance that captures your heart immediately. We are so pleased to share this Treasure with you! Enjoy!

Ingredients   Serves 4~6

Butter Almond	3/4	Lb. of Butter (Sweet & Lightly Salted)
Sauce	3	Tablespoons of Olive Oil
	1	Fresh Lemon (Use Juice Only)
	4	Tablespoons of Capers (Large Size)
		(Finely Chop 3 Tablespoons for Sauce)
		(Save 1 Tablespoon of Whole Capers for Garnish)
	1	Pinch of Salt
	1	Pinch of Pepper
	1	Pinch of Sugar (Granulated)
	1	Teaspoon of Almond Extract
	1/4	Cup of Slivered Almonds
The Pasta	1	Lb. of Vermicelli Pasta (Cooked Al Dente)
		(Follow Cooking Instructions on the Package)
The Garnish	1/4	Bunch of Fresh Parsley
	1/4	Cup of Romano Cheese (Grated)

Preparation ~ Butter & Almond Caper Sauce

1. In a Large Skillet, Heat The Butter on Medium Heat,
   Until it Melts and Bubbles, About 2 Minutes.
2. Add The Olive Oil to The Melted Butter, and Stir in Well.
   Heat on Medium for 2 Minutes More.
3. Add The Lemon Juice, Chopped Capers, Salt, Pepper,
   Sugar and Almond Extract. Stir Together Well.
   Heat All on Medium Heat for About 3~4 Minutes.
4. Add The Whole Capers and The Slivered Almonds. Stir In.
5. Cover Pan. Reduce Heat. Simmer The Sauce for 5 Minutes.
   Serve This Sauce Immediately, While It Is Hot!

Serving Suggestion

On a Heated Decorative Platter, Spoon some Sauce across The Platter. Arrange Vermicelli Pasta over The Sauce. Spoon more Sauce over Pasta. Toss Together Gently. Sprinkle The Top Lightly with Grated Romano Cheese. Arrange Parsley Sprigs and The Whole Capers for a Perfect Presentation! Serve with Caesar Salad, Hot Cheese Bread and Rose Wine! Enjoy!

Oil & Garlic Sauce, Olives & Pine Nuts

Olio Aglio Salsa Pinola

This Very Delicious Mama Lena's Sauce was Grandma's Recipe. Grandpa Matteo would get Fresh Olives, Garlic and Pine Nuts at The Market, and Grandma Anna would prepare This Delicious Sauce for him. This is a Wonderful Sauce to use over any Pasta. We heard Grandpa liked it on Vermicelli, with some hot Italian Bread and a glass of Chianti Wine! Our Guests just loved This Delightful Recipe! We know you will, too! Enjoy!

Ingredients   Serves 4~6

Oil & Garlic	1	Cup of Olive Oil
Sauce	3	Tablespoons of Butter (Sweet & Lightly Salted)
	5	Cloves of Garlic (Cut into Quarters)
The Olives &	1/4	Lb. of Large Green Olives
Pine Nuts		(Pitted and Sliced Thin)
	1/4	Lb. of Pine Nuts
The Pasta	1	Lb. of Pasta (Cooked Firm ~ Al Dente)
		(Follow Cooking Instructions on the Package)
The Garnish	1/4	Bunch of Fresh Parsley
	1/4	Cup of Parmesan Cheese (Grated)

Preparation ~ Oil & Garlic Sauce, Olives & Pine Nuts

1. **In a Large Skillet, Heat The Olive Oil to Medium.**
   Saute Garlic, Until a Light Brown, About 1 Minute.
   Remove Garlic with a Slotted Spoon. Discard The Garlic.
2. **Add The Butter to The Olive Oil, and As Soon As The Butter Melts,**
   Add The Large Green Olives. Saute for About 2 Minutes.
3. **Remove The Skillet from The Heat.**
4. **Add The Pine Nuts to The Sauteed Green Olives and**
   The Garlic~Flavored Olive Oil. Mix Together Quickly.
5. **Serve This Sauce Immediately, While It Is Hot!**

Serving Suggestion

Arrange Hot Pasta on a Large Warmed Platter. Spoon on This Hot Sauce over The Pasta, A Little At A Time. (So it will not lump up in one spot). Then Lightly Toss The Pasta. Sprinkle with Grated Parmesan Cheese and Garnish with Parsley Sprigs. Serve with our Tomato, Scallion & Red Onion Salad and Asiago Cheese Dressing, warm Italian Bread for The Sauce and a Chianti Wine ~ Just as Grandpa had it ~ You will love it, too! Enjoy!

White Cream Sauce Supreme

Krema Bianco Salsa Suprema

Our Beautiful White Cream Sauce is a Smooth and Creamy Sauce, with a very fragrant cheese aroma. This Special Sauce can be prepared in a Lighter or Richer Style, according to your preference. The Delicacy of This Lovely Sauce is a perfect compliment to any Pasta, Fish, Veal or Poultry Dish. At Mama Lena's, we often prepared a Richer Version of This Luscious Sauce and served it on Ribbon Pastas, Fettucine or Tagliatelle ~ Spinach, Tomato or Plain Ribbons! We think you will love it that way, as our Guests did! Enjoy!

Ingredients   Serves 4~6

The	1/2	**Lb. of Butter (Sweet & Lightly Salted)**
Cream Sauce	1	**Pint of Heavy Cream**
		(For a Lighter Sauce, Use Half & Half)
	2	**Eggs (Lightly Beaten) (Use Egg Whites Only)**
	2	**Pinches of Sugar (Granulated)**
	1/2	**Cup of Parmesan Cheese (Grated)**
The Pasta	1	**Lb. of Ribbon~Style Pasta (Cooked ~ Al Dente)**
		(Fettucine or Tagliatelle) (Tomato, Spinach, Plain)
The Garnish	1/2	**Cup of Parmesan Cheese**
		(The White Sauce Needs Extra Cheese)
	1/4	**Bunch of Fresh Parsley**

Preparation ~ White Cream Sauce Supreme

1. **In a Cold Bowl, with a Whisk, Beat 2 Egg Whites Only, for 2 Minutes.**
2. **Add Cream & Sugar to The Eggs. Beat 2 Minutes, Until Light & Fluffy.**
3. **In a Large Skillet, Heat The Butter on Medium, Until Melted.**
4. **Slowly, Add The Cream~Sugar~Egg Mixture to The Melted Butter.**
   Stir Constantly with a Whisk to keep The Mixture Smooth,
   Until All Combined. Then, Continue to Stir for 5 Minutes More.
5. **Slowly, Add The Parmesan Cheese. Stir Constantly for 2~3 Minutes,**
   Until The Cream Sauce is Perfectly Smooth.
6. **If Sauce is Lumpy, Strain it. Then, Return it to The Skillet, and**
   Continue to Stir Constantly, Until Sauce is "Perfectly Smooth."

Serving Suggestion

On a Heated Decorative Platter, Spoon 1 Cup of White Cream Sauce. Arrange Pasta and Pour 1 Cup more of Sauce on Top. Toss Gently. Sprinkle Lightly with Parmesan Cheese. Arrange Parsley Sprigs to Nicely Garnish. Serve extra Sauce in a Heated Gravy Bowl. Accompany with our Caesar Salad, Garlic & Sweet Onion Bread and White Wine! Enjoy!

Red Cream Sauce Supreme

Krema Pomodoro Salsa Suprema

Mama and Salvino thought a Red Cream Sauce would be a nice compliment to many of
The Mama Lena's Pastas and Entrees. So, they worked to develop This Delectable Sauce.
Mama Lena's Red Cream Sauce Supreme is a Lovely Combination Sauce! The Taste and
Texture is a combination of the Bold Spicy Taste of our Basic Tomato Sauce with the
Smooth, Creamy Taste of our White Cream Sauce. Mama Lena's Guests fell in love with
This Delicious Sauce, especially when we served it over the Rigatoni Pasta. It also makes
a Nice Topping for Fish or Chicken Dishes. You will love to prepare and serve This Sauce!
Our Red Cream Sauce Supreme really makes every Dish a Festive One!   Enjoy!

Ingredients   Serves 4~6

The **Tomato Sauce**	2	Cups of Mama Lena's "Quick" Basic Tomato Sauce (See Recipe ~ Chapter Five)
The **Cream Sauce**	1/2	Lb. of Butter (Sweet & Lightly Salted)
	1	Pint of Heavy Cream (For a Lighter Effect ~ Use Half & Half)
	2	Egg Whites Only (Lightly Beaten)
	2	Pinches of Sugar (Granulated)
	1/2	Cup of Parmesan Cheese (Grated)
The Pasta	1	Lb. of Rigatoni Pasta (Large~Size) (Cooked to a Semi~Soft Texture) (Follow Cooking Instructions on the Package)
The Garnish	1/4	Cup of Parmesan Cheese (Grated) (To Use for Topping)
	1/4	Bunch of Fresh Parsley

Preparation ~ Red Cream Sauce Supreme

The
Tomato Sauce

1. *In a Large Pan (8 Qt.), Prepare 1 Recipe of*
   Mama Lena's "Quick" Basic Tomato Sauce.
2. *When The Tomato Sauce is Cooking, and is in*
   The 20~Minute Simmer, then
   Prepare The Cream Sauce.

The
Cream Sauce

1. *In a Chilled Bowl, and with a Large Metal Whisk,*
   Beat The 2 Egg Whites Only, for About 2 Minutes.
2. *Add The Cream and Sugar to The Eggs.*
   Beat All Together for 2 Minutes More,
   Until The Texture is Light and Fluffy.
3. *In a Large Skillet, Heat The Butter on Medium,*
   Just Until Butter is Melted.
4. *Slowly, Add In The Cream~Sugar~Egg Mixture*
   to The Melted Butter. Stir Constantly with Whisk,
   Keeping Texture Smooth, Until Well Combined.
   Then, Continue to Stir for 2 Minutes More.
5. *Slowly, Add The Parmesan Cheese. Stir Constantly,*
   Keeping Smooth, For About 2~3 Minutes More,
   Until The Cream Sauce is "Perfectly Smooth."

The
Tomato & Cream Sauces
~ Combine ~

1. *Once The Cream Sauce is Perfectly Smooth,*
   Add it to The Tomato Sauce in The Large Pan.
2. *If The Cream Sauce is Not Smooth, then*
   Pour It through Strainer into The Tomato Sauce.
3. *Stir The Sauces Together Well. Cover Pan.*
   Let The Combined Sauces Simmer Together
   for About 10 Minutes. Stir Often.
4. *Then, Uncover Pan. Continue to Stir The Sauce Often,*
   Until You Are Ready To Serve The Sauce!

Serving Suggestion

On a Large Deep Heated Platter, Pour 1 Cup of The Sauce. Place The Rigatoni Pasta and Top with 1 Cup More of Sauce. Toss Together Gently. Sprinkle Lightly with Parmesan Cheese. Garnish Platter with Parsley Sprigs. Place Extra Sauce in a Gravy Bowl. Serve This Special Dish with our Antipasto & Italian Salad Supreme, our Hot Cheese Bread and a Nice Dry Red Wine. Finish with our Anisette & Vanilla Biscotti and Coffee for Dessert! You will love this simple, yet Very Festive Dinner, as our Guests did! Enjoy!

Variations for
Tomato Sauces & Cream Sauces

Restos Pomodo Krema Salsas

At Mama Lena's Italian Kitchen, we often enhanced our Special Sauces by adding Fresh Vegetables when they were in Season to honor Grandpa, who had worked his whole life with the Fresh Vegetables. Also, we added Sweet or Dry Wines to honor Papa Frank, who had made Homemade Wine, as a boy with his Father in Sicily, and believed it was a welcome addition to the Sauce! And, to Always Honor our Two Most Excellent Cooks ~ Mama Lena and her Dear Mother, Grandma Anna ~ we added various Meats & Cheeses to the Sauces, as they favored! So, for a New Adventure and a New Taste, try one of our Mama Lena's Variations in the measurements below! Choose a Vegetable, Meat, Cheese or Wine from your kitchen ~ Start Now ~ Try a Mama Lena's Variation Recipe!   Enjoy!

Vegetable Variations In The Tomato Sauces

Measures & Instructions

Asparagus
Broccoli (Flowers Only)
Carrots
Celery
Green Peppers
Sweet Red Onions
Zucchini

Use 1/2 Cup of The Fresh Vegetables
    of Your Choice. Wash and Drain Well.
Heat 1/2 Cup of Olive Oil in a
    Large Skillet on Medium Heat, and
Saute The Vegetables 3 Minutes. Drain Well.
Add Vegetables to The Basic Tomato Sauce
    for The Last 15 Minutes of Cooking.

Vegetable Variations In Cream Sauces

Measures & Instructions

Asparagus
Broccoli (Flowers Only)
Capers
Red Pimento Peppers
Shallots
Sweet Peas
Sweet Red Onions
White Mushrooms
Zucchini

Use 1/2 Cup of The Fresh Vegetables
    of your Choice. Wash and Drain Well.
Heat 1/2 Cup of Olive Oil in a
    Large Skillet on Medium Heat.
Saute Vegetables 3 Minutes. Drain of The Oil.
Add to The White Cream Sauce,
    At Final 5 Minutes of Cooking. ~ <u>OR</u> ~
Add to The Red Cream Sauce,
    At Final 10 Minutes of Cooking
Stir Often to Keep Sauce Smooth.

126

Variations For ~ Tomato Sauces & Cream Sauces

Meat Variations
In Tomato & Cream Sauces

1 Lb. Of Mixed Ground Meat
(1/3 Lb. of Beef, Pork & Veal)
(All Ground Together)

Add 1 Onion & 1 Clove Garlic
(Finely Chopped)
1 Pinch of Cayenne Pepper
1 Pinch of Salt

Measures & Instructions

In a Large Skillet, Heat 1/2 Cup
of Olive Oil to Medium Heat.
Saute The Onion for 3 Minutes.
Add The Garlic. Saute 1 Minute More.
Add Seasoned Ground Meat, and
Saute, Until Brown, 3~5 Minutes.
Drain The Meat. Discard The Oil.
Add The Browned Meat to The Sauce,
for The Final 5 Minutes of Cooking.

Cheese Variations
In Tomato & Cream Sauces

Fontinella Cheese (Grated)
Parmesan Cheese (Grated)
Romano Cheese (Grated)

Ricotta Cheese (Fresh)

Measures & Instructions

Slowly, Add 1/2 Cup of Grated Cheese
(Fontinella, Parmesan or Romano)
During The Last 5 Cooking Minutes.
Constantly Whisk Sauce to Keep Smooth.
Add 1 Cup of The Fresh Ricotta Cheese to
Sauce at Final 10 Minutes of Cooking.

Wine Variations
In Tomato & Red Cream Sauces

Cream Sherry Wine
(Not Cooking Sherry)
Dry or Sweet Red Wine
Dry or Sweet White Wine

Measures & Instructions

Add 1/2 Cup of The Wine to The Sauce.
Add The Wine During The Final
10 Minutes of Cooking The Sauce.
Blend Into Sauce with a Large Whisk.
Stir The Sauce Often.

Wine Variations
In the White Cream Sauces

Champagne or Spumanti
Cream Sherry Wine
Rose Wine
Soft White Wine
Sweet or Dry White Wine

Measures & Instructions

After The Sauce is Completely Cooked,
Add 1/2 Cup of Wine, and
Blend into The Sauce with a Whisk.
Simmer for 10 Minutes More.
Stir Often to Keep The Sauce Smooth.

Now, that you have used a Mama Lena's Variation Recipe, you can see how easy it is to have a new and different sauce, as you choose! Select one of Mama Lena's Pastas, Salads, Breads and a Nice Wine to Compliment your Brand New Sauce! Garnish your Platter Nicely. Time to Try Out Your Delicious New Sauce! Enjoy!

~ *Chapter Six* ~
Fish & Seafood Entrees

Pages 129 ~ 139

Lemon Oregano Tuna, Broiled

Tono Lessato Limone Oreganato

Papa Frank learned to appreciate Fresh Fish from his Sicilian parents. This recipe was a special favorite of Papa's Father, Grandpa Antonio. Of course, it became Papa's favorite, too! Whenever Papa was thinking of his Father and his childhood, , he would stop after work at The Fresh Fish Store and buy a 5 Lb. Whole Tuna and bring it home wrapped in white butcher paper. Papa would cut the head and tail off, so we couldn't see the tuna's eyes, and Mama would wash the Tuna with cold water and lemon, wrap it in wax paper and immediately put it in the Ice Box! We kids just couldn't wait for the next day to see what would happen with that Tuna! And, the next day when Papa arrived home from work, there was a beautiful Broiled Lemon Oregano Tuna waiting for him! Once you try this Treasure, prepared Mama's way, you'll know why it was Papa's Favorite! Enjoy!

Ingredients   Serves 4~6

The Fresh Tuna	2~1/2	Lbs. of Fresh Tuna (Six 6 ~7 Oz. Filets)
		(Have Cut to Size at The Market)
The Basting Mixture	1/2	Cup of Olive Oil
	3	Cloves of Garlic (Minced)
	2	Lemons (Fresh) (Use The Juice Only)
	3	Pinches of Oregano
	1	Pinch of Salt
	1	Pinch of Coarse Black Pepper
The Vegetable Mixture	1/4	Cup of Olive Oil
	1	Clove of Garlic (Minced)
	1	Small White Onion (Finely Minced)
	1	Fresh Tomato (Finely Chopped)
	1	Stalk of Celery (Finely Chopped)
	1	Fresh Green Pepper (Finely Chopped)
	12	Large Green Olives (Pitted and Cut in Slivers)
	1	Pinch of Salt
	1	Pinch of Freshly Ground Pepper
	1	Pinch of Sugar (Granulated)
	2	Pinches of Fresh Oregano
The Garnish	1	Whole Lemon (Cut into Thin Slices)
	1	Lb. of Fresh Broccoli (Flowers Only)

Preparation ~ Lemon Oregano Tuna, Broiled

The Fresh Tuna
~ Prepare ~

1. Wash The Tuna with Cold Water. Pat Dry with Paper Towels.
2. Brush The Broiling Pan Lightly with Olive Oil.
3. Set The Tuna over The Oil on The Pan. Set Aside.

The
Basting Mixture

1. In a Large Bowl, Combine The Olive Oil, Garlic, Lemon Juice, Oregano, Salt & Pepper. Mix Together Well.
2. You will need a Vegetable Basting Brush to Baste The Tuna. Or, Like Mama, Swab The Tuna with A Lettuce Leaf.
3. Keep The Basting Mixture and The Tuna Aside, While you make The Vegetable Mixture.

The
Vegetable Mixture

1. In a Large Skillet, Heat 1/4 Cup of Oil on Medium Heat. Add The Onions, and Saute, Until Transparent.
2. Add The Garlic. Saute Onions & Garlic for 1 Minute More.
3. Now, Add Tomatoes, Celery, Green Peppers, & Olives. Stir In.
4. Add The Salt, Pepper, Sugar and Oregano. Continue to Stir. Saute All on Medium for 3~4 Minutes More. Cover Pan.
5. Remove The Vegetable & Seasonings Mixture from The Heat. Set Aside, Until Ready to Spoon under The Broiled Tuna.

The
Broccoli & Lemon
Slices

1. Wash The Broccoli under Cold Water. Cut Off Only The Stems. (Use Broccoli Flowers Only).
2. In a 2 Qt. Pan, Add 2 Cups of Water and 1 Pinch of Salt, and Bring to a Full Boil. Reduce Heat to Medium. Add The Broccoli. Cover Pan. Steam Broccoli for 3~4 Minutes, Until The Broccoli is Tender, but Firm.
3. Slice a Fresh Lemon into 10~12 Thin Slices for Garnish.
4. Set Aside Broccoli & Lemon Slices, Until The Tuna is Broiled.

The Fresh Tuna
~ Broiling ~

1. Place Tuna on a Broiler Pan in Oven ~ Second Shelf from Top.
2. Broil The Tuna on Each Side for 5 Minutes.
3. Baste Occasionally with The Basting Mixture. Turn Only Once.
4. Finish Test ~ Touch Tuna with a Fork ~ See If Tuna Flakes To The Touch ~ Tuna should be Lightly Flaky, yet Moist.

Serving Suggestion

On a Heated Decorative Platter, Spoon on Sauteed Vegetables First. Place The Broiled Tuna on Top of The Mixed Vegetables. Surround The Broiled Tuna Filets with Broccoli Flowers, and Place Lemon Slices on each Filet for Final Garnish. Papa Frank would have This Dish with his favorite salad of Tomato, Scallion & Red Onions, Mama's warm Italian Bread and Red Wine. A White Wine would be our suggestion at Mama Lena's. Sweetly Finish This Delightful Meal, with Papa's favorite Chocolate Spice Cookies & Coffee! May you enjoy This Wonderful Dish ~ A Dish So Special to our Family and to our Guests, too!   Enjoy!

Mussels in Sherry Sauce

Cozza Shere Salsa

Our Mama Lena's Mussels Cooked in Sherry Sauce was a Recipe created by Salvino for our Mama Lena's Italian Kitchen Guests. He wanted a Sauce that would be a delicate compliment to the Mussels, but one with such flavor that it stood out and delighted the pallet. This was such a favorite with our Guests, and it was requested on our private party menus for years! You will enjoy Mussels like never before, once you try Salvino's very special recipe! Enjoy!

Ingredients   Serves 6~8

The Mussels	5	**Dozen Mussels (In Their Shells)**
The Sherry Sauce	1/4	**Cup of Olive Oil**
	2	**Cloves of Garlic (Sliced Thin)**
	1	**Small Onion (Finely Chopped)**
	1	**Small Green Pepper (Finely Chopped)**
	2	**Stalks of Celery (Finely Chopped)**
	10	**Large Green Olives (Pitted & Sliced into Slivers)**
	4	**Large Fresh Tomatoes (Chopped) ~ OR ~**
	1	**Large Can of Plum Tomatoes, Crushed in Puree (Large Can ~ 28 Oz. Size)**
	3	**Cups of Hot Water**
	2	**Tablespoons of Basil**
	2	**Tablespoons of Oregano**
	2	**Tablespoons of Parsley**
	1	**Tablespoon of Paprika**
The Capers & Sherry	3	**Tablespoons of Capers**
	1	**Cup of Cream Sherry Wine**
* To Taste *		*** Add Salt and Pepper to Your Own Taste ***
** For Spicy Hot **		**** Optional ~ If You Prefer A Hot & Spicy Flavor **** **Add 2 Pinches of Red Pepper Flakes or Cayenne Pepper.**
The Pasta	1	**Lb. of Vermicelli Pasta (Cooked Firm ~ Al Dente)** **(Follow Cooking Instructions on the Package)**
The Garnish	1/4	**Bunch of Fresh Parsley**
	1/2	**Cup of Parmesan Cheese (Grated)**

Preparation ~ Mussels in Sherry Sauce

**The
Sherry Sauce
~Prepare ~**

1. *In an 8 Qt. Large Pan, Heat The Olive Oil to Medium.
   Add The Garlic, and Saute for 1 Minute.*
2. *Add The Onions. Saute Together for 2 Minutes More.*
3. *Now, Add The Green Peppers, Celery and Green Olives to
   The Garlic, Onions & Oil. Saute for 3 Minutes More.*
4. *Add The Chopped Tomatoes ~OR~ Canned Tomatoes,
   And 3 Cups of Hot Water. Stir In Well.*
5. *Add The Seasonings of Basil, Oregano, Parsley, and
   Paprika, Salt, Black Pepper. Stir In Well.*
6. *If you Prefer Spicy Hot, Add The Red Pepper Flakes,
   Or The Cayenne Pepper Now. Stir In Well.*
7. *Leave Pan Uncovered. Cook The Sauce for 20 Minutes,
   Until Sauce reaches a Full Boil. Stir Often.*
8. *Cover Pan. Reduce Heat. Simmer Sauce for 30 Minutes.*
9. *Uncover Pan. Add The Cream Sherry and The Capers.
   Simmer Entire Sauce for 5 Minutes More.*

**The Mussels
~ Cooking ~**

1. *First, Clean and Scrub The Mussels, Cutting The Beards.
   Check to be sure The Shells are completely Closed.
   *If Any Shells are Open Before Cooking ~
   Pinch Them Closed.
   *If The Shells Stay Open, They are Not Good ~
   Discard Shells that Remain Open Before.*
2. *Set The Cleaned Mussels into The Sauce. Cover Pan.
   Simmer The Mussels & Sauce for 5~7 Minutes,
   Until All Closed Shells Have Opened in Cooking ~
   After The Simmer, Turn Heat Off.*
3. *Let The Mussels and The Sauce Sit with Pan Covered,
   Until Ready to Serve.*
4. *Remember ~
   The Mussel Shells must be Closed Before Cooking.
   After Cooking, All Shells should be Open. If Not,
   Discard Any Shells That Did Not Open in Cooking.*

Serving Suggestion

On a Large Deep Decorative Platter, Spoon some Sauce across The Platter. Place The Vermicelli Pasta and More Sauce on Top. Toss Gently. Sprinkle Lightly with Parmesan Cheese. Arrange The Mussels on Top of Pasta. Place Parsley Sprigs all around The Platter. Serve with our Caesar Salad, our Mama Lena's Tomato Cheese Bread and Nice White Wine. Anisette & Vanilla Biscotti and Coffee for Dessert make a Sweet Finish to This Delicious Dish! Salvino is Very Proud of This Very Special Recipe! It's a True Treasure! Enjoy!

Shrimp & Scallops, Marinara

Gamberetti Marinara Conchiglie

Salvino created this Wonderful and Zesty Dish especially for Mama Lena's Italian Kitchen. It was one of our Seafood Entrees that Guests loved best. This Delightful Seafood Dish is just So Delicious, and was a Favorite of Mama Lena and Papa Frank, too! They both loved Fish and Seafood from their Childhood Days. Mama Lena always loved Shrimp and Papa Frank loved Scallops, so this Salvino Dish was a great one for both of them! We hope This Very Flavorful Dish will be a favorite of yours also! Enjoy!

Ingredients   Serves 4~6

The Shrimp & Scallops	1	Lb. of Medium Shrimp (Shelled and De~veined)
	1	Lb. of Sea Scallops
The Breading Mixture	1	Recipe of Mama Lena's Bread Crumbs (Italian Seasoned) (See Recipe ~ Chapter Ten)
	2	Large Eggs (Lightly Beaten) (To Dip Shrimp & Scallops for Breading)
	1/2	Cup of Olive Oil
The Seafood Marinade	1/2	Cup of Cream Sherry
	2	Pinches of Salt
	2	Pinches of Black Pepper
	1	Clove of Garlic (Minced)
	1	Small White Onion (Finely Chopped)
	1/4	Cup of Olive Oil
	1	Pinch of Cayenne Pepper (If You Prefer Spicy Hot)
The Marinara Sauce	1	Recipe of Mama Lena's Marinara Sauce (See Recipe ~ Chapter Five)
	1/2	Cup of Cream Sherry (To Add To The Sauce)
The Linguine Pasta	1	Lb. of Linguine Pasta (Cooked Firm ~ Al Dente) (Follow Cooking Instructions on the Package)
The Garnish	1/2	Cup of Parmesan Cheese (Grated)
	1/4	Bunch of Fresh Parsley

Preparation ~ Shrimp & Scallops, Marinara

**The
Shrimp & Scallops
~ Marinate ~**

1. In a Large Bowl, Combine The Sherry Marinade Mixture ~
   Mix Together The Cream Sherry Wine, The Salt,
   Black Pepper, Minced Garlic, Chopped Onion,
   Olive Oil and, if you wish, Cayenne Pepper.
   Allow The Mixture to Sit, While you Clean Seafood.
2. Rinse The Shrimp and Scallops Thoroughly in Cold Water.
   Set on Paper Towels, Allowing Excess Water to Drain.
3. Place All The Shrimp and The Scallops into
   The Marinade Mixture, Covering Each Well.
4. Seal The Bowl Airtight with Plastic, and Refrigerate.
   Allow The Mixture to Marinate for 30 Minutes.
5. Place The Shrimp and Scallops in a Colander to Drain
   Off the Marinade Liquid. Save The Marinade
   Liquid to put into The Mama Lena's Marinara Sauce.

**The
Shrimp & Scallops
~ Bread & Fry ~**

1. Dip The Shrimp & Scallops into Lightly Beaten Eggs.
   Coat Each Piece Well with The Bread Crumbs.
2. Allow Breading to Dry Well on Seafood ~ About 3 Minutes.
3. In a Skillet, Heat 1/2 Cup of Olive Oil to Medium Heat.
   Place The Breaded Shrimp & Scallops into The Oil.
4. Let The Shrimp & Scallops Brown Lightly on All Sides,
   for About 2~3 Minutes. Remove with a
   Slotted Spoon to Allow The Oil to Drain Off.
5. Place Browned Seafood on Paper Towels to Drain and Dry.

**The
Marinara Sauce
~ Prepare ~**

1. Prepare 1 Recipe of Mama Lena's Marinara Sauce.
   (See Recipe ~ Chapter Five)
2. To The Marinara Sauce, Add 1/2 Cup of Cream Sherry
   and The Marinade Liquid you saved.
   (Sherry Flavor will Compliment Sauce & Seafood).
3. Continue to Simmer & Stir The Sauce, Until Ready to Use.
4. Cook The Linguine Pasta to Al Dente, As Instructed.
5. Heat a Platter in Oven to Serve The Pasta and Sauce Hot.

Serving Suggestion

*Arrange on a Deep Heated Platter ~ 1 Cup Sauce, then The Pasta and 1 Cup of Sauce and
Toss Lightly. Arrange Shrimp & Scallops across The Top of Tossed Pasta. Drizzle The
Sauce over Shrimps & Scallops. Sprinkle Lightly with Grated Parmesan Cheese, and
Place Parsley Sprigs Attractively over Dish. This Dish makes a Beautiful Presentation.
We served This Dish with our Italian & Antipasto Salad Supreme and Hot Cheese Bread.
Serve a Side Bowl of Marinara Sauce. Dry White Wine is a Nice Compliment to This Dish.
Mama & Papa would have Mama Lena's Cannoli and Coffee for a Grand Finish! Enjoy!*

Swordfish in Lemon Sauce, Baked

Pesce Forno Limone Salsa

This Lovely Fish Baked in Lemon Sauce is a Very Delicately Prepared Dish. Mama Lena and Salvino created This Delicious Dish for Mama Lena's Italian Kitchen Guests. And, our Guests absolutely loved these Very Beautifully Prepared Swordfish Filets, with the Special Seasonings, Assorted Peppers, Green Grapes and Rose Wine Sauce! This Recipe is so lovely that you can almost taste This Delicious Dish as you read through the Recipe! Everyone looks forward to this Very Special Dish that has such Great Flavors and Aroma. Be sure to try this one just for yourself. We know you'll be very pleased! Enjoy!

Ingredients   Serves 4~6

The Swordfish Filets	2~1/2	Lbs. of Fresh Swordfish (Six 6~7 Oz. Filets) (Have Cut at The Market)
The Lemon Sauce	1/2	Cup of Olive Oil
	1/4	Lb. of Butter (Sweet & Lightly Salted)
	3	Cloves of Garlic (Minced)
	1	Large Onion (Finely Chopped)
	3	Large Lemons (Use The Juice Only)
	2	Pinches of Salt
	2	Pinches of Pepper
	2	Pinches of Tarragon
	1	Pinch of Thyme
	1/2	Lb. of Seedless Green Grapes
	1	Cup of Rose Wine
The Mixed Peppers	2	Large Green Peppers
	2	Large Yellow Peppers
	2	Large Red Pimento Peppers
	1/2	Cup of Olive Oil
	3	Large Pinches of Sugar (Granulated)
	2	Pinches of Salt
	2	Pinches of Black Pepper
The Garnish	1	Lemon (Thinly Sliced)

136

Preparation ~ Swordfish in Lemon Sauce, Baked

The Lemon Sauce
~ Prepare ~

1. *Rinse The Swordfish Filets Very Well in Cool Water.*
   Set on Paper Towels to Dry.
2. *In a Large Skillet, Heat The Olive Oil to Medium.*
   Add The Onions, and Saute for 3 Minutes.
3. *Add The Garlic. Saute Onions & Garlic for 1 Minute More.*
4. *Add The Lemon Juice, Salt, Pepper, Tarragon and Thyme.*
   Stir In. Bring to a Boil. Remove Pan from Heat.
5. *Pour The Lemon Sauce into a Bowl. Set Aside.*

The Swordfish
~ Prepare ~

1. *Wipe The Skillet Clean with Paper Towels. Do Not Wash.*
2. *Melt The Butter & 1 Tablespoon of Olive Oil on Medium.*
3. *Saute The Swordfish Filets, 4 Minutes on Each Side.*

The Fish & Sauce
~ Combine & Bake ~

1. *In a Large Roaster Pan, Pour Half of The Lemon Sauce*
   Across The Bottom of The Pan.
2. *Arrange The Swordfish Filets on Top of The Lemon Sauce*
   in Roaster Pan. Cover Filets with All The Rose Wine.
3. *Add The Remaining Lemon Garlic Sauce, Pouring Gently*
   Across the Top. Place The Grapes on Top of Sauce.
4. *Cover Pan Airtight with Foil, and Bake in a*
   Preheated 300 Degree Oven for 20~25 Minutes.
5. *The Fish should Flake, When Touched with A Fork ~*
   If not, Seal Pan and Bake Fish, About 5 Minutes More.

The Vegetables
~ Saute ~

1. *Wash and Clean The Green, Yellow and Pimento Peppers.*
   Remove and Discard The Stems, Seeds & Pulp.
2. *Cut Each Pepper in Half. Sugar Inside of Each Pepper.*
   Next, Salt & Pepper Each Pepper.
3. *After Seasoning, Cut Pepper Halves into 3 Pieces Each.*
   (A Nice Size, and Yields 36 Pepper Pieces)
4. *In a Large Skillet, Heat The Olive Oil to Medium.*
   Saute The Mixed Peppers for About 4 Minutes.

Serving Suggestion

Serve on a Large White Platter, Arranging Lemon Sauce, then Swordfish Filets, and then Peppers all around The Filets. Place The Grapes over Top of The Filets. Drizzle on more Sauce over The Grapes. Add The Lemon Slices for a Nice Garnish. Your guests will appreciate the Nice Presentation, as well as the Delightful Tastes and Aroma of This Dish! Serve with Vermicelli Pasta and Butter Parsley Sauce and warm Herbs & Spices Bread. A Soft White Wine will compliment perfectly. Sweetly Finish This Divine Dish with Cannoli & Coffee! Mama & Salvino would love to join you for This Dish! Enjoy!

Vermouth Sole,
Sauteed Vegetables, Baked

Vermouth Sogliola Verdura

Once you read This Special Recipe, you will see that Mama's Father, Grandpa Matteo, was the Inspiration for The Recipe, which uses the Fish he loved and all the wonderful Vegetables from His Wagon. This Recipe was truly loved by Mama's Family and was a Special Favorite of Mama Lena's Guests. It brings the History of Grandpa and Sicily to the Table all at once. We hope you treasure This Special Dish as we do! Enjoy!

Ingredients   Serves 4~6

The Filets of Sole	2~1/2	Lbs. of Fresh Sole (Six 6~7 Oz. Filets)
The Vermouth Sauce	1	Cup of Vermouth (Dry)
	2	Lemons (For Juice Only)
	2	Cloves of Garlic (Finely Minced)
	1/2	Cup of Olive Oil
	2	Pinches of Salt
	2	Pinches of Pepper
	2	Pinches of Thyme
The Sauteed Vegetables	1/4	Cup of Olive Oil
	1	Small White Onion (Finely Chopped)
	1	Scallion (Finely Chopped, Including Green Stems)
	1	Large Red Pepper (Cut into Chunks)
	2	Stalks of Celery (Chop into Small Pieces)
	10	Large Green Olives (Pitted and Sliced Thin)
	3	Large Zucchini (Sliced into 1" Pieces)
	1/2	Lb. of White Mushrooms (Sliced into Halves) ~OR~
	1	Large Can of Mushroom Halves ~ Drained
	2	Large Fresh Tomatoes (Chopped Small) ~OR~
	1	Large Can (28 Oz.) Plum Tomatoes, Crushed in Puree
	2	Pinches of Salt
	2	Pinches of Pepper
	2	Pinches of Oregano
	1	Large Can of Artichoke Hearts (Drain and Cut into Halves)
	2	Tablespoons of Capers (Rinsed in Cool Water)
	2	Bay Leaves to Set on Very Top of Vegetables
The Garnish	1/4	Bunch of Fresh Parsley
	1	Fresh Lemon (Cut into Thin Slices)

Preparation ~ Vermouth Sole with Sauteed Vegetables, Baked

The
Sole & Vermouth Sauce
~ Prepare & Bake ~

1. Rinse Filets in Cool Water. Dry on Paper Towels.
2. In a Sauce Pan, Combine The Dry Vermouth,
   Olive Oil, Juice of 2 Lemons, Minced Garlic,
   Salt, Pepper, Parsley and Thyme. Mix Well.
   Bring All to a Boil, and Turn Heat Off.
3. Pour One~Half of The Sauce Mixture across
   The Bottom of Large Deep Roaster Pan.
4. Arrange The Filets of Sole Carefully on Top of
   The Sauce Mixture. Gently Pour Remaining
   Vermouth Sauce over The Top of Each Filet.
5. Seal Top of The Roaster Pan Airtight with Foil.
6. Bake in a Preheated 350 Degree Oven for 20 Minutes.
7. While Sole & Sauce Bakes, Prepare The Vegetables,
   To Combine with Filets after 20 Minutes' Baking.

The Vegetables
~ Saute ~

1. In a Large Skillet, Heat The Olive Oil to Medium.
2. Saute The White Onion, Scallions, Red Peppers,
   and Celery for 5 Minutes.
3. Add In The Green Olives. Saute for 3 Minutes More.
4. Remove, The Onions, Scallions, Red Peppers, Celery
   and Olives from The Oil. Set Aside.
5. Now, To Same Oil, Add Zucchini. Saute 3 Minutes.
   Add Mushrooms. Saute Together 2 Minutes More.
6. Add Tomatoes, Salt, Pepper, & Oregano. Mix Well.
   Cover Pan. Simmer All for 3 Minutes.
7. Now, Add in The Artichokes and Capers, as well as
   The Onions, Scallions, Peppers and Olives that
   you had set aside. On Top, Place Bay Leaves.
8. Cover Skillet. Simmer All Vegetables 3 Minutes More.

The
Sole, Sauce & Vegetables
~ Combine & Bake ~

1. Carefully, Open Foil Cover on The Roaster Pan.
2. Evenly Spoon The Sauteed Vegetables over
   The Baked Sole Filets and Vermouth Sauce.
3. Seal Foil Again. Place The Roaster Pan Back in Oven.
4. Continue to Bake for 10 Minutes More at 350 Degrees.

Serving Suggestion

Onto a Deep Heated Platter, Spoon on some Vermouth Sauce. Arrange The Filets of Sole, and surround The Filets attractively with The Vegetables. (Discard The Bay Leaves). Drizzle Vermouth Sauce over Top of The Sole and Vegetables. Place Lemon Slices and Parsley Sprigs to Garnish. We served This Fabulous Dish with our Caesar Salad, Angel Hair Pasta in Marinara Sauce, and Hot Cheese Bread. Try our Zabaione Marsala with Fresh Fruit to Sweetly Finish. Grandpa would be singing, and you will, too! Enjoy!

~ Chapter Seven ~
The Chicken Entrees

Pages 141 ~ 151

Chicken in Marsala Wine

Pollo di Petto Marsala

This was known, when we were children, as The Celebration Chicken. When Mama took the Marsala Wine out to cook with, we knew there was something special to celebrate, especially for Grandma & Grandpa and Papa Frank! Marsala Wine is a wonderful product of Sicily, and it was a sign of pride for them to enjoy a Wine so special to each of them, having come from Sicily. Each time we served this Dish at the Restaurant, we thought of it as a special Celebration of Them! Our Guests always welcomed it with great celebration, too! Once you have tasted this Very Special and Very Delicious Recipe, you will be searching for your own special occasions to use it again and again! Enjoy!

Ingredients   Serves 4~6

The Chicken Breasts	8	Large Chicken Breasts (Double Breasts) (Boneless & Skinless)
To Saute	1/2	Cup of Olive Oil
	1/4	Lb. of Butter (Sweet & Lightly Salted)
The Marsala Sauce	1	Large Can of Plum Tomatoes, Crushed in Puree (Large Can ~ 28 Oz. Size)
	3	Cups of Marsala Wine (Dry)
	2	Large White Onions (Finely Chopped)
	2	Pinches of Salt
	2	Pinches of Pepper
	2	Pinches of Sugar (Granulated)
	2	Pinches of Tarragon
	1	Pinch of Thyme
	1	Pinch of Anise Seed
	1/8	Cup of Bread Crumbs (Italian Seasoned) (See Recipe ~ Chapter Ten)
The Farfalle Pasta	1	Lb. of Farfalle Pasta (Butterfly Pasta) (Cooked) (Follow Cooking Instructions on the Package)
The Garnish	1/4	Cup of Romano Cheese (Grated)
	1/4	Bunch of Fresh Parsley

142

Preparation ~ Chicken in Marsala Wine

**The
Marsala Sauce**

1. *In a Sauce Pan, Combine The Plum Tomatoes,
    The Marsala Wine and The Onions.*
2. *Add 1 Pinch Only of Each of The Following ~
    Salt, Pepper, Tarragon, Thyme, and Anise Seed.*
3. *Add 2 Pinches of Sugar. Mix All Together Well.*
4. *Bring to a Boil. Turn Off, and Set Aside.*

**The
Chicken Breasts
~ Saute ~**

1. *Rinse The Chicken Breasts in Cool Water, and
    Place on Paper Towels to Drain. Pat Dry.*
2. *Sprinkle Each Chicken Breast with
    1 Pinch Each of Salt, Pepper & Tarragon.*
3. *In a Large Skillet, Heat The Olive Oil to Medium.
    Brown The Seasoned Chicken on Both Sides,
    for About 2~3 Minutes Each Side*
4. *Once, The Chicken is Browned on Both sides,
    Brush Butter over The Chicken in The Olive Oil.*
5. *Lower Heat to Simmer. Cover Pan. Cook for 3 Minutes.*
6. *Remove The Sauteed Chicken from The Olive Oil.
    Place on Paper Towels to Drain.*

**The
Chicken Breasts & Sauce
~ Combine & Bake ~**

1. *In a Large Roaster Pan, Pour Half of
    The Prepared Sauce Across The Bottom of Pan.*
2. *Place The Chicken Breasts on Top of The Sauce.
    Pour Other Half of Sauce over Top of Chicken.*
3. *Sprinkle The Top of The Chicken and Sauce Evenly,
    with Bread Crumbs, to Completely Seal Top.*
4. *Seal The Roaster Pan Airtight with Foil.*
5. *Bake in a Preheated 350 Degree Oven for 1 Hour.*
6. *Turn Off Oven. Let The Sealed Pan Sit in Oven,
    Until You Are Ready To Serve.*

Serving Suggestion

On a Large Decorative Heated Platter, Spoon on 1 Cup of Marsala Wine Sauce across Platter. Place The Farfalle Pasta, and 1 Cup More of Marsala Wine Sauce over The Pasta. Toss Together Gently. Then, Place The Chicken Breasts on Top and Spoon more Marsala Wine Sauce over The Chicken. Sprinkle The Entire Dish Lightly with Romano Cheese and Parsley Sprigs for a Nice Garnish. Serve with a Lettuce Salad with Anchovy & Capers Dressing, Hot Cheese Bread, and a Rose Wine. Salvino's Rum Cassata and Cappuccino makes for a Very Delightful and Sweet Finish! Let The Celebration Begin! Enjoy!

Chicken Breast, Eggplant Sauce

Pollo Al Forno Melanzane Salsa

At Mama Lena's Italian Kitchen, one of our very favorite ways to serve The Chicken was the way they serve it in Sicily ~ with The Eggplant. Our Recipe calls for our very special Caponata di Melanzane, which is in our Appetizer Chapter One. Mama told us that her Mother had told her, as a girl, that the Eggplant Appetizer got its name ~ Caponata ~ because it was almost always served with the Chicken ~ The Capon! This Story is one of many Charming Stories Salvino entertained Mama Lena's Guests with prior to dinner. This Delightful Dish has the Rich, especially Spicy, Tastes of the Sicilian Countryside! Mama Lena's Guests were thrilled with This Dish and your family will be, too! Enjoy!

Ingredients   Serves 6~8

The Chicken Breasts	8	**Large Chicken Breasts (Double Breasts) (With the Bone Split in Half)**
The Caponata Sauce	2	**Large Cans of Plum Tomatoes, Crushed in Puree (28 Oz. Each Can)**
	2	**Large Onions (Finely Chopped)**
	3	**Pinches of Salt**
	2	**Pinches of Pepper**
	2	**Pinches of Basil**
	1	**Pinch of Mint**
	3	**Pinches of Sugar (Granulated)**
	3	**Cups of Mama Lena's Caponata di Melanzane (See Recipe ~ Chapter One)**
	1/2	**Cup of Mama Lena's Bread Crumbs (Italian Seasoned) (See Recipe ~ Chapter Ten)**
The Angel Hair Pasta	1	**Lb. of Angel Hair Pasta (Cooked ~ Al Dente) (Follow Cooking Instructions on the Package)**
The Garnish	1/4	**Cup of Parmesan Cheese (Grated)**
	1/4	**Bunch of Fresh Parsley**

Preparation ~ Chicken Breast, Eggplant Sauce

**The
Chicken & Sauce
~ Prepare ~**

1. *Prepare The Following Ingredients In Advance ~*
   ~ The Caponata ~ Needs Time to Marinate Well.
   ~ The Bread Crumbs ~ Great to Have Ready.
   ~ The Pasta ~ Prepare As Baking Finishes.
2. *Rinse The Chicken Breasts Very Well in Cold Water.*
   Drain on Paper Towels. Pat Dry.
3. *In a Sauce Pan, Combine 2 Cans of Plum Tomatoes,*
   Crushed in Puree, with The Chopped Onions,
   The Salt, Pepper, Basil, Mint and Sugar.
   Mix All Well. Bring to a Boil. Turn Heat Off.
4. *Gently, Fold in The Caponata di Melanzane with*
   The Plum Tomatoes, Onions & Seasonings.
5. *Pour One~Half of The Sauce Mixture into*
   The Bottom of a Large Roaster Pan.
   Place Chicken, Standing Side by Side,
   (Make Sure the Plump Side is Down in Roaster).
6. *Gently Pour Remaining Sauce Over the Tops of*
   The Chicken Breasts.
7. *Sprinkle Top of The Chicken and The Sauce Evenly,*
   with The Bread Crumbs to Completely Seal Top.

**The
Chicken & Sauce
~ Baking ~**

1. *Seal The Top of The Roaster Pan Airtight with Foil,*
   Allowing Chicken and Sauce to Steam Better.
2. *Bake in a Preheated 350 Degree Oven for 1 Hour.*
3. *Check The Chicken Breasts with a Fork ~*
   Chicken should be Tender and Separate Easily.
   If not, Seal Foil, and Bake for 15 Minutes More.

Serving Suggestion

On a Large Deep Heated Platter, Spoon Sauce to Cover Platter. Then, Place Angel Hair Pasta and Spoon on More Sauce. Toss Gently. Arrange Chicken Breasts on Top of Pasta, and Place The Remaining Sauce over The Chicken and The Pasta. Lightly Sprinkle with Grated Parmesan Cheese. Place Parsley Sprigs Around to Garnish. Serve with our Caesar Salad and our Garlic & Sweet Onion Bread. A White Wine will nicely compliment. Try Mama Lena's Zabaione Marsala and Coffee for Dessert. This Special Dish has Such Very Unique Tastes and a Great Presentation, as in the Tradition of True Sicilian Cooking! Mama Lena & Papa Frank & Family would love to join you for this Dinner! Enjoy!

Chicken in Amaretto Rice

Pollo di Petto con Amaretto Riso

Mama always said Salvino had a Special Touch in using Wines and Liqueurs to cook with. This Very Special Dish is prepared with Salvino's Favorite ~ Amaretto, The Liqueur of Italy. This Recipe was a Mama Lena's Recipe that Mama and Salvino adapted from one of Grandma's recipes, which originally was prepared with Grandpa's homemade wine. But, Salvino and Mama felt The Amaretto would really compliment this Filled Chicken Dish and please the tastes of our Guests in a very special way. Needless to say, it turned out to be a Sensational Dish ~ Different & Delightful ~ A Special Dish loved by our Guests and one that Mama truly loved, too! We think you will agree with Mama on this Great Dish! Enjoy!

Ingredients   Serves 4-6

The Chicken Breasts	6	**Large Chicken Breasts (Boneless & Skinless)** **(Purchase Double Breasts, Not Split, So You Can Fill)**
	2	**Pinches of Salt**
	2	**Pinches of Pepper**
To Saute	1/2	**Cup of Olive Oil**
	2	**Cloves of Garlic (Sliced Thin)**
The Amaretto Rice Filling	1/4	**Lb. of Italian Dry Black Olives** **(Pit Olives & Cut into Slivers)**
	2	**Cups of White Rice (Cooked)** **(Mix Into Cooked Rice ~ 2 Tablespoons of Butter,** **1 Pinch of Salt and 1 Tablespoon of Lemon Juice)**
	2	**Large Eggs (Lightly Beaten)**
	1/4	**Cup of Amaretto Liqueur (For Filling)**
	1/2	**Cup of Mama Lena's Bread Crumbs (Italian Seasoned)** **(See Recipe ~ Chapter Ten)**
	1/4	**Lb. Stick of Pepperoni** **(Remove The Casing & Cut into Thin Strips)**
The Amaretto Sauce	1	**Recipe of Mama Lena's "Quick" Basic Tomato Sauce** **(See Recipe ~ Chapter Five)**
	2	**Pinches of Rosemary (Ground) (Add to The Sauce)**
	1/4	**Cup of Amaretto Liqueur (Add to The Sauce)**
To Seal	24	**Toothpicks to Seal Filled Chicken Breasts** **(4 Toothpicks ~ Per Chicken Breast)**
The Garnish	1/4	**Bunch of Fresh Parsley**
	1/4	**Cup of Romano Cheese (Grated)**

146

Preparation ~ Chicken in Amaretto Rice

The Chicken
~ Prepare ~

1. Rinse The Chicken Very Well in Cool Water.
   Let Drain on Paper Towels. Pat Dry.
2. Salt & Pepper The Chicken, and Place on A Platter.

Garlic & Onion
~ Saute ~

1. In a Large Skillet, Heat The Olive Oil to Medium.
   Add The Garlic, and Saute for 1 Minute.
   Remove Garlic from Oil. Discard The Garlic.
2. Add The Sliced Olives to The Oil. Saute for 2 Minutes.
   Remove The Olives from Oil. Save Olives for Filling.
3. Turn Off Heat. Set The Oil Aside to Brown Filled Chicken.

The
Amaretto Filling
~ Prepare ~

1. In a Large Bowl, Combine The Sauteed Olives, Eggs,
   Cooked Rice, and Bread Crumbs. Mix Well.
2. Add 1/4 Cup of Amaretto Liqueur to Mix and Blend.
3. Evenly, Fill Each Chicken Breast with
   The Amaretto Rice Filling. Set 1 Piece of
   Pepperoni on Each Side of The Rice.

The Chicken
~ Seal & Brown ~

1. Tightly Seal Each Chicken Breast with 4 Toothpicks.
2. Take Large Skillet with The Garlic Olive Oil, you saved,
   and Heat It to Medium.
3. Brown Each Chicken Breast for 3 Minutes on Each Side.

The
Amaretto Sauce

1. Prepare Mama Lena's "Quick" Basic Tomato Sauce.
   (See Recipe ~ Chapter Five)
2. Add 2 Pinches of Rosemary, and
   1/4 Cup of Amaretto Liqueur. Mix In Well.

The
Chicken Breasts & Sauce
~ Combine & Bake ~

1. In a Large Roasting Pan, Pour Half of The Warm
   Amaretto Sauce Across The Bottom of The Pan.
2. Gently Place Filled Chicken Breasts on Top of The Sauce.
   Cover Chicken Breast Tops with Remaining Sauce.
3. Seal The Pan Airtight with Foil. Bake in a
   Preheated 350 Degree Oven for 1 Hour.
4. Remove Pan from Oven. Let Pan Stand for 15 Minutes,
   Allowing Textures to Settle.

Serving Suggestion

Nicely Arrange These Beautifully Filled Chicken Breasts on a Large Deep Heated Platter. (Remove All Toothpicks). Spoon The Amaretto Sauce Over The Chicken Breasts. Sprinkle Lightly with Romano Cheese. Place Parsley Sprigs. We served this Beautiful Dish with a Lettuce & Tomato Salad & Asiago Cheese Dressing, a Pasta with our Butter Parsley Sauce, and our Herbs & Spices Bread. The Tastes in This Dish are So Exquisite and Flavorful, that a perfect compliment is a Soft White Wine. Mama Lena's Amaretto Cream Puffs & Coffee for a Very Sweet Finish! A Very Special Meal will bring a Very Special Evening to You! Enjoy!

Chicken Oregano, Orange Sauce

Chicken Oreganato Arancia

Mama and Salvino were always working to perfect dishes that would delight our Guests. This wonderfully Delicious Dish is one of their perfected dishes, with a Sauce by Salvino of Grand Marnier Liqueur, Oranges & Spices ~ It's a Dish truly inspired by Grandpa Matteo. Mama loved This Dish, as it not only reminded her of Grandpa, but she also had a very real fondness for Chicken Dishes. Papa Frank really loved The Chicken Oregano, too, because, like Grandpa, he loved the Oranges & Spices. This Very Special Dish turned out to have such a distinct and divine taste that our Guests were absolutely delighted and called it a favorite! Definitely, one of the Lighter Dishes on our Menu, but one of the most flavorful and delicious!. It's also very easy to prepare. We hope it becomes one your favorites, too! Enjoy!

Ingredients   **Serves 4~6**

The		
Chicken Breasts	6	Large Chicken Breasts (Boneless & Skinless) (Purchase Double~Size Chicken Breasts ~ Have Them Split into Half ~ 12 Pieces)
The		
Orange Sauce	1/2	Cup of Olive Oil
	1	Large Onion (Finely Chopped)
	1	Clove of Garlic (Minced)
	3	Pinches of Salt
	2	Pinches of Pepper
	3	Pinches of Oregano
	2	Pinches of Parsley
	2	Pinches of Mint
The		
Grand Marnier	4	Oz. of Grand Marnier Liqueur
Mixture	1	Cup of Fresh Orange Juice
	2	Pinches of Sugar (Granulated)
The Garnish	2	Oranges (Cut into Thin Round Slices) (Simmer Orange Slices in The Olive Oil ~ Later Use Slices on The Serving Platter To Garnish The Chicken Dish)
	1/4	Cup of Romano Cheese (Grated)
	1/4	Bunch of Fresh Parsley

Preparation ~ Chicken Oregano, Orange Sauce

**The
Grand Marnier Sauce
~ Prepare ~**

1. *In a Large Deep Skillet, Heat The Olive Oil to Medium.
   Saute The Chopped Onions for 3 Minutes.
   Add Garlic, and Saute for 1 Minute More.*
2. *Place Orange Slices on Top of The Onion and Garlic.
   Lower The Heat and Simmer The Oranges, and
   Onion and Garlic for 1~2 Minutes More.*
3. *Remove The Orange Slices from Pan. Set Aside.
   Use Orange Slices Later to Garnish Chicken.*
4. *With a Slotted Spoon, Remove Onion & Garlic from Oil.
   Save The Oil to Saute The Chicken.*
5. *In a Large Bowl, Combine The Grand Marnier Liqueur,
   The Orange Juice and 2 Pinches of Sugar. Mix Well.
   Add The Sauteed Onion & Garlic and Parsley & Mint.
   Mix The Entire Orange Sauce Very Well.*
6. *Set Aside The Orange Sauce. Allow Flavors to Settle In.*

**The
Chicken Breasts
~ Season & Saute ~**

1. *Rinse The Chicken Very Well in Cold Water, and
   Drain on Paper Towels. Pat Dry.*
2. *Season The Chicken Breasts with 3 Pinches of Salt,
   2 Pinches of Pepper and 3 Pinches of Oregano.*
3. *Heat The Skillet with The Olive Oil to Medium Again.
   Saute Each Seasoned Chicken Breast.*
4. *Brown The Chicken Breasts on Both Sides Thoroughly,
   About 3~4 Minutes, for Each Side to Brown Nicely.*

**The
Chicken & Sauce
~ Combine & Cook ~**

1. *Once The Chicken Breasts have been Browned,
   Take Orange Sauce, that has Settled. Stir Well.*
2. *Then, Slowly Pour The Entire Orange Sauce
   Over The Browned Chicken & Olive Oil.*
3. *On Medium, Let The Sauce Boil Lightly. Reduce Heat.*
4. *Cover Pan. Simmer The Chicken Breasts, Olive Oil
   And Orange Sauce for About 30 ~40 Minutes,
   Until Chicken "Flakes" when Tested with a Fork.*

A Special Note

1. *If Liquid Evaporates, Mix 1/2 Cup of Orange Juice,
   1/4 Cup of Hot Water and 2 Oz. Grand Marnier.
   Add This to Pan, and Simmer 5 Minutes More.*

Serving Suggestion

On a Large Warmed Platter, Spoon some Orange Sauce across The Platter. Arrange The Chicken Breasts, and Spoon more Orange Sauce over The Chicken. Sprinkle Lightly with Grated Romano Cheese. Place The Orange Slices and Parsley Sprigs to Garnish. We served This Dish with our Caesar Salad, Parsley Cheese Potatoes and our Herbs & Spices Bread. Compliment with a White Wine. To Sweetly Finish and in keeping with Sicilian Tradition, try Mama's Fig Cookies ~ Cucidati ~ and Coffee! A Perfect Meal & Perfect Finish! Enjoy!

Chicken Tarragon, Spumante Sauce

Tarragon Pollo Spumante

Chicken Tarragon in Spumante Sauce was a Dish created by Salvino, using two ingredients that both he and Margo love ~ Sweet Asti Spumante Sparkling Wine and Angel Hair Pasta. Guests at Mama Lena's also fell in love immediately with this fabulous Dish! This Special Dish of Lovely Flavors is a wonderful Holiday Dish with The Sparkling Spumante Sauce! This Lightly Sweet and Flavored Chicken makes a Festive Dish in Taste and in Appearance. Don't wait for the Holidays to prepare This Delight! We know you can find many occasions that call for a Light, Romantic Dish, like this wonderful one! We are sure you will fall in love with This Lovely Dish the very first time, just as our Mama Lena's Guests did! Enjoy!

Ingredients   Serves 4~6

The Chicken Breasts	4	**Large Chicken Breasts (Boneless & Skinless)** **(Double Breasts ~ Split in Half for 8 Pieces)**
	2	**Pinches of Salt**
	1	**Pinch of Pepper**
	3	**Pinches of Tarragon**
To Saute	1/4	**Cup of Olive Oil**
	1/2	**Lb. of Butter (Sweet & Lightly Salted)**
The Spumante Sauce	1	**Large Onion (Finely Chopped)**
	1/2	**Cup of White Pearl Onions (Whole)**
	2	**Pinches of Salt**
	1	**Pinch of Pepper**
	1	**Pinch of Thyme**
	3	**Cups of Asti Spumante Wine**
The Angel Hair Pasta	1	**Lb. of Angel Hair Pasta (Cooked ~ Al Dente)** **(Follow Cooking Instructions on the Package)**
The Garnish	1/4	**Cup of Pine Nuts**
	1/4	**Cup of Asiago Cheese (Finely Grated)**
	1/4	**Bunch of Fresh Parsley**

Preparation ~ Chicken Tarragon, Spumante Sauce

**The
Spumante Sauce
~ Prepare ~**

1. *In a Large Skillet, Heat The Olive Oil to Medium.
Saute The Chopped Onions for About 3 Minutes.*
2. *Add The Pearl Onions, and Saute for 1 Minute More.*
3. *Remove Chopped Onions and Pearl Onions from
The Olive Oil. Set The Oil Aside to Saute Chicken.*
4. *In a Large Saucepan, Combine The Sauteed
Chopped Onions and The Sauteed Pearl Onions
with 2 Pinches of Salt, 1 Pinch of Pepper,
and 1 Pinch of Thyme. Stir Together.*
5. *Add 3 Cups of Asti Spumante Wine to The Ingredients,
and Stir In for 1 Minute, Bringing All to a Boil.*

**The
Chicken Breasts
~ Saute ~**

6. *Turn Heat Off. Cover Sauce Pan. Let Sauce Set Up.*

1. *Rinse Chicken Thoroughly with Cold Water, and
Place on Paper Towels to Drain. Pat Dry.*
2. *Season The Chicken Breasts with 2 Pinches of Salt,
1 Pinch of Pepper and 3 Pinches of Tarragon,
Patting The Seasonings into The Chicken.*
3. *On Medium, Heat The Olive Oil you saved, and
Add The 1/2 Lb. of Butter Now. Melt In with The Oil.*
4. *Brown Chicken Breasts for 3~4 Minutes ~ Each Side.*

**The
Chicken & Sauce
~ Combine & Bake ~**

1. *In a Large Roaster, Pour Half of The Spumante Sauce
Across The Bottom of The Roaster Pan.*
2. *Place The Sauteed Chicken Breasts on Top of Sauce.
Pour Oil & Butter Sauce over The Chicken Breasts.*
3. *Now, Pour All Remaining Spumante Sauce over The Top.*
4. *Seal Roaster Pan Airtight with Foil.*
5. *Bake in a Preheated 325 Degree Oven for 1 Hour.*
6. *At 30 Minutes, Take Pan Out of Oven. Do Not Open Foil.
Just Gently Shake Pan to Allow Sauce to Settle Well.*
7. *Return Pan to Oven for Final 30 Minutes of Baking.*
8. *After Baking, Remove Pan. Allow Pan to Sit 15 Minutes,
And Let Textures Settle Before Opening and Serving!*

Serving Suggestion

On a Large Deep Heated Decorative Platter, Spoon a little Spumante Sauce across Platter. Place The Pasta and Spoon more Sauce on Pasta. Toss Together Gently. Arrange The Chicken on Top of Tossed Pasta. Then, Spoon Remaining Spumante Sauce over Top of The Chicken. Sprinkle Chicken Tops with Pine Nuts & Grated Asiago Cheese. Place Parsley Sprigs over The Chicken and Angel Hair Pasta to Garnish. Serve with Artichoke & Bibb Lettuce Salad, Herbs & Spices Bread and a Nice Rose Wine. A Lovely Finish to This Superb Dish is Our Cassata ~ Chocolate & Vanilla, with Salvino's Vanilla Rum Sauce and an Italian Cappuccino! A Dinner like this can only bring Romance to your Table! Enjoy!

Chapter Eight
The Meat Entrees

Pages 153 ~ 193

Braciola Steak, Breaded

Bistecca Braciola Pannato

Our Fall Menu at Mama Lena's was never complete without our Unique and Delicious Breaded Braciola. Our Guests were ready for something a bit heartier with the "Crisp" Chicago Wind starting to stir the leaves from the Trees. And Our Tender Braciola, with our Very Special Filling smoothly topped by our Mama Lena's Tomato Sauce, was just the Entree to warm their hearts and take their chills away! We very much enjoyed serving This Dish and watching our Guests uncover each surprise taste and treat unfolding with every bite. You will want to make this a Regular on your Fall & Winter Menu, too!   Enjoy!

Ingredients   Serves 4~6

The Braciola Steak	2	Lbs. of Boneless Sirloin Tip (Have Sliced into Eight 1/4 Lb. Steak Pieces)
The Braciola Filling	1/2	Cup of Olive Oil
	2	Cloves of Garlic (Minced)
	1	Medium Green Pepper (Finely Chopped)
	1	Medium White Onion (Finely Chopped)
	3	Stalks of Celery (Finely Chopped)
	3	Eggs (Large) (Hard Boil, Cool & Finely Chop)
	1/2	Cup of Mama Lena's Bread Crumbs (Italian Seasoned)
	2	Tablespoons of Capers (Whole)
	1/4	Cup of Parmesan Cheese (Grated)
The Seasonings	2	Large Pinches of Salt
	2	Large Pinches of Pepper
	1	Large Pinch of Marjoram
	1	Large Pinch of Mint
The Bread Crumbs	1	Recipe of Mama Lena's Bread Crumbs (Italian Seasoned) (See Recipe ~ Chapter Ten)
	2	Eggs (Lightly Beaten) (To Dip Steaks for Breading)
The Tomato Sauce	1	Mama Lena's "Quick" Basic Tomato Sauce Recipe (See Recipe ~ Chapter Five)
For Sealing	32	Toothpicks (To Hold Rolled Steaks Together)
The Garnish	1/4	Cup of Asiago Cheese (Grated)
	1/4	Bunch of Fresh Parsley

Preparation ~ Braciola Steak, Breaded

**The
Filling for Steaks
~ Prepare ~**

1. In an Extra~Large Skillet, Heat The Olive Oil to Medium.
   Add The Green Pepper, Chopped Onions & The Celery.
   Add 1 Pinch of Salt and 1 Pinch of Pepper.
   Saute for About 3~4 Minutes.
2. Add The Garlic, and Saute All Together for 1 Minute More.
3. With a Slotted Spoon to Drain, Remove All from The Oil.
   Place in Large Bowl. Save The Skillet & Oil for Frying.
4. In The Large Bowl, Combine The Sauteed Green Peppers,
   Onions, Celery, Garlic with 1 Pinch More of Salt,
   1 Pinch More of Pepper, 1 Pinch of Marjoram,
   1 Pinch of Mint. Mix Together Well.
5. Add The 3 Chopped Eggs, 1/2 Cup of Bread Crumbs,
   The Capers and Parmesan Cheese. Mix Together Well.
   The Texture should now be Firm and Moist.
   If Texture is Too Dry, Add 1 Tablespoon of Olive Oil.

**The Steaks
~ Stuff, Roll & Seal ~**

1. On a Sheet of Wax Paper, Place The Sirloin Steaks.
2. Spoon The Filling on Each Flat Steak, Covering a
   Generous Portion of The Steak Center.
   Add Two Whole Green Pimento Olives to Top of Filling.
3. Roll Each Steak, Securing The Filling in The Center.
   Tuck in Each End and Bind Steak with 4 Toothpicks.

**The
Steaks & Sauce
~ Bread, Fry & Bake ~**

1. Egg The Rolled Steaks and Coat Each with Bread Crumbs.
   Set Breaded Steaks on Paper Towels to Dry Breading.
2. In The Large Skillet, Heat to Medium The Oil you saved.
   Evenly Brown The Steaks, About 2 Minutes Each Side.
3. In a Large Roaster Pan, Pour Across Bottom of The Pan ~
   1 Cup of "Warm" Mama Lena's "Quick" Tomato Sauce.
4. Place The Browned Steaks on Top of The Warm Sauce.
   Cover The Steaks with 2 More Cups of Warm Sauce.
5. Seal Pan Top Airtight with Foil.
6. Bake in a Preheated 350 Degree Oven for 1 Hour.

Serving Suggestion

*Serve The Braciola on a Large Deep Heated White Platter, Spooning Sauce across Bottom
of The Platter. (Remove All Toothpicks and Discard Them). Arrange Braciola Attractively.
Spoon Remaining Sauce over The Braciola Tops. Sprinkle Lightly with Asiago Cheese.
Place Parsley Sprigs for a Nice Touch! We served our Very Special Braciola with our
Italian & Antipasto Salad Supreme, Pasta & Butter Parsley Sauce and Hot Cheese Bread.
A Soft Red Wine compliments This Special Dish ~ One of Mama Lena's Best! Enjoy!*

Meat Balls With Cream Sherry

Polpette con Shere

As children, all we had to see was the Big Black Cast Iron Skillet and the Ground Chuck out in the morning, and we would all be flying home in the afternoon to taste Mama's Meat Balls! Mama would be waiting for us. As she turned, to place some of her fresh Italian Bread on the Table, we kids, who just could not wait, would each snatch a Meatball right out of the Skillet! At Mama Lena's Italian Kitchen, we served our Meatballs on our Party Menus only. We had to double the recipe every time, using one Recipe for Sandwiches with Sauce on the Side, and we needed a second Recipe to cook The Meatballs in Mama Lena's Sauce to serve on Pasta! Our Restaurant Guests loved our Very Delicious Mama Lena's Meat Balls as much as we did! You just cannot resist a Mama Lena's Meat Ball ~ You'll see!   Enjoy!

Ingredients   Serves 6~8

The Ground Meat	2	Lbs. of Ground Chuck Beef (85 % Lean) (Have The Meat Ground Medium)
To Saute With The Meat	1/2	Cup of Olive Oil
	1	Large Onion (Finely Chopped)
	1	Large Green Pepper (Finely Chopped)
	1	Clove of Garlic (Minced)
The Seasonings	3	Pinches of Salt
	2	Pinches of Pepper
	3	Pinches of Oregano
	2	Pinches of Basil
	3	Pinches of Parsley
	1	Pinch of Mint
The Special Additions	1/4	Cup of Parmesan Cheese
	4	Eggs (Large) (Lightly Beaten)
	1/8	Cup of Mama Lena's Italian Dressing Supreme (See Recipe ~ Chapter Three)
	1/4	Cup of Cream Sherry
The Tomato Sauce	1	Recipe of Mama Lena's "Quick" Basic Tomato Sauce (See Recipe ~ Chapter Five)
The Bread Crumbs	1	Cup of Bread Crumbs (Italian Seasoned) (See Recipe ~ Chapter Ten)
The Garnish	1/4	Cup of Parmesan Cheese (Grated)
	1/4	Bunch of Fresh Parsley

Preparation ~ Meat Balls with Cream Sherry

**The
Saute Mixture**

1. In a Large Skillet, Heat The Olive Oil to Medium.
   Saute The Onions and Green Peppers for 3 Minutes.
2. Add The Garlic, and Saute for 1 Minute More.
3. Remove The Onions, Green Peppers & Garlic from Oil.
   Place All in Bowl, and Set Aside to Add Later.
   Save The Olive Oil for Browning Meat Balls Later.

**The Meat Mixture
~ Combine ~**

1. In a Large Bowl, Place The Ground Chuck, and Salt
   Pepper, Oregano, Basil, Parsley & Parmesan Cheese.
2. Mix Together with a Wooden spoon, Or Like Mama ~
   Use The Hands to Feel The Texture of The Mixture.
3. Add Eggs, Italian Dressing & Cream Sherry. Mix Well.
4. Now, Add Sauteed Onions, Peppers & Garlic. Mix Gently.
5. Lastly, Add Mama Lena's Italian Seasoned Bread Crumbs.
   Gently Mix In for About 2~3 Minutes.
6. If The Mixture is Too Soft, Add More Bread Crumbs,
   A Little At A Time ~ Texture Should Not be Too Firm.

**The Meat Balls
~ Shape ~**

1. First, Shape The Meatballs by Using an Ice Cream Scoop.
   Using The Scoop to Shape, This Recipe will
   Yield About 12 to 14 Nicely~sized Meat Balls.
2. Rub Hands with The Olive Oil, You Set Aside Above.
   Roll Each Meat Ball in Your Hands to Make It Tight.
3. The Meat Balls should be Evenly Shaped and Firmed ~
   Perfect for Browning, and A Picture to Serve!

**The Meat Balls
~ Brown ~**

1. In a Large Skillet, Heat The Saved Olive Oil to Medium.
2. Brown Meat Balls, Until Evenly Browned on Both Sides.

**The Meat Balls
~ And Sauce ~**

1. When Serving The Meat Balls in The Tomato Sauce,
   Brown Only Lightly ~ They Cook More in The Sauce.
2. Once The Sauce is Cooking, Add The Meat Balls for
   Only The Last 20 Minutes of Cooking.

Serving Suggestions

To Serve as Sandwiches ~ *Place The Delicious Meat Balls, with the Marvelous Aroma, into a Large Heated Decorative Bowl. Serve with a Basket of Mama's Baguette Style Bread, a Side Dish of our Tomato Sauce to Spoon On, and some Fontinella Cheese, Olives & Wine! Enjoy!*

To Serve in Sauce with Pasta ~ *On a Heated Platter, Spoon some Sauce on Platter. Place The Pasta and Spoon on More Sauce. Toss Gently. Place The Meat Balls on Top of Pasta and Top with More Sauce. Sprinkle with Parmesan Cheese and Garnish with Parsley Sprigs. Serve with our Italian & Antipasto Salad Supreme, our warm Italian Bread and a Soft Red Wine. Such a Simple Mama Lena's Treat, but a Simply Great One! A Delicious Delight! Enjoy!*

Steak, Ground & Stuffed With Rice Filling

Orrinchini ala Madonna

When we were children, Grandma would make a Sicilian Dish called Arancini, which was Small Flavored Rice Balls with a Meat Filling. For The Restaurant, Mama & Salvino wanted A Dish with Rice that would be Very Special for our Guests. While, Mama loved the Arancini Grandma had made, Papa thought that we should serve More Meat and Less Rice. So, Salvino created a Superb Ground Round Steak, with The Most Delightful Rice Filling imaginable, and topped it with Mama Lena's Tomato Sauce. While This Dish was inspired by Grandma's Arancini ~ Salvino had truly created a unique new Mama Lena's Dish, called by our Guests, "Orrinchini." Try it now ~ " Orrinchini ala Madonna!" Enjoy!

Ingredients   Serves 6~8

"Orrinchini"		
Steak Mixture	2	Lbs. of Round Steak (Ground Fine ~ 85% Lean)
	4	Eggs (Large) (Lightly Beaten)
	1	Cup of Mama Lena's Bread Crumbs (Italian Seasoned)
	2	Pinches of Salt
	2	Pinches of Pepper
	2	Pinches of Parsley
	2	Pinches of Romano Cheese (Grated)
	1/2	Cup of Dry Vermouth
	1/2	Cup of Olive Oil
"Orrinchini"		
Rice Filling	2	Cups of White Rice (Prepare & Use Cooked)
	1/4	Cup of Mama Lena's Bread Crumbs (Italian Seasoned)
	1/8	Cup of Grated Orange Rind
	1	Large White Sweet Onion (Finely Chopped)
	2	Stalks of Celery (Finely Chopped)
	1	Large Red Pepper (Finely Chopped)
	3	Scallions (Finely Chopped)
	12	Large Green Olives (Pitted and Chopped)
	2	Pinches of Romano Cheese (Grated)
	2	Pinches of Salt
	2	Pinches of Black Pepper
	2	Pinches of Mint
	1/4	Cup of Pine Nuts
The		
Tomato Sauce	1	Recipe of Mama Lena's "Quick" Basic Tomato Sauce (See Recipe ~ Chapter Five)
The Garnish	1/4	Cup of Romano Cheese (Grated)
	1/4	Bunch of Fresh Parsley
	1	Orange (Sliced into Thin Rounds)

Preparation ~ Steak, Ground & Stuffed, with Rice Filling ~ Orrinchini

The Rice Filling
~ Prepare ~

1. In a Large Skillet, Heat The Olive Oil to Medium.
   Saute The Red Peppers for 2 Minutes.
2. Add The Onions and Celery. Saute for 2 Minutes More.
3. Add Scallions, Green Olives, 1 Pinch of Salt & Pepper.
   Mix In Well. Cover Pan. Simmer for 3 Minutes.
4. With a Slotted Spoon, Remove Sauteed Vegetables
   for The Filling. Save The Oil to Brown Meat.

The Rice Filling
~ Combine ~

1. In a Large Bowl, Mix The Cooked Rice, Bread Crumbs,
   Grated Orange Rind, Romano Cheese, Pine Nuts,
   1 Pinch of Salt & Pepper and 2 Pinches of Mint.
2. Slowly, Add The Sauteed Vegetables to The Mixture.
   Mixture should be Moist & Firm. If Mixture is
   Too Dry, Add 1 Tablespoon of The Oil you saved.

The
Steak Mixture
~ Prepare ~

1. In a Large Bowl, Combine Ground Round Steak, Eggs,
   1/2 Cup of Bread Crumbs, Salt, Pepper, Parsley,
   Romano Cheese and 1/4 Cup Dry Vermouth.
2. Mix Together Well with Hands, Until Moist and Firm.
   If Texture is Too Soft, Add Bread Crumbs to Firm.
3. Divide Meat Mixture into 8 Equal~sized Balls of Meat.
4. Put Wax Paper Over Meat. Press The Balls of Meat Flat.

The
Steak & Filling
~Combine~
~Brown & Bake~

1. Spoon Equal Amounts of The Filling onto Meat Center.
   Fold The Edges of The Meat Together.
   Rub Hands with Oil. Shape Meat into Oval Shape.
2. Heat The Olive Oil you saved, and Brown Each
   Filled Steak on All Sides, Until Evenly Browned.
3. Place on Paper Towels to Let The Oil Drain Off.
4. In a Large Roaster Pan, Pour 1 Cup of "Warm"
   Mama Lena's "Quick" Basic Tomato Sauce.
5. Place The 8 Orrinchini on Top of Warm Sauce.
   Pour 1/4 Cup of Dry Vermouth Over Orrinchini.
   Now, Top All with 2 Cups More of The Sauce.
6. Seal the Roaster Pan Airtight with Foil.
7. Bake in a Preheated 350 Oven for 30 Minutes.

Serving Suggestion

Serve Salvino's Specialty on a Large Heated Platter. Spoon Sauce across Bottom of Platter. Arrange The Orrinchini, and Spoon Remaining Sauce over The Tops. Sprinkle Lightly with Romano Cheese. Place Parsley Sprigs and Slices of Oranges on Platter for Nice Garnish. Accompany with a Caesar Salad, a Pasta & White Cream Sauce and warm Italian Bread. A Soft Red Wine would be the proper compliment to allow you to concentrate on the truly captivating aroma and lovely special flavors of The "Orrinchini ala Madonna."   Enjoy!

Steak with Lemon Oregano Sauce

Bistecca con Limone

Our Mama Lena's Steak, with the Lemon and Oregano Sauce, originated with Mama's Father. Grandpa Matteo loved for Grandma Anna to use his Fruits and Vegetables at every chance. At that time, they served Steak only for very special occasions. So one time, as Grandma and Grandpa were preparing for Mama's Birthday ~ a very special occasion ~ they decided upon this wonderful recipe, using Grandpa's Lemons, Garlic, Oregano, Mint, Mushrooms and Onions ~ all the products he very lovingly selected each day at the Market for His Wagon. This very Treasured Recipe always had Very Special Memories for Mama and was always appreciated by our Guests! We know you will love This Special Dish as we all do!   Enjoy!

Ingredients   Serves 4~6

The		
Dinner Steaks	2~1/2	Lbs. of Beef Tenderloin (Six 6~7 Oz. Filets)
		(Have Cut to Equal Size at The Market)
The		
Lemon Oregano	2	Lemons (Use The Juice Only)
Sauce	2	Cloves of Garlic (Minced)
	1/2	Cup of Olive Oil
	3	Large Pinches of Oregano
	2	Large Pinches of Coarse Black Pepper
	1	Pinch of Mint
Season		
After Broiling	2	Large Pinches of Salt
		(Sprinkle onto Steaks, After Broiling)
Topping		
For Broiled Steaks	1/2	Lb. of White Mushrooms (Slice into Halves)
	2	Large White Onions (Sliced Thin)
	2	Tablespoons of Butter
	4	Tablespoons of Olive Oil
	2	Large Pinches of Salt
	2	Large Pinches of Black Pepper
The Garnish	1/8	Cup of Asiago Cheese (Grated)
	1	Lemon (Cut into Thin Rounds)
	1/4	Bunch of Fresh Parsley

160

Preparation ~ Steak with Lemon Oregano Sauce

**The
Dinner Steaks
~ Marinate ~**

1. In a Large Bowl, Combine The Juice of 2 Lemons,
   The Garlic, Olive Oil, Oregano, Black Pepper,
   and Mint. Mix Together Well. Set Aside.
   Allow The Lemon Sauce To Marinate for 15 Minutes.
2. Then, Place The Tenderloin Steaks into The Bowl.
   Cover The Steaks Completely with Marinade Sauce.
3. Cover The Bowl Airtight with Plastic. Set Aside.
   Allow The Steaks & Sauce to Marinate for 30 Minutes.

**The
Marinated Steaks
~ Broil ~**

1. Preheat Oven to 400 for 5 Minutes. Turn to Broil Setting,
   Just Prior to Placing The Steaks into The Oven.
   The Oven is Heated & Broils More Evenly This Way.
2. Remove The Steaks from The Marinade Sauce.
   Place Them Evenly Apart on The Broiler Pan.
   Broiler Pan should be on Second Shelf from The Top.
3. Broil to Your Preference ~ (Oven Has Been Preheated)
4. Medium Broiled Steaks ~ Broil 2 Minutes First on One Side.
   Brush with Marinade Sauce. Broil ~1 Minute More.
   (One Side is Finished)
   Turn Steak, Broil 2 Minutes on The Other Side.
   Brush with Marinade. Broil Again ~ 1 Minute More.
   (Other Side is Finished)
5. For Rare Steaks   ~ Do First Broil Each Side ~ 1 Minute.
6. Well~Done Steaks ~ Do First Broil Each Side ~ 3 Minutes.

**The
Broiled Steaks
~ Add Topping ~**

1. In a Large Skillet, Slowly Heat The Butter to a Melt.
   Add The Olive Oil. Heat on Medium for 1 Minute More.
2. Saute Onion 4 Minutes. With a Slotted Spoon, Remove Onion.
3. Saute The Mushrooms for 2 Minutes , and
   Then Season The Mushrooms with Salt and Black Pepper.
4. Add The Onions Back into The Mushrooms, Salt and Pepper.
   Saute All Together for 3 Minutes More.
5. Turn Off Heat. Cover Pan. Let The Pan Stand, Until
   You Finish Broiling and Remove The Steaks from Oven.

Serving Suggestions

Arrange The Broiled Steaks on Large Heated Decorative Platter. Spoon Topping over Steaks, Covering Well. Sprinkle Lightly with Asiago Cheese. Garnish with Lemon Slices & Parsley Sprigs for a Nice Finish! Serve This Superb Steak Entree with our Caesar Salad, Vermicelli Pasta with Marinara Sauce and our Tomato Cheese Bread. Zabaione and Coffee for Dessert. A Soft Red Wine is a perfect compliment to This Delicious Dish of Special Memories! Enjoy!

Steak Pizzaiola

Bistecca Pizzaiola

Mama Lena's Steak Pizzaiola is a Treasure close to our hearts, as this Recipe was perfected by Mama and Salvino together for the Restaurant, and it became one of the most favored dishes to our Mama Lena's Guests. Mama's Mother had made a lovely Breaded Steak that remained in Mama's mind. Mama made Grandma's Breaded Steak, while Salvino enhanced the Dish with a luscious Red Wine Sauce with some lovely spices and the special addition of our Caponata di Melanzane ~ ala Madonna. This Divine Dish turned out to be So Exquisite! As soon as you try This Very Delicious Dish, you will see why it joined the Top of The List as an All~Time Favorite of Mama Lena's Guests and Mama and Family, too!   Enjoy!

Ingredients   Serves 4~6

The Dinner Steaks	2~1/2	Lbs. of Rib~Eye Steak (Six 6~7 Oz. Steaks) (Have Cut to Size at Market)
The Base for Sauce	1/2	Cup of Olive Oil
	1	Large Onion (Finely Chopped)
	3	Cloves of Garlic (Slivered)
	1	Cup of Dry Red Wine
	1	Large Can of Plum Tomatoes, Crushed in Puree (Large Can ~ 28 Oz. Size)
	1	Large Can of Hot Water
The Seasonings	1	Large Pinch of Red Pepper Flakes (Saute)
	2	Large Pinches of Salt
	2	Large Pinches of Pepper
	2	Large Pinches of Sugar (Granulated)
	2	Large Pinches of Basil
	2	Large Pinches of Oregano
The Cheese	1/2	Cup of Romano Cheese (Grated)
The Bread Crumbs	1	Recipe of Mama Lena's Bread Crumbs (Italian Seasoned) (See Recipe ~ Chapter Ten)
	2	Eggs (Lightly Beaten) (Dip Meat Prior to Breading)
The Caponata	1	Recipe of Caponata di Melanzane (Eggplant Relish) (See Recipe ~ Chapter One) ~ OR ~
	1	Large Can of Commercial Caponata (10 Oz. Can Size) (Purchase At Italian Store)
The Garnish	1/4	Cup of Romano Cheese (Grated)
	1/4	Bunch of Fresh Parsley

Preparation ~ Mama Lena's Steak Pizzaiola

The **Saute Mixture**	**1.**	**In a Large Skillet, Heat The Olive Oil to Medium.** **Add The Chopped Onions, and Saute for 3 Minutes.** **Add The Slivered Garlic and The Red Pepper Flakes.** **Saute All Together for 1 Minute More.**
	2.	**Remove The Onions and Garlic from The Olive Oil.** **Set Aside The Olive Oil for Browning Steaks Later.**

The
Red Wine Sauce

1. **In a Large Saucepan, Combine The Plum Tomatoes and**
   Water, Onions and Garlic, and Salt, Pepper,
   Sugar, Basil and Oregano.
2. **Bring The Entire Mixture to a Boil, Stirring Often.**
3. **Lower The Heat to Medium. Add The Dry Red Wine.**
   Let The Sauce Cook for 2~3 Minutes More.
4. **Add The Caponata to The Sauce. Simmer for 5 Minutes.**
5. **Turn Sauce Off. Set Aside, Until Ready to Bake.**

The Steaks
~ Bread & Brown ~

1. **Dip The Steaks in The Beaten Egg, and**
   Coat with The Italian Seasoned Bread Crumbs.
2. **Let The Steaks Sit & Allow Breading to Dry, About 3 Minutes.**
3. **Meanwhile, Heat The Olive Oil to Medium Heat.**
4. **Then, Brown The Breaded Steaks for 2 Minutes on Each Side.**
5. **Place The Browned Steaks on Paper Towels to Drain.**

The
Steaks & Sauce
~ Combine & Bake ~

1. **In a Large Roaster, Pour 1 Cup of The Wine Sauce**
   Across The Bottom of The Roaster Pan.
2. **Lightly, Place The Breaded Steaks on Top of The Sauce.**
3. **Slowly, Pour The Remaining Sauce over The Steaks.**
4. **Sprinkle Entire Top of The Sauce with Romano Cheese.**
5. **Seal The Roaster Top Airtight with Foil.**
6. **Bake in a Preheated 350 Degree Oven for 1 Hour.**

Serving Suggestion

On a Lovely Deep Heated Platter, Pour about 1 Cup of The Steak Pizzaiola Sauce onto Platter. Arrange The Steaks Pizzaiola on The Sauce. Spoon The Remainder of The Sauce Over The Steaks ~ The Tomatoes and The Caponata will make an Attractive and Appealing Topping. Sprinkle Lightly with Romano Cheese. Place Parsley Sprigs to Garnish. This Dish has such wonderful character, so we accompanied it simply with Our Artichoke & Bibb Lettuce Salad, Pasta & Butter Parsley Sauce and Herbs & Spices Bread. Finish Sweetly ~ Biscotti & Coffee. Soft Red Wine perfectly compliments This Dish, so loved by all Mama Lena's Guests! Enjoy!

Lamb Chops
in Sweet & Sour Sauce

Agnello~Cotolette di Agro~ Dolce

The Mama Lena's Lamb Chops in Sweet & Sour Sauce is a Dish that would always draw applause. The Flavorful Sauce is absolutely Captivating and Perfectly Compliments the Sauteed Chops. This Delicious Sauce has just the Right Combination of Sweetness and Sharpness that a Lamb Dish needs. This Delightful Dish is also so very simple to prepare! We know you will love This Treasure as our Mama Lena's Guests always did! Enjoy!

Ingredients   Serves 4~6

The **Lamb Chops**	2	Lbs. of Lamb Chops (4 Large, Or 6 Medium Chops)
To Saute	1/4	Cup of Olive Oil
	2	Cloves of Garlic (Large Slices)
The **Sweet & Sour Sauce**	1	Large Can of Plum Tomatoes, Crushed in Puree (Large Can ~ 28 Oz. Size)
	1/2	Can of Hot Water (14 Oz.)
The **Seasonings**	2	Pinches of Salt
	2	Pinches of Pepper
	4	Pinches of Mint
	1/4	Cup of White Vinegar
	1/4	Cup of Sugar (Granulated)
The **Marinated Apricots**	1	Dozen Dried Apricots (Cut into Halves)
	1/2	Cup of White Wine (Marinate Apricots)
	1/8	Cup of Sugar (Granulated)
The **Bread Crumbs**	1/2	Cup of Mama Lena's Bread Crumbs (Italian Seasoned) (See Recipe ~ Chapter Ten)
The Garnish	1/4	Cup of Asiago Cheese (Grated)
	1/4	Bunch of Fresh Parsley

Preparation ~ Lamb Chops, Sweet & Sour Sauce

The *Apricots in Wine* *~ Marinate ~*	1. **Place The Apricot Halves into a Bowl, and Sugar Them.**
	2. **Pour The White Wine over Sugared Apricots. Stir Gently.**
	3. **Seal Bowl Airtight with Plastic. Set Aside to Marinate.**

The *Lamb Chops*

1. **In an Extra~Large Skillet, Heat The Olive Oil to Medium. Saute Garlic, Until Lightly Brown, About 1 Minute. Remove The Garlic from The Oil. Discard Garlic.**
2. **In The Oil, Brown The Lamb Chops 2~3 Minutes Each Side. Place The Lamb Chops on Paper Towels to Drain.**

The *Sweet & Sour Sauce*

1. **In a Large Sauce Pan, Combine Tomatoes, Water, Salt, Pepper, and Mint. Bring to a Boil, Stirring Often.**
2. **When The Sauce Boils, Add The White Vinegar and Sugar. Bring Sauce to a Second Full Boil.**
3. **At The Second Boil, Lower Heat. Cook on Low Heat for 15 Minutes More. (Keep Covered Full 15 Minutes)**
4. **Remove Sauce from Heat. Let Sauce Set Up for 5 Minutes.**

The *Lamb Chops & Sauce* *~ Combine & Bake ~*

1. **In a Large Roaster Pan, Pour 1 Cup of Sweet & Sour Sauce Across The Bottom of The Pan.**
2. **Arrange The Lamb Chops on Top of The Sauce, and Slowly Add All Remaining Sauce to Top of Chops.**
3. **Add The Apricot Halves and The White Wine Marinade to The Top of The Sauce.**
4. **Sprinkle All of The Italian Bread Crumbs over the Top of The Sauce to Seal It During Baking.**
5. **Seal Top of Pan Airtight with Foil.**
6. **Bake 50 Minutes in a Preheated 350 Degree Oven.**
7. **You can Immediately Serve This Delightful Dish!**

Serving Suggestion

Arrange The Lamb Chops on Deep Heated Decorative Platter. Spoon Sweet & Sour Sauce onto Platter. Place The Lamb Chops over The Sauce. Spoon more Sauce onto Lamb Chops. Arrange Apricots over The Lamb Chops. Sprinkle Asiago Cheese on Tops and Place Parsley Sprigs to Garnish. Serve extra Sauce in a Heated Gravy Bowl. Accompany This Delicious Dish with Artichoke & Bibb Lettuce Salad with White Wine Vinaigrette Dressing, Fettucine Pasta with Butter Almond Caper Sauce. Soft Blush Wine compliments perfectly! Sweetly Finish with a Cassata Amaretto with Pine Nuts and a nice Flavored Coffee. Mama Lena's Guests were enchanted with This Meal and your family will be, too! Enjoy!

Lamb Cutlets in Marsala Wine

Agnello Costolette Marsala

We personally love The Dishes Cooked with Marsala Wine ~ there's such a lovely aroma and flavor to These Dishes and an Old~World Romance about them! The Marsala Wine is The Wine produced in Sicily. Whenever we use it in our Cooking, it seems to impart some sort of Romance of the Past! This Wine captures a Unique Taste that Grandma conveyed to Mama and Mama conveyed to us. We think you will agree with us, as you prepare our Recipes that include The Marsala Wine. You will find yourself appreciating the wonderful results produced with these exceptional wines which come in Dry, Sweet & Other Flavors. This Recipe calls for Dry Marsala Wine! Be Prepared for a Romantic Dish! Enjoy!

Ingredients   Serves 4~6

The Lamb Cutlets	2~1/2	Lbs. of Lamb Cutlets (Six 6~7 Oz. Cutlets) (Have Cut from The Sirloin End of The Leg)
The Seasonings	3	Pinches of Salt
	2	Pinches of Pepper
	1	Pinch of Rosemary (Ground)
	1	Pinch of Thyme
	1	Pinch of Basil
To Saute	1/2	Cup of Olive Oil
	1	Clove of Garlic (Sliced)
The Mushrooms	1	Lb. of Fresh Mushrooms (Sliced) (Saute Separately for Sauce)
The Marsala Sauce	1/4	Lb. of Butter (Sweet & Lightly Salted)
	1	Cup of Marsala Wine (Dry)
	1/2	Cup of Seedless White Raisins (Marinated in Marsala Wine First)
The Garnish	1/4	Cup of Pine Nuts
	1/4	Cup of Asiago Cheese (Grated)
	1/4	Bunch of Fresh Parsley

Preparation ~ Lamb Cutlets in Marsala Wine

The
Raisin Marinade

1. **Place White Raisins into The Marsala Wine. Mix Well.**
2. **Cover Airtight with Plastic. Set Aside to Marinate, While You Prepare Lamb Cutlets.**

The
Lamb & Mushrooms
~ Saute ~

1. **Place The Lamb Cutlets between Two Pieces of Wax Paper. Using a Mallet, Pound The Cutlets Until Flat & Thin.**
2. **Season The Lamb Cutlets on Both Sides with Salt, Pepper, Rosemary, Thyme and Basil.**
3. **In a Large Skillet, Heat The Olive Oil to Medium. Lightly Brown The Garlic for About 1 Minute. Remove The Garlic from The Oil. Discard Garlic.**
4. **Place The Lamb Cutlets into The Garlic~flavored Oil. Saute Cutlets for 2 Minutes on Each Side. Take Cutlets from Oil. Set on Paper Towels to Drain.**
5. **In the Same Oil, Saute The Sliced Mushrooms for About 2~3 Minutes. Remove The Mushrooms, and Place in a Strainer to Drain Oil. Set Them Aside.**

The
Lamb & Marsala Sauce
~ Cook ~

1. **Discard The Olive Oil from The Large Skillet, and Wipe Skillet Clean with a Paper Towel.**
2. **Slowly, Heat The Butter in The Skillet to a Melt.**
3. **Set The Lamb Cutlets into The Butter. Turn Cutlets Over, so Butter is on Both Sides of The Cutlets.**
4. **Spoon Sauteed Mushrooms on Top of The Buttery Cutlets.**
5. **Slowly, Pour The Marsala Wine through a Strainer, and Keep The Marinated Raisins Aside to Add Later.**
6. **Cover Pan. Cook The Lamb Cutlets with The Mushrooms, And The Marsala Wine & Butter Sauce on Medium Heat, for About 10 Minutes.**
7. **After 10 Minutes, Add The White Raisins. Cover The Pan. Cook Again for 5 Minutes More on Low Heat.**

Serving Suggestion

On a Large, Heated Platter, Spoon The Marsala Wine Sauce. Arrange Lamb Cutlets and cover Tops with The Marsala Wine Sauce, Raisins and Mushrooms. Sprinkle Pine Nuts across Top of Dish. Sprinkle Lightly with Asiago Cheese. Place Parsley Sprigs to Garnish. This is a Dish of Exceptional Tastes and Appearance. Accompany with our Caesar Salad, Pasta with White Cream Sauce & Hot Cheese Bread! Sweetly Finish ~ Zabaione Marsala. You will love The Romantic Tastes of This Dish, as our Mama Lena's Guests did! Enjoy!

Lamb Stew
With Macaroni

Agnello Stuffato Maccheroni

Our Mama Lena's Lamb Stew is a hearty and tasty dish, which especially pleased our Guests during those cold Chicago Winter months. The Macaroni Pasta always makes it even heartier and is fun to serve as well. There's something happy about the Macaroni in the Lamb Stew! Our Guests could hardly wait to enjoy this Dish. Some have said it was those blustery Chicago Winds blowing the Guests into Mama Lena's all Winter long, but we know better! After you have prepared This Dish yourself, you will know better, too! We think you and your family will love Mama Lena's Lamb Stew, as we all do! Enjoy!

Ingredients   **Serves 4~6**

The Lamb Meat	1~1/2	Lbs. of Lamb Shoulder (Boneless) (Cut into 2" Pieces for Stew)
	3	Pinches of Salt
	3	Pinches of Pepper
	1/4	Cup of Flour (To Flour The Lamb Pieces)
	4	Tablespoons of Olive Oil
The Vegetable Broth	2	Quarts of Vegetable Broth (See Recipe ~ Chapter Two) ~ OR ~
	2	Quarts of Water and 3 Vegetable Bouillon Cubes
	2	Pinches of Salt
	1	Pinch of Pepper
	2	Pinches of Parsley
	2	Pinches of Mint
	1	Bay Leaf (For Flavor Only)
	1	Cup of Cream Sherry
The Vegetables	3	Large Potatoes (Cut into Quarters ~ Makes 12 Pieces)
	4	Large Carrots (Cut into 1" Pieces)
	3	Stalks of Celery (Cut into 1" Pieces)
	1	Large Onion (Finely Chopped)
The Macaroni Pasta	1/2	Lb. of Imported Italian Macaroni (Small Shells) (Follow Cooking Instructions on the Package)
The Garnish	1/4	Cup of Parmesan Cheese (Coarsely Grated)
	1/4	Cup of Chopped Chives (Garnish over Cheese)

Preparation ~ Lamb Stew with Macaroni

**The
Lamb Stew Meat
~ Prepare ~**

1. Spread The Lamb Pieces out on a Cutting Board, and
   Add 1 Pinch of Salt and 1 Pinch of Pepper.
2. Then. Generously Flour Each Lamb Piece.
3. In a Large Skillet, Heat Oil to Medium, and
   Brown Each Lamb Piece Thoroughly.
4. Remove Pan from Heat. Discard The Olive Oil.
   Place The Meat on Paper Towels to Drain.

**The
Broth & Meat &
Vegetables
~ Combine ~**

1. In a Large Stockpot, Bring Following to a Full Boil ~
   2 Qts. of Vegetable Broth   ~ <u>OR</u> ~
   2 Qts. of Water with 3 Vegetable Bouillon Cubes.
2. Add Salt, Pepper, Parsley, Mint, and Bay Leaf.
   Stir All into Boiling Liquid.
3. Add Lamb to The Broth & Seasonings. Reduce Heat.
4. Cover Pan. Simmer for 1~1/2 Hours. Stir Often.
5. After One Hour, Add The Vegetables and Cream Sherry.
6. Cover Pan Again. Simmer for 30 Minutes More.

**The
Italian Macaroni
~ Prepare ~**

1. While The Lamb, The Vegetables, The Broth and
   Cream Sherry are in The Final Simmer,
   Prepare Imported Italian Macaroni.
   (Follow Cooking Instructions on the Package)
2. Drain The Pasta, But Do Not Rinse Pasta.

**The Pasta
~ Add to Broth ~**

1. After The Final Simmer of The Lamb, and
   Vegetables, Broth and Cream Sherry, then
   Add The Cooked Pasta to The Stockpot.
2. Turn Heat Off in The Stockpot, and
   Let The Entire Mixture Sit for 5~10 Minutes,
   Allowing The Flavors to Settle and Blend with Pasta.

Serving Suggestion

Serve This Colorful & Hearty Dish in a Large Soup Tureen with Ladle. Spoon into Dinner Soup Dishes or Pasta Dishes. Sprinkle Lightly with Parmesan Cheese & Chives. Serve This Flavorful Dish with Mama Lena's Italian Salad Supreme and an Extra Serving of our Hot Cheese Bread. A Dry Red Wine compliments. Anisette & Vanilla Biscotti for Dessert. Just like our Mama Lena's Guests in Chicago, you will warm up to This Delightful Dish the first time you try it! Papa would like to join you for this one! Enjoy!

Lamb & Zucchini Meatballs

Agnello Zucchini Polpette

The Mama Lena's Lamb & Zucchini Meatballs Dish is one we always delighted in serving! The Meatballs have a very light and delicate taste, filled with the Zucchini & Seasonings! This Dish is perfectly complimented by our Mama Lena's Red Cream Sauce with Zucchini! It is truly a surprise of many lovely tastes! Once you have tried This Delicious Dish, you will find it easy to make it one of your favorites, as our Mama Lena's Guests did! Enjoy!

Ingredients   Serves 4~6

The Lamb Meat	2	Lbs. of Lamb (Ground from Shoulder)
The Zucchini Filling	1	Large Zucchini (Cut into 1~1/2" Pieces)
	1	Medium Onion (Finely Chopped)
	2	Cloves of Garlic (Crushed)
	1/4	Cup of Olive Oil
	4	Large Eggs (Lightly Beaten)
The Seasonings	2	Large Pinches of Salt
	2	Large Pinches of Pepper
	2	Large Pinches of Parsley
	2	Large Pinches of Tarragon
	2	Large Pinches of Oregano
The Bread Crumbs	1	Cup of Mama Lena's Bread Crumbs (Italian Seasoned) (See Recipe ~ Chapter Ten)
The Marmalade	1	Fresh Lemon (Cut into Tiny Pieces ~ Cook with Skin) (A Fresh Orange could be substituted)
	2	Large Pinches of Sugar
	1/4	Cup of Water
The Zucchini Sauce	1	Recipe of Mama Lena's Red Cream Sauce (See Recipe ~ Chapter Five)
	1	Zucchini (Chop, Saute & Drain ~ Add to Sauce During Final 10 Minutes of Cooking Sauce)
The Pasta	1	Lb. of Angel Hair Pasta (Cooked) (Follow Cooking Instructions on the Package)
The Garnish	1/4	Cup of Romano Cheese (Grated)
	1/4	Bunch of Fresh Parsley

Preparation ~ Lamb & Zucchini Meatballs

**The
Marmalade**

1. Press Lemon Pieces in a Strainer to Extract All Juice.
2. Into a Sauce Pan, Pour Lemon Juice, Pulp & Rind,
   Water and Sugar. Bring to a Boil, Stirring Often.
3. Reduce Heat. Simmer, Until It Thickens into A Paste.
   Remove from Heat and Let Cool. Set Aside.

**Saute
Onions, Garlic
& Zucchini**

1. In a Large Skillet, Heat The Olive Oil to Medium.
   Saute Onions for 2 Minutes or Until Transparent.
   Add Garlic & Saute for 1 Minute More. Remove Onion
   and Garlic from Oil with a Slotted Spoon. Set Aside.
2. In Same Oil, "Saute" The Zucchini for About 2 Minutes,
   Just Until Tender. Remove from Oil, and Set Aside.
   Save Oil to "Fry" The Zucchini for The Sauce.

**The
Lamb Mixture
~ Prepare ~**

1. In an Extra~Large Bowl, Combine The Ground Lamb,
   Salt, Pepper, Parsley, Tarragon & Oregano. Mix Well.
2. Add Sauteed Onion and Garlic, and Blend Well.
3. Add Bread Crumbs, Parmesan Cheese & Eggs. Mix Well.
4. Add The Lemon Marmalade, and Blend In Gently.
5. Mixture should be a Softer Texture. But, If Too Soft,
   Slowly Add Bread Crumbs to Firm Up, But Not Dry.

**The
Lamb Mixture
~ Fill & Bake ~**

1. With a Large Knife, Divide Lamb Mixture into 8~10 Pieces.
   Place Between Wax Paper, and Press Pieces Flat.
2. Spoon 2 Tablespoons of Sauteed Zucchini onto
   The Center of Each Lamb Piece.
3. Moisten Hands with a little Olive Oil. Shape and Fold
   Each Divided Lamb Piece into a Small Oval Meatball.
4. Place Meatballs into Baking Pan on a Trivet. Remove Cover.
   Bake in a Preheated 350 Degree Oven for
   15 to 20 Minutes, Or Until Meat is Firm to Touch.

**The
Sauce & Pasta
~ Prepare ~**

1. As Meat Bakes, Prepare Mama Lena's Red Cream Sauce.
2. In Olive Oil, Saute 1 More Chopped Zucchini. Drain of Oil.
   Add Chopped Zucchini to Sauce for Final 10 Minutes.
3. Now, Cook The Pasta. Drain Pasta, but Do Not Rinse.

Serving Suggestion

Spoon some Zucchini Sauce across A Large Deep Heated Platter. Set The Angel Hair Pasta on The Sauce and Toss Gently.   Place The Baked Lamb & Zucchini Meatballs over Pasta. Cover Meatballs & Pasta with Remaining Zucchini Sauce. Sprinkle The Dish Lightly with Romano Cheese. Place Parsley Sprigs to Garnish.   Serve with a Lettuce & Tomato Salad and Asiago Cheese Dressing, Hot Cheese Bread and a Soave Bolla Wine. Your family will delight at This Very Delicate and Tasteful Dish, just as Mama Lena's Guests did!   Enjoy!

Roasted Leg of Lamb
in Vermouth Sauce

Arrosto Agnello Vermouth

Mama Lena's Roasted Leg of Lamb in Vermouth Sauce was a True Favorite of our Guests. The Vermouth Sauce is a simply superb finish to the preparation of this very special dish! This Sauce on The Lamb was also one of Papa Frank's favorites, as he liked a Dish with Orange and Citrus Flavors ~ It reminded him of the Orange and Lemon Groves near Palermo when he was a boy. Mama served Roasted Leg of Lamb only for special occasions at home. At our Mama Lena's, we would often serve This Dish for the special occasion parties, too! Hope you have a Holiday or a Very Special Occasion to use our Treasured Recipe soon ~ It's really a Very Simple, but a Truly Special Treat! Enjoy!

Ingredients   Serves 6~8

The		
Leg of Lamb	6	Lbs. of Sirloin Half Leg of Spring Lamb (Boned And Tied)
	1/4	Cup of Olive Oil
	3	Pinches of Salt
	3	Pinches of Pepper
The		
Vermouth Sauce	2	Cups of Dry Vermouth
	2	Lemons (Fresh) (Use The Juice Only)
	2	Oranges (Fresh) (Use The Juice Only)
	2	Pinches of Salt
	2	Pinches of Pepper
	1	Pinch of Rosemary (Finely Ground)
	1	Pinch of Thyme
	2	Pinches of Ginger
	2	Pinches of Mint
The		
Vermouth Garlic	3	Cloves of Garlic (Cut into 15 Slivers) (Marinate in Vermouth Sauce)
The		
Raw Onions	2	Large Onions (Finely Chopped) (Use Raw)
The Garnish	1/2	Bunch of Fresh Parsley
	1	Lemon (Cut Lemon into Thin Slices)
	1	Orange (Cut Orange into Thin Slices)

Preparation ~ Roasted Leg of Lamb in Vermouth Sauce

**The
Vermouth Sauce**

1. In a Large Bowl, Combine The Dry Vermouth,
   The Lemon Juice and The Orange Juice.
2. Add The Salt, Pepper, Ground Rosemary, Ginger,
   and Mint. Stir In Very Well.
3. Add The Sliced Garlic to This Mixture, and
   Let Garlic Marinate in The Vermouth Sauce,
   While You Prepare The Roast.

**The
Lamb Roast
~ Prepare ~**

1. As The Roast is Sitting with The Fat Side Up,
   Slice 15 Slits of About 1" to 2" Deep throughout
   The Entire Roast to Insert The Marinated Garlic.
2. After Inserting The Marinated Garlic Slices into The Roast,
   Rub The Roast with The Olive Oil, Salt & Pepper.
3. Place The Roast into a Large Roaster Pan, on a Trivet.
4. Very Gently, Pour The Vermouth Sauce over The Roast.
5. Slowly, Pat The Chopped Onion over The Roast and Sauce.

**The
Leg of Lamb
~ Roasting ~**

1. Insert a Meat Thermometer into Meat, Away from Fat Part.
   (The Lamb Roast Timing is 20 Minutes Per Pound).
2. Cover The Entire Roast Loosely with Foil.
   Leave The Bottom of Foil Open to Let Roast Drain.
   Foil Tent prevents The Roast from Browning Quickly.
   (Make a Slit in Foil to View Thermometer).
3. Bake Without a Pan Cover ~ Just with The Foil Tent ~
   In a Preheated 350 Degree Oven for 2 Hours.
   Baste The Roast Frequently.
4. At End of The 2 Hours of Baking, Remove The Foil Tent.
   Baste The Entire Roast with The Vermouth Sauce.
5. Put The Roast Back into The Oven.
   Bake 20~30 Minutes More ~ Check Thermometer.
6. Remove The Roast. Baste with The Vermouth Sauce Again.
   Let Roast Sit at Room Temperature for 10~15 Minutes.
   First, Remove String, and Then Slice The Roast.
7. Slice The Lamb Roast into 1~1/2" Even Slices for Serving.

Serving Suggestion

Spoon some Vermouth Sauce onto a Deep Heated Decorative Platter. Arrange Sliced Lamb over The Sauce. Spoon All The Remaining Vermouth Sauce and The Onions & Garlic Pieces across The Sliced Lamb. Arrange Lemon & Orange Slices and Parsley Sprigs to Garnish. Accompany This Special Dish with our Caesar Salad, our Specially Baked Herb Potatoes and Garlic & Sweet Onion Bread. A Rose Wine will perfectly compliment This Lovely Dish! Finish with Salvino's Chocolate & Vanilla Rum Cassata & Coffee! A Dinner Divine! Enjoy!

Pork Chops ~ Sicilian Style

Bistecca Maiale Vino

There's nothing like a Delicious Breaded Pork Chop, Sauteed in Olive Oil, but then to be baked in Special Chianti Wine Sauce ~ Oh My, Mama Lena! Mama's Breaded Pork Chop was a true favorite of Papa Frank. It was Papa Frank who actually inspired The Sauce that Salvino perfected for the Special Pork Chop Dish with Berries as a Special Garnish! This Divine Dish was also a "Very Special" Favorite with our Guests at our Restaurant. We think you will love this marvelous Dish so much, you will be saying, with every bite, "What a Delicious Mama Lena's Pork Chop!" You will love Salvino's Sauce, too! Enjoy!

Ingredients   **Serves 4~6**

The Pork Chops	2	Lbs. of Pork Chops (Trimmed of Fat) (4 Large Chops ~ <u>OR</u> ~ 6 Medium Chops)
	1/2	Cup of Olive Oil
The Breading Mixture	1~1/2	Cups of Mama Lena's Bread Crumbs (Italian Seasoned) (See Recipe ~ Chapter Ten)
	2	Eggs (Lightly Beaten) (Dip Chops Before Breading)
	1	Pinch of Salt
	1	Pinch of Pepper
The Chianti Sauce	1	Large Can of Plum Tomatoes, Crushed in Puree (28 Oz. Size Can)
	2	Large Onions (Sliced into Quarter Sections)
	2	Large Green Peppers (Sliced into Quarter Sections)
	2	Cloves of Garlic (Minced)
	2	Pinches of Salt
	2	Pinches of Pepper
	2	Pinches of Oregano
	2	Pinches of Basil
	4	Pinches of Sugar (Granulated)
	1	Cup of Chianti Wine
The Raspberries	1	Cup of Large Raspberries (Marinate in Sugar and Wine)
	1/4	Cup of Sugar (Granulated) (To Marinate Berries)
	1/4	Cup of Chianti Wine (To Marinate Berries)
The Garnish	1/4	Cup of Romano Cheese (Grated)
	1/4	Bunch of Fresh Parsley

Preparation ~ Pork Chops, Sicilian Style

The Raspberries

1. *Wash The Raspberries. Drain Thoroughly in Colander.*
2. *Place The Clean Raspberries in a Large Bowl.*
   Add 1/4 Cup of Sugar to The Berries. Blend Gently.
   Pour 1/4 Cup of Chianti Wine over Berries. Gently Stir.
3. *Seal The Bowl Airtight with Plastic, and*
   Marinate The Berries, Until Ready to Use as Garnish.

The Pork Chops

1. *Place 2 Fresh Eggs in a Deep Bowl, and*
   Add 1 Pinch Each of Salt and Pepper. Lightly Beat.
2. *Dip and Coat The Pork Chops with The Egg Mixture.*
3. *Bread All the Dipped Pork Chops, Covering Thoroughly.*
   Set Them Aside for 5 Minutes to Allow Breading to Dry.
4. *In an Extra-Large Skillet, Heat Olive Oil to Medium.*
   Saute The Breaded Pork Chops on Both Sides,
   Until Nicely Browned, About 3 Minutes Each Side.

The Chianti Sauce

1. *In a Large Sauce Pan, Combine The Tomato Halves,*
   The Onions and Green Peppers and Garlic, and
   The Salt, Pepper, Oregano, Basil. Stir In Well.
2. *Add 4 Pinches of Sugar and 1 Cup of Chianti Wine.*
   Mix In Well. Bring Mixture to a Boil. Remove from Heat.
3. *In a Roaster Pan, Pour Half of Warm Sauce on Bottom of Pan.*
   Arrange The Browned Pork Chops on Top of Sauce.
   Pour Remaining Half of Sauce Over The Browned Chops.
   Evenly Sprinkle Bread Crumbs Across Entire Top of Sauce.
4. *Seal The Pan Top Airtight with Foil.*
5. *Bake in a Preheated 350 Degree Oven for One Hour.*
   (Depending on Thickness of The Pork Chops,
   More Baking Time May Be Needed ~
   At One Hour, Carefully Open The Foil Away from You.
   Check Tenderness of Chops for Need of More Baking Time.
   If Needed, Seal Foil. Bake 15 Minutes More. Check Again).

Serving Suggestion

On a Large Deep Heated Decorative Platter, Spoon some Chianti Sauce Across Platter. Arrange Pork Chops Attractively. Spoon more Sauce over The Chops. Sprinkle with Romano Cheese & Parsley Sprigs to Garnish. Serve extra Sauce in a Heated Gravy Bowl. Now, Place The Marinated Raspberries around Platter for a Very Delightful Presentation! Serve Dish with our Italian Green Beans, Onions & Tomatoes, Baked in Romano Cheese, our Specially Baked Herb Potatoes, and warm Italian Bread. Soft Red Wine compliments! Our Happy Guests had Mama Lena's Cannoli & Coffee for a Sweet Finish!   Enjoy!

Pork Loaf,
Baked in White Wine

Maiale Formato Bianco

This Mama Lena's Recipe is one which sounds so simple ~ A Pork Loaf ~ and actually it is simple to make. However, our completed dish is far from simple in taste or appearance! Our Pork Loaf Baked in White Wine becomes one of the most delightful, attractive and aromatic dishes you could ever ask for! It was a dish Mama's Mother used to make and one Mama liked to make, too! Our Mama Lena's Italian Kitchen Guests just loved this unique dish and were always trying to figure the wonderful ingredients, too! We know you will find this a very pleasing surprise to add to your personal menu also! Enjoy!

Ingredients   Serves 4~6

The Pork Meat	2	Lbs. of Ground Pork (Medium Ground)
The Breading Mix	1	Recipe of Mama Lena's Bread Crumbs (Italian Seasoned) (See Recipe ~ Chapter Ten)
	3	Pinches of Asiago Cheese (Grated)
	4	Eggs (Large) (Lightly Beaten)
To Saute	1/4	Cup of Olive Oil
	1	Medium Onion (Finely Chopped)
	1	Medium Red Pepper (Finely Chopped)
	1	Large Red Firm Tomato (Finely Chopped)
The Seasonings	2	Pinches of Salt
	2	Pinches of Pepper
	2	Pinches of Oregano
	2	Pinches of Parsley
	2	Pinches of Mint
The Special Additions	4	Slices of Italian Salami (Cut into Very Small Strips) (Use Sweet, Mild, Or Hot Salami, As You Prefer)
	1	Dozen Large Green Pimento Olives (Finely Chopped)
	3	Tablespoons of Pine Nuts
The White Wine	1	Cup of Dry White Wine (To Flavor Pork Loaf) (Use in Roaster Only During Baking)
The Garnish	1/4	Cup of Asiago Cheese (Grated)
	1/4	Bunch of Fresh Parsley
	1/4	Bunch of Mint Leaves

Preparation ~ Pork Loaf, Baked in White Wine

The Vegetables
~ Saute ~

1. In a Large Skillet, Heat The Olive Oil to Medium.
   Add The Chopped Onions, Red Peppers and
   Tomatoes. Saute All for 3~5 Minutes.
2. Remove The Vegetables from The Oil with a Slotted Spoon.
   Set Them Aside. Discard The Olive Oil.

The Pork Loaf
~ Mixing ~

1. In a Large Bowl, Combine The Ground Pork & Eggs, and
   1 Cup of Bread Crumbs with The Asiago Cheese.
   Mix All Together Gently.
2. Season with Salt, Pepper, Oregano, Parsley and Mint.
3. Add The Sauteed & Seasoned Vegetables. Mix In Gently.
4. Add The Special Addition Ingredients ~ One at Time ~
   Salami, Green Olives and Pine Nuts. Mix In Gently.
5. Mixture should be Firm Enough to Hold ~
   If Mixture is Too Soft, Add More Bread Crumbs ~
   A Tablespoon at a Time ~ To Firm Up The Mixture.

The Pork Loaf
~ Baking ~

1. Turn The Large Bowl Upside Down to Release
   The Pork Mixture into The Roasting Pan.
2. Moisten your hands with Warm Water, and
   Shape The Pork Mixture into a Nice Oblong Loaf.
3. Pour The Dry White Wine Over The Pork Loaf.
4. Bake Uncovered in Preheated 350 Degree Oven for 1 Hour.

The
Final Steps

1. After 1 Hour of Baking, Turn The Oven Off.
   Let The Roaster Pan Sit for 10 Minutes More,
   Allowing The Pork Loaf to Firm Up for Slicing.
2. Remove The Baked Pork Loaf from The Roaster Pan.
   Cut The Pork Loaf into 1 Inch Slices.
3. Discard All Wine and Fat Drippings ~
   They are Only Used to Flavor Loaf During Baking.

Serving Suggestion

The Pork Loaf Slices are a Picture with the wonderful Vegetables, Seasonings and Special Additions all baked in! Arrange the Slices attractively on a Heated Decorative Platter. Sprinkle Lightly with Asiago Cheese. Place Parsley Sprigs and Mint Leaves to Garnish. Serve This Dish with our Parsley Cheese Potatoes, a Lettuce & Tomato Salad with our Sweet & Sour Dressing, and our warm Italian Bread. Compliment This Delightful Dish with a Light White Wine. For a Sweet Finish, try our Anisette & Vanilla Biscotti & Coffee. You will be experiencing something special that Mama Lena's Guests enjoyed so much. And Mama & Grandma Anna would be Smiling! Enjoy!

Pork Roast, Pizzaiola

Maiale Arrosto Pizzaiola

Our Mama Lena's Pork Roast Pizzaiola is an Exceptional Dish, beaming with the Delightful Flavors of The Caponata Filling, The Cream Sherry Marinara Sauce and Topped with The Asiago Cheese. Mama and Salvino created this one just for Mama Lena's Italian Kitchen and our Guests were so very grateful! Once you have tried this Recipe, we are sure you will want to serve it often for your family and guests. It's a Dish with such Unusual and Satisfying Tastes and such An Appealing Presentation, that it's always welcome at The Dinner Table. We are so happy to share this Mama Lena's Treasure with you! Enjoy!

Ingredients   Serves 4~6

The		
Pork Roast	2	Lbs. of Pork Tenderloin (One Piece Tenderloin)
	1/4	Cup of Olive Oil
	1	Pinch of Salt
	2	Pinches of Cayenne Pepper
	2	Pinches of Rosemary (Ground)
	2	Pinches of Thyme
	2	Pinches of Sage
	2	Pinches of Oregano
The		
Caponata Filling	2	Cups of Mama Lena's Caponata di Melanzane
		(Eggplant Relish Appetizer)
		(See Recipe ~ Chapter One)
	1/4	Cup of Mama Lena's Bread Crumbs (Italian Seasoned)
		(See Recipe ~ Chapter Ten)
		(Gently Mix The Bread Crumbs with
		The Caponata for A Firm Filling)
Marinara		
Sherry Sauce	1	Recipe of Mama Lena's Marinara Sauce
		(See Recipe ~ Chapter Five)
	1	Cup of Cream Sherry
		(Add to Our Marinara Sauce Recipe)
Seal Roast	12	Toothpicks to Seal Filled Pork
The		
Cheese Topping	1/4	Lb. of Asiago Cheese (Thinly Sliced)
The Garnish	1/4	Cup of Asiago Cheese (Grated)
	1/4	Bunch of Fresh Parsley

178

Preparation ~ Pork Roast, Pizzaiola

**The
Pork Tenderloin
Roast**

1. *Place The Pork Tenderloin with The Fat Side Up.
On One Side, Slice into The Center of The Loin
for The Entire Loin Length to Provide
One Long Pocket for The Caponata Filling.*
2. *Fill The Pocket Completely with The Caponata and
Bread Crumb Mixture. Seal with 12 Toothpicks.*
3. *Rub The Filled Pork Tenderloin with Olive Oil, and
Season Pork Loin with Salt, Cayenne Pepper,
Rosemary, Thyme, Sage and Oregano.*
4. *Place Pork Tenderloin on a Trivet and into a Roaster
(Fat Side Up). Pour 2 Cups of Hot Water into Pan.*
5. *Seal Pan Airtight with Foil, so Steam does not escape.*
6. *Bake in a Preheated 325 Degree Oven for 30 Minutes.*

**The
Marinara Sauce**

1. *Prepare 1 Recipe of Mama Lena's Marinara Sauce.*
2. *Add 1 Cup of Cream Sherry to The Marinara Recipe.*

**The
Second Bake**

1. *In a Second Roaster Pan, Pour Half of The Marinara
Sauce Across The Bottom of The Pan.*
2. *Remove Only Pork Tenderloin from The First Roaster.
(Discard Drippings from First Pan ~ Do Not Use).*
3. *Move Pork Tenderloin onto Sauce in Second Roaster.
Place Sliced Asiago Cheese over The Tenderloin.*
4. *Slowly, Spoon Remaining Half of Marinara Sauce onto
Asiago Sliced Cheese and The Pork Tenderloin.*
5. *Seal Pan Airtight with Foil.*
6. *Bake Again in 325 Degree Oven for 30 Minutes.*

**The
Finishing Steps**

1. *Remove Roaster from Oven. Do Not Open The Foil.
Let Roaster Stand & Roast Settle for 15 Minutes.*
2. *Carefully, Take Baked Tenderloin from The Roaster.*
3. *Remove All Toothpicks from The Tenderloin.*
4. *Slice Tenderloin into Even 1 Inch Serving Pieces.*
5. *Gently Move The Serving Pieces with a Large Spatula,
Keeping The Caponata Filling All Intact.*

Serving Suggestion

*This Entree makes a Very Lovely Presentation. Take a Deep Heated Decorative Platter and
Spoon The Marinara Sherry Sauce to cover Bottom of Platter. Carefully Move The Cut
Serving Slices, and Place Them Attractively on Top of The Sauce. Spoon Remaining Sauce
onto Tenderloin Slices. Sprinkle Lightly with Asiago Cheese and Parsley Sprigs to Garnish.
We served this with our Mama Lena's Vegetable Salad & White Wine Vinaigrette Dressing,
a Vermicelli Pasta with Butter & Almond Caper Sauce and our Herbs & Spices Bread.
Rose or Dry White Wine is a perfect compliment to This Very Delectable Mama Lena's Dish!
Cassata Amaretto & Cappuccino for a Sweet Finish to This Divine Dinner! Enjoy!*

Sausage,
with Brown Sugar Peppers

Salsiccia Bruna Castag Pepe

Salvino remembers fondly Mama's stories of The Great Italian Feast, which is held each year in the Late Summer. She told of how her Father lead the Procession, and how her Mother had worked so hard on the Feast, helping with all the Planning and the Cooking. The Children could not wait to go to the Feast ~ some of them were Angels in The Procession. Everyone had Special Memories of the Feast. But Salvino remembered mostly how the Air was filled with the Aroma of the Sausage and Peppers! Luckily, Mama prepared her Sausage and Peppers all year long! At the Restaurant, Salvino mixed the Peppers for an attractive presentation and a more versatile taste. He also made a very delicious Brown~Sugar Sauce to compliment Mama's Sausage. Here we share with you, our Treasured Recipe that we served to our Guests for years! This Delicious Dish always made our Guests feel like they were at the Italian Feast! You will, too! Enjoy!

Ingredients   Serves 4~6

The Italian Sausage	3	**Lbs. of Italian Sausage (1 Piece*)** **(Sweet, Mild Or Hot, As You Prefer)** ***Cut Sausage Only After Cooking, and When Ready to Serve ~ Cook in a One~Piece Coil***
To Saute	1/2	**Cup of Olive Oil**
The Peppers & Onions	4	**Large Peppers (1 Red, 1 Yellow & 2 Green Peppers)** **(Cut into Quarter Sections ~ Makes 16 Pieces)**
	1	**Large White Onion (Cut into Quarter Sections)**
The Cream Sherry	1	**Cup of Cream Sherry Wine**
The Seasonings	1	**Pinch of Salt**
	1	**Pinch of Pepper**
	3	**Pinches of Oregano**
The Brown Sugar	4	**Pinches of Brown Sugar** **(Soften with Cream Sherry, If Needed)**
The Garnish	1/2	**Bunch of Fresh Parsley**

Preparation ~ Sausage, with Brown Sugar Peppers

**The
Peppers & Onions
~ Saute ~**

1. The Mixed Peppers ~ Remove Cores & Seeds and Discard.
   Wash Peppers and Cut Them Into Quarter Sections.
2. The White Onion ~ Peel Shell & Core Onion, and Discard.
   Wash Onion and Slice into Quarter Sections.
3. In an Extra~Large Skillet, Heat The Olive Oil on Medium.
4. Saute The Mixed Peppers and Onions, About 3~4 Minutes.
   Remove from Oil with a Slotted Spoon. Set Aside.

**The Sausage
~ Saute ~**

1. In The Same Oil, Place The Sausage (1 Piece Coil), and
   Brown Sausage for 3~4 Minutes on Each Side, Or
   Until The Sausage is a Medium Brown.

**The Sausage
~ First Bake ~**

1. In a Large Baking Pan, First Place The Sausage and Oil.
2. Pour The Cream Sherry Over The Sausage & Oil, and
   Sprinkle Top with The Salt, Pepper and Oregano.
3. Seal The Pan Airtight with Foil.
4. Bake in a Preheated 325 Degree Oven for 30 Minutes.

**The Sausage
~ Second Bake ~**

1. Carefully Open Foil Top Away from You. Let Steam Out.
2. Add in The Sauteed Peppers & Onions over The Sausage.
3. Sprinkle All of The Brown Sugar Evenly Over
   The Entire Top of The Peppers and Onions.
4. Re~Seal Foil on Pan Airtight.
5. Bake The Sausage Again for 30 Minutes More,
   In the Preheated 325 Degree Oven.

**The
Finishing Steps**

1. Turn Off Oven Heat. Let Pan Sit Sealed in The Oven,
   For 15 Minutes to Allow The Sauce & Flavors to Settle
   Nicely Into The Sausage, Peppers & Onions!

Serving Suggestion

On a Large Heated Platter, Place Sausage Decoratively in an Open Coil (Cut into 8 Pieces). Arrange The Colorful Peppers and The Onions over The Sausage. Then, Top by Spooning The Brown Sugar Sauce over Top of The Dish. Garnish Dish Nicely with Parsley Sprigs. Serve This Very Delicious Dish with Our Parsley Cheese Potatoes, and Our Appetizer of Breaded Zucchini with Orange Sauce. Also, Serve A Basket of Our warm Italian Bread, some Fontinella Cheese & Sicilian Olives, and Red Wine. Now, It's Time for A Real Feast! Our Homemade Sweet Cream Cannoli and Coffee for Dessert would be a Sweet Finish! Close Your Eyes, Smell The Aroma, and Imagine You Are At The Italian Feast!   Enjoy!

Sicilian Pork Cutlets, Stuffed

Siciliano Maiale Costoletta Ripieno

Our Stuffed Sicilian Pork Cutlets were always a pleasure to make and to serve at our Restaurant! Mama and Salvino would pound and chop and saute and simmer while singing one of their favorite songs~ one which Mama's Father used to sing to her Mother ~ O Solo Mio! It really made for a happy time while they prepared this delightful Treasure. Before Dinner, Salvino would entertain our Guests, telling them how he and Mama had sang that day. As our Guests would taste our delicious Stuffed Sicilian Pork Cutlet, they would start singing, O Solo Mio! Your guests will sing after their first taste, too! Enjoy!

Ingredients   Serves 4~6

The Pork Cutlets	2	Lbs. of Pork Tenderloin (Cut to Eight ~ 4 Oz. Cutlets) (Pound to Flat Even Pieces)
	2	Pinches of Salt
	2	Pinches of Pepper
The Filling	*1/2	Cup of Olive Oil
* 4~Part *	1	Medium Onion (Diced)
	1/2	Cup of Celery (Diced)
	1	Cup of Green Peppers (Diced)
	1/2	Cup of Pimento Olives (Cut into Halves)
	1/4	Cup of White Raisins (Seedless)
	* 1	Cup Mama Lena's Bread Crumbs (Italian Seasoned) (See Recipe ~ Chapter Ten)
	3	Pinches of Romano Cheese
	1	Pinch of Fennel
	2	Pinches of Pepper
	* 1/2	Cup of Dry White Wine (Lightly Beat with Egg)
	1	Egg (Large) (Lightly Beat with Wine)
	* 1/4	Cup of Pine Nuts (Add to Filling Last)
The Prosciutto	8	Thin Slices of Prosciutto Ham (Very Salty Taste)
To Seal	24	Toothpicks (Seal Cutlets with 3 Picks per Cutlet)
The Dry White Wine	1	Cup of Dry White Wine (To Steam the Cutlets & Flavor the Apples)
The Garnish	2	Medium Apples (Core and Slice for Apple Rings)
	2	Pinches of Cinnamon Sugar (To Garnish Apples)
	1/4	Cup of Romano Cheese (Grated)
	1/4	Bunch of Fresh Parsley

Preparation ~ Sicilian Pork Cutlets, Stuffed

The Filling *Part 1*	* 1. **In a Large Skillet, Heat 1/4 Cup of Olive Oil to Medium.**
	2. **Saute The Onions, Celery & Green Peppers for 3 Minutes.**
	3. **Add The Pimento Olives and The White Raisins, and Saute for 2 Minutes More.**
	4. **Remove All from Oil with a Slotted Spoon to Drain Oil. Place All in a Large Bowl. Allow to Cool.**
	5. **Remove Pan from Heat. Use This Oil Later to Saute Pork.**
The Filling *Part 2*	* 1. **After Onions, Celery, Peppers, Olives & Raisins are Cool, Add In The Italian Seasoned Bread Crumbs, Romano Cheese, Fennel and Pepper. Mix Well.**
The Filling *Part 3*	* 1. **Combine 1/2 Cup of White Wine & The Egg. Lightly Beat.**
	2. **Add Beaten Wine & Egg to Make Mixture a Firm Texture. (If Too Soft, Add Bread Crumbs, A Little At A Time, To Firm Mixture). Blend The Entire Mixture Again.**
The Filling *Part 4*	* 1. **Add The Pine Nuts to The Entire Mixture. Blend In Well. Now, Set The Filling Aside, While Preparing Cutlets.**
The Pork Cutlets ~ Season ~	1. **Place The Slices Between Two Sheets of Wax Paper.**
	2. **With a Mallet, Pound The Cutlets to Flat Even Pieces.**
	3. **Place The Pork Cutlets on a Platter. Rub Both Sides with a Little Oil. Then Salt and Pepper The Cutlets.**
The Pork Cutlets ~ Stuff ~	1. **Place One Prosciutto Ham Slice on Each Cutlet.**
	2. **Add 2 Tablespoons of Filling on Top of Prosciutto Ham.**
	3. **Roll Each Cutlet. Seal with 3 Toothpicks per Cutlet.**
The Pork Cutlets ~ Saute ~	1. **Add Remaining Olive Oil to Oil in Skillet. Heat to Medium.**
	2. **Brown Cutlets on All Sides ~ About 5 Minutes.**
The Pork Cutlets ~ Simmer ~	1. **Add 1 Cup of White Wine to Oil. Place Apple Rings on Top.**
	2. **Lower The Heat. Cover Pan. Simmer for 25 Minutes, Or Just Until Tender. Do Not Overcook.**

Serving Suggestions

On a Large Deep Heated Platter, Spoon some White Wine Sauce across The Platter. (Remove All Toothpicks). Arrange The Stuffed Pork Cutlets on Top of Sauce. Spoon The Remaining Sauce over Tops of Cutlets. Sprinkle Lightly with Grated Romano Cheese. Place The Apple Rings & Parsley Sprigs. Sprinkle Cinnamon Sugar over The Apple Rings! Serve with a Lettuce & Tomato Salad with White Wine Vinaigrette Dressing, Rotini Pasta with White Cream Sauce and Hot Cheese Italian Bread. Compliment with a Rose Wine! Now, you will be ready to sing like Grandpa, Mama and Salvino ~ O Solo Mio!   Enjoy!

Brochettes, Stuffed Veal

Vitello Spiedo

Our Mama Lena's Stuffed Veal Cutlets on Brochettes was a Dish that Mama liked to make at home for Special Occasions. Salvino told our Mama Lena's Guests about The Dish and that it was one of our favorite Special Occasion Dishes. So, our Guests would call to book Special~Occasion Parties just to experience This Very Special Dish! Needless to say, by very popular demand, Mama Lena's had to add This Delightful Dish to The Regular Menu! We know This Delicious Dish will be just as special to your family and guests! Enjoy!

Ingredients   Serves 4~6

The Veal	12	Veal Cutlets (4 Oz. Each) (Cut from The Veal Leg) (Have Cut & Pounded to 1/2" Thick At Market)
	2	Cups of Cream Sherry (For Steaming Veal)
For The Brochette	1	Large White Onion (12 Large Chunks)
	12	Bay Leaves (Whole)
	1	Cup of Olive Oil (To Saute Brochettes)
The Tomato Cheese Filling	2	Cups of Mama Lena's Bread Crumbs (Italian Seasoned) (See Recipe ~ Chapter Ten) (Toast Bread Crumbs)
	3	Tablespoons of Parmesan Cheese (Mix with Crumbs & Nuts)
	3	Tablespoons of Pine Nuts (Mix with Cheese & Crumbs)
	1	Lb. of Fresh Ripe Tomatoes (Seeded) (Finely Chopped) ~OR~
	1	Medium Can (15 Oz.) Plum Tomatoes (Whole) (Chopped) (Do Not Use The Juice of The Tomatoes)
	1	Large White Onion (Finely Chopped)
	2	Pinches of Salt __and__ 2 Pinches of Pepper
	2	Pinches of Parsley
Italian Rice Mixture	1	Cup of White Rice (Use The Instant)
	1	Teaspoon of Lemon Juice
	1	Cup of Cream Sherry
	2	Tablespoons of Butter (Sweet & Lightly Salted)
	1	Pinch of Salt
	1	Pinch of Mint
Extra Items	6	Brochette Skewers (Each One Holds 2 Stuffed Cutlets)
	36	Toothpicks (3 Picks Per Cutlet)
The Garnish	1/4	Cup of Romano Cheese (Grated)
	1/4	Bunch of Fresh Parsley
	1	Lemon (Slice into Thin Rounds to Garnish Plate)

Preparation ~ Brochettes, Stuffed Veal

**The
Tomato Cheese
Filling**

1. In a Skillet, Heat 2 Tablespoons of Olive Oil to Medium.
2. Add Bread Crumbs & Stir into Oil, Until Toasted Brown.
   Remove Toasted Bread Crumbs. Set Aside.
3. Wipe Skillet with a Paper Towel. Add 2 New Tablespoons
   of Olive Oil, and Heat to Medium.
4. Saute The Chopped White Onions for About 2 Minutes.
5. Stir In Tomatoes, Salt, Pepper & Parsley with The Onions.
6. Cover Pan. Reduce Heat to Medium and Cook 10 Minutes,
   Stirring Often. Remove from Heat.
7. Separately, Mix Together Toasted Bread Crumbs,
   Parmesan Cheese and Pine Nuts. Add Half to Skillet.
   Save Other Half of The Mixture for The Rice).
8. The Filling Mixture should be Soft and Firm.
   (If Too Soft, Slowly, Add Bread Crumbs to Firm).

**The Veal Cutlets
~ Stuff ~**

1. Brush a Little Olive Oil on Both Sides of Each Veal Cutlet.
2. Place One Tablespoon of Stuffing on Each Veal Cutlet.
3. Roll Stuffed Cutlets. Toothpick Seal Both Ends & Center.
   (Insert Skewer Next to Center Toothpick.)

**The Brochettes
~ Prepare ~**

1. In Order, Place One Piece of Onion, One Whole Bay Leaf,
   and One Stuffed Cutlet on Each Skewer and Repeat.
   (Each Skewer has 2 Onions, 2 Bay Leafs & 2 Cutlets).

**The Brochettes
~ Saute ~**

1. In a Skillet, Heat Olive Oil to Medium High.
2. Add Brochettes to Oil. Brown Each Side for 1~2 Minutes.
3. Add 2 Cups of Cream Sherry and Lower The Heat.
4. Cover Pan. Simmer for 12~15 Minutes, Until Tender.

**The Italian Rice
~ Prepare ~**

1. In a Sauce Pan, Mix The Lemon Juice, Cream Sherry,
   Butter, Salt & Mint. Bring Mixture to a Full Boil.
2. Slowly Stir In The Instant Rice into The Boiling Mixture.
3. Cover Pan & Turn Off. Remove Pan from The Heat.
   Let Rice Set 7 Minutes. Then, Lightly Fluff with Fork.
4. Add To The Rice, The Remaining Bread Crumbs and
   Cheese and Pine Nut Mixture. Mix In Well.
5. Cover Pan. Let Pan Sit, Until Ready to Serve.

Serving Suggestion

On a Heated Decorative Platter, Spread The Italian Rice Mixture Across The Platter. (Remove Skewer and Discard Toothpicks). Arrange Brochettes Nicely on Top of The Rice. Spoon Sauce over Each Brochette. Sprinkle Lightly with Romano Cheese. Place Lemon Slices & Parsley Sprigs for Garnish. Serve with our Caesar Salad and a Ribbon Pasta with White Cream Sauce and our Garlic & Sweet Onion Bread. A Dry White Wine will compliment This Lovely Dish and will make Your Evening a Special Occasion! Enjoy!

Veal Chops, Marsala Wine Sauce

Vitello Dolci Marsala Salsa

Salvino really loved our Delightful Mama Lena's Veal Chops with a Sweet Marsala Sauce, a Special Dish he worked hard to perfect. Salvino loved working with The Marsala Wines. And Veal Dishes, as we mentioned, were a special favorites of his and Mama's to make. This Lovely Recipe has Salvino's Special "Marsala Capers." This Recipe is simple and easy to prepare, but it delivers the Most Tender and Flavorful Veal Dish you can imagine! It's one of the recipes that highlights Salvino's true love of cooking and attention to detail. Mama Lena's Guests just delighted each time we served This Treasure of Lovely Flavors! Mama and Papa loved This Very Special Dish, too! We think you will, too! Enjoy!

Ingredients   Serves 4~6

The Veal Chops	6	Veal Chops (Have Cut to 1 Inch Thickness)
	2	Pinches of Salt
	2	Pinches of Pepper
To Saute	1/4	Cup of Olive Oil
	3	Cloves of Garlic (Cut into Thin Slices)
The Marsala Capers	1	Cup of Marsala Wine (Sweet) (To Marinate Capers and Then Add to Sauce)
	1/4	Cup of Capers (Whole) (Marinate Capers in Sweet Marsala Wine)
The Marsala Wine Sauce	1	Can of Plum Tomatoes, Crushed in Puree (Large Can ~ 28 Oz. ~ Size)
	2	Pinches of Salt
	2	Pinches of Pepper
	3	Pinches of Tarragon
	3	Pinches of Oregano
	3	Pinches of Parsley
	3	Pinches of Thyme
To Seal	1/2	Cup of Mama Lena's Bread Crumbs (Italian Seasoned) (See Recipe ~ Chapter Ten)
The Garnish	1/4	Cup of Asiago Cheese (Grated)
	1/4	Bunch of Fresh Parsley

Preparation ~ Veal Chops, Marsala Wine Sauce

The
Sauteed Garlic

1. **In an Extra~Large Skillet, Heat The Olive Oil to Medium.**
   Add The Garlic. Saute Garlic for About 1 Minute,
   Just Until The Garlic is a Light Brown.
2. **Remove Garlic from The Oil with a Slotted Spoon.**
   Save The Garlic to Mix with Capers & Marsala Wine.
   Save The Oil to Saute The Veal Chops.

The
Marsala Capers

1. **In a Large Bowl, Combine The Whole Capers and**
   The Sweet Marsala Wine with The Sauteed Garlic.
   Mix All Together Well.
2. **Cover The Bowl Airtight with Plastic, and Set Aside.**
   Allow Capers to Marinate, while Preparing The Sauce.

The
Marsala Wine Sauce

1. **In a Large Saucepan, Combine The Plum Tomatoes,**
   Salt, Pepper, Tarragon, Oregano, Parsley and Thyme.
   Bring to a Boil. Reduce Heat. Simmer for 15 Minutes.
2. **Now, Add The Marinade of Capers Marsala Wine & Garlic.**
   Cover Pan. Simmer for 15 Minutes More.

The
Sauteed Veal Chops

1. **Season Veal Chops with 2 Pinches Each of Salt & Pepper.**
2. **In Same Skillet, Bring Garlic~Flavored Oil to Medium.**
3. **Add The Veal Chops to The Hot Olive Oil, and**
   Saute Chops, Until Brown, 2~3 Minutes on Each Side.

The
Veal Chops & Sauce
~ Combine & Bake ~

1. **In a Large Roaster Pan, Pour Half of The Warm Sauce**
   Across The Bottom of The Pan.
2. **Arrange The Veal Chops on Top of The Sauce, and**
   Pour Remaining Half of Warm Sauce Over The Chops.
3. **Sprinkle Bread Crumbs Thoroughly Across Top of Sauce.**
4. **Seal Pan Airtight with Foil.**
5. **Bake in a Preheated 350 Degree Oven for 45 Minutes.**

Serving Suggestion

On a Large Deep Heated Platter, Spoon some Sweet Marsala Sauce across The Platter. Attractively Arrange Baked Veal Chops on The Sauce. Spoon More Sauce on The Chops. Sprinkle with Asiago Cheese and Garnish with Parsley Sprigs. This is a Beautiful Dish, with The Marsala Capers, in Taste and Presentation! Serve with our Caesar Salad, Farfalle Pasta with our Butter Parsley Sauce and a Basket of our Herbs & Spices Bread. A Soft Red Wine perfectly compliments This Very Special Salvino Dish! A Sweet Finish ~ Our Cream Puffs Amaretto & Coffee for Dessert! A Dinner of Delightful Treats! Enjoy!

Veal Cutlets & Sweet Peppers

Vitello Dolci Pepe

Mama Lena's Veal Cutlets & Sweet Peppers is one of the Most Tender & Delicious Dishes we ever served! The Wonderful Sauce from Olive Oil & Sweet Peppers is just captivating! Our Guests just could not get enough of This Very Delightful Mama Lena's Veal Entree! Salvino loved preparing Veal Dishes, so they Always were extra delicious. And he was so great with Sauces ~ This Recipe shows just the right touch with The Peppers & Olive Oil. Guests gave him Applause on the Preparation of This Treasure! It's Delectable Dish! You will love This Delicious Mama Lena's Dish, just as our Guests did!   Enjoy!

Ingredients   Serves 4~6

The Veal Cutlets	12	Veal Cutlets (About 4 Oz. Each ~ Cut from The Leg) (Have Cut and Pounded Thin At The Market)
	2	Pinches of Salt
	2	Pinches of Pepper
The Breading Mix	2	Cups of Mama Lena's Bread Crumbs (Italian Seasoned) (See Recipe ~ Chapter Ten)
	4	Pinches of Parmesan Cheese
	1	Pinch of Parsley
	1	Pinch of Mint
	2	Large Eggs (Lightly Beaten) (Dip & Coat Veal Cutlets)
	1	Cup of Flour (All Purpose)
To Saute	1	Cup of Olive Oil (1/2 Cup to Saute Peppers & Onions) (1/2 Cup More to Saute Veal Cutlets)
The Sweet Pepper Mix	6	Large Peppers (2 Green, 2 Yellow & 2 Pimento Peppers) (Core, Clean & Cut Peppers into 8 Pieces Each)
	2	Pinches of Salt
	2	Pinches of Pepper
	2	Large White Onions (Chopped)
	1	Tablespoon of Sugar (Granulated)
	1	Tablespoon of Sugar (Brown)
The Garnish	1/4	Cup of Parmesan Cheese (Grated)
	1/4	Bunch of Fresh Parsley

Preparation ~ Veal Cutlets & Sweet Peppers

**The
Veal Cutlets
~ Bread ~**

1. **In a Large Bowl, Blend Mama Lena's Bread Crumbs
   with The Parmesan Cheese, Parsley and Mint.**
2. **Season The Veal Cutlets with Salt and Pepper.**
3. **Lightly Beat Eggs in a Deep Dish.**
4. **Dip Each Veal Cutlet into Eggs, Coating Both Sides.**
5. **Bread Each Cutlet Well. Place on Paper Towels to Dry.**

**The
Sweet Peppers
~ Prepare ~**

1. **In a Large Skillet, Heat 1/2 Cup of Olive Oil to Medium.**
2. **Add The Mixed Peppers, and Saute for 4 Minutes.
   Season Sauteed Peppers with The Salt and Pepper.**
3. **Add The Chopped Onions, and Saute for 3 Minutes More.**
4. **Sprinkle The White Sugar and The Brown Sugar Over
   The Sauteed Peppers & Onions.**
5. **Reduce Heat. Cover Pan. Now Simmer for 5 Minutes.**
6. **Remove The Peppers & Onions with a Slotted Spoon.
   Set Aside, While You Saute Cutlets.**

**The
Veal Cutlets
~ Saute ~**

1. **Add The Remaining 1/2 Cup of Olive Oil to The Skillet.
   Heat The Olive Oil to Medium High.**
2. **Saute The Breaded Veal Cutlets to Light Golden Brown on
   Each Side ~ About 1/2 Minute on Each Side.**
3. **Set The Sauteed Cutlets on a Large Platter.**
4. **Remove The Skillet and The Olive Oil from The Heat.**

**The
Veal Cutlets & Peppers
~ Combine & Bake ~**

1. **In a Roaster Pan, Spoon Half of The Oil from The Skillet
   Across The Bottom of The Roaster Pan, and
   Place The Veal Cutlets Evenly Over The Oil.**
2. **Top The Veal Cutlets with The Peppers and Onions.**
3. **Cover Top of The Veal, Peppers and Onions with
   The Other Half of The Olive Oil from The Skillet.**
4. **Seal Pan Airtight with Foil.**
5. **Bake in a Preheated 350 Degree Oven for 20 Minutes.**

Serving Suggestion

*Serve on a Large Decorative Heated Platter. Spoon some Sauce across The Platter.
Arrange The Breaded & Baked Veal Cutlets Attractively on The Sauce. Top The Veal with
The Sugared Peppers & Onions. Gently Top The Veal & Peppers with Remaining Sauce.
Sprinkle Lightly with Grated Parmesan Cheese, and Place Parsley Sprigs for Garnish.
What a Pretty Platter with Lightly Brown Veal, Colorful Peppers & Sweet Olive Oil Sauce!
Our Guests couldn't wait ~ the Aroma was so enchanting, too! Serve This Special Dish
with Lettuce & Tomato Salad & Asiago Cheese Dressing, Vermicelli with Marinara Sauce,
and Mama Lena's Tomato Cheese Bread. A Soft White Wine was the perfect compliment!
Salvino knows you will get rave reviews for This Fabulous Mama Lena's Dinner! Enjoy!*

Veal Parmesan, Vermouth Sauce

Vitello Parmigana Vermouth

Our Mama Lena's Veal Parmesan with Sweet Vermouth Sauce was a Delicious Dish that our Guests gladly welcomed any time, but especially during the Chicago Winter Months. Served with Pasta and Delicious Vermouth Sauce, it is more robust than any of our other Veal Dishes. This Wonderful Combination of Flavors and Tastes just cannot be matched. It's A Delightful Dish of Many Satisfying Flavors and also a Colorful Dish that makes a Beautiful Presentation at your table. You are in for a Very Special Treat with This Dish! Mama and Papa both loved This Dish as much as our Guests did! You will, too! Enjoy!

Ingredients   Serves 4~6

The Veal Cutlets	12	**Veal Cutlets (4 Oz. Each ~ Cut from The Leg)** *(Have Cut and Pounded to 1/2" Thick At Market)*
	2	**Pinches of Salt**
	2	**Pinches of Pepper**
The Breading	2	**Cups of Mama Lena's Bread Crumbs (Italian Seasoned)** *(See Recipe ~ Chapter Ten)*
	1/4	**Cup of Parmesan Cheese (Finely Grated)**
	3	**Eggs (Lightly Beaten) (Dip and Coat Veal Cutlets)**
To Saute	1/2	**Cup of Olive Oil (To Saute Breaded Cutlets)**
The Vermouth Sauce	1	**Recipe of Mama Lena's "Quick" Basic Tomato Sauce** *(See Recipe ~ Chapter Five)*
	1	**Cup of Sweet Vermouth** *(Add to Sauce for Last 20 Minutes of Simmer)*
The Cheese Slices	12	**Thin Slices of Mozzarella Cheese** *(Place Over Cutlets & Sauce for Broiling)*
The Pasta	1	**Lb. of Imported Farfalle Pasta (Medium Butterfly Pasta)** *(Follow Cooking Instructions on the Package)*
The Garnish	1/4	**Cup of Parmesan Cheese (Finely Grated)**
	1/4	**Bunch of Fresh Parsley**

Preparation ~ Veal Parmesan, Vermouth Sauce

The
Vermouth Sauce

1. *Prepare Mama Lena's "Quick" Basic Tomato Sauce,*
2. *After The "Basic Tomato Sauce" has come to a Boil,*
    Add The Sweet Vermouth to Sauce. Stir in Well.
3. *Cover Pan. Simmer Sauce for 20 Minutes. Stir Often.*

The Cutlets
~ Bread ~

1. *Blend Bread Crumbs and 1/4 Cup of Parmesan Cheese.*
2. *Season The Veal Cutlets with Salt and Pepper.*
3. *Lightly Beat The Eggs in a Deep Dish.*
4. *Dip Each Veal Cutlet into The Eggs, Coating Both Sides.*
5. *Bread Each Cutlet Well. Allow to Dry for 3 Minutes.*

The Cutlets
~ Saute ~

1. *In a Large Skillet, Heat The Olive Oil to Medium High.*
2. *Saute The Breaded Cutlets to Light Golden Brown on*
    Each Side ~ About 1/2 Minute Each Side.
3. *Remove The Pan from The Heat.*
4. *Take Cutlets from Skillet with a Slotted Spoon to Drain.*
5. *Place The Sauteed Cutlets on Paper Towels to Dry.*

Cutlets & Sauce
~ Bake ~

1. *In a Large Roaster Pan, Pour Half of The "Warm"*
    Sweet Vermouth Sauce Across The Bottom of The Pan.
2. *Arrange The Veal Cutlets Over The Sauce.*
3. *Gently, Pour 2 Cups More of The Sweet Vermouth Sauce*
    over The Tops of The Breaded Cutlets.
4. *Seal Roaster Pan Airtight with Foil.*
5. *Bake in a Preheated 375 Degree Oven for 20 Minutes.*

Cheese Topping
~ Broil ~

1. *After Baking Time, Remove Pan from Oven & Remove Foil.*
2. *Place 12 Slices of Mozzarella Cheese Over The Top of Veal.*
3. *Place Pan Back into Oven. Set The Oven on Broil Setting.*
4. *Broil Carefully. Remove The Pan from Oven, as Soon as*
    Mozzarella Topping Turns a Light Brown & Bubbles.
5. *Cover Across Pan Top with The Baking Foil, and*
    Allow Topping to Set for 5 Minutes Before Serving.

Serving Suggestion

Use a Large Deep Heated Platter. Spoon some Sauce from The Pan, while not disturbing The Cheese Topping. Spoon The Sauce across The Platter. Place The Butterfly Pasta over The Sauce. Top Pasta with a Little More Sauce. Gently Toss. Carefully, Transfer The Veal Cutlets to The Platter, Keeping The Broiled Cheese Topping Intact. Arrange The Cutlets on Top of The Tossed Butterfly Pasta. Gently Spoon on any Remaining Sauce. Sprinkle Lightly with Grated Parmesan Cheese, and Place Parsley Sprigs to Garnish. Serve with our Italian & Antipasto Salad Supreme and a Basket of Tomato Cheese Bread. A Light White Wine will compliment this Fabulous Dish! Sweetly Finish This Delicious and Delightful Dinner with Sweet Cream Cannoli & Coffee! It's a True Feast! Enjoy!

Veal Superb
Sweet Onion Sauce

Vitello Superba Cipolla

Our Mama Lena's Veal Superb with Sweet Onion Sauce is a Very Delightful Veal Dish of Sweet and Unique Flavors. Mama and Salvino loved to prepare The Veal Dishes, with their delicate texture and tastes ~ This Special Recipe shows how versatile they could be. It has a Spicy, Sweet Blend of Flavors that truly compliment the subtle taste of the Veal. Our Mama Lena's Guests always found this to be a very fascinating and delicious Dish! It was one of our Guests' "Special All~Time Favorites." We know you will just love this Mama Lena's Italian Kitchen Delicious Dish, as our Guests always did!   Enjoy!

Ingredients   Serves 4~6

The Veal Cutlets	12	Veal Cutlets (4 Oz. Each ~ Cut from The Leg)
		(Have Cut and Pounded Thin At The Market)
	2	Pinches of Salt
	2	Pinches of Pepper
The Breading Mix	2	Cups of Mama Lena's Bread Crumbs (Italian Seasoned)
		(See Recipe ~ Chapter Ten)
	1/8	Cup of Asiago Cheese (Grated)
	2	Pinches of Parsley
	3	Large Eggs (Lightly Beaten) (Dip & Coat Veal Cutlets)
To Saute	1~1/2	Cups of Olive Oil (1 Cup to Saute 3 <u>Lbs</u>.* Onions)
		(1/2 Cup to Saute The Breaded Cutlets)
The Sweet Onion Sauce	1	Recipe of Mama Lena's Marinara Sauce
		(See Recipe ~ Chapter Five)
	3	<u>Lbs</u>.* of White Onions (Sliced Medium)
		(This Very Generous Amount of Onions is Correct)
	3	Pinches of Sugar (Granulated)
	1/4	Cup of Prosciutto
		(Buy A Slice, 1/2" Thick, & Dice to Small Pieces)
		(Prosciutto is Salty ~ Use Recipe Amount Only)
The Garnish	1/4	Cup of Asiago Cheese (Grated)
	1/4	Bunch of Fresh Parsley

Preparation ~ Veal Superb, Sweet Onion Sauce

**The
Sweet Onion
Sauce**

1. *Prepare 1 Recipe of Mama Lena's Marinara Sauce.*
2. *Saute Sliced Onions while Marinara Sauce is Cooking.*
3. *In a Large Skillet, Heat 1 Cup of Olive Oil to Medium. Saute 3 Lbs. of Onions, Until Transparent in Color. This Should take About 15 Minutes, and The Onions will be Ready when The Sauce is Ready.*
4. *Remove Pan from Heat. Remove Sauteed Onions with a Slotted Spoon to Drain Oil. Save The Oil for Veal.*
5. *Add The 3 Lbs. of Sauteed Onions, Diced Prosciutto, and 3 Pinches of Sugar to Marinara Sauce. Stir Well.*
6. *Cover Pan. Simmer The Sauce for 20 Minutes. Stir Often.*

**The Cutlets
~ Bread ~**

1. *Blend The Bread Crumbs with 1/8 Cup of Asiago Cheese.*
2. *Season The Veal Cutlets with Salt and Pepper.*
3. *Lightly Beat The Eggs in a Deep Dish.*
4. *Dip Each Veal Cutlet into The Eggs, Coating Both Sides.*
5. *Bread Each Cutlet Well. Place on Paper Towels to Dry.*

**The Cutlets
~ Saute ~**

1. *In Same Skillet, to The Oil you Sauteed The Onions in, Add 1/2 Cup More of Oil. Heat Oil to Medium High.*
2. *Saute The Breaded Cutlets to a Light Golden Brown on Each Side ~ About 1/2 Minute on Each Side.*
3. *Remove The Veal Cutlets with a Slotted Spoon, and Place on Paper Towels to Drain.*

**The
Cutlets & Sauce
~ Combine & Bake ~**

1. *In a Large Roaster, Pour Half of Warm Marinara Sauce, with The Onions & Prosciutto, across Bottom of Pan.*
2. *Arrange The Veal Cutlets Over The Sauce.*
3. *Gently, Spoon Last Half of Sauce Over Top of Veal Cutlets.*
4. *Seal The Roaster Pan Airtight with Foil.*
5. *Bake in a Preheated 375 Degree Oven for 20 Minutes*
6. *Remove from Oven. Keep Sealed & Let Sit for 15 Minutes.*

Serving Suggestion

On a Large Heated Decorative Platter, Spoon 1 Cup of Sweet Onion Sauce Across Platter. Arrange The Cutlets Attractively. Spoon More Sauce, Onions & Prosciutto onto Cutlets. Sprinkle Dish Lightly with Asiago Cheese. Place Parsley Sprigs to Nicely Garnish Platter! Serve with our Vegetable Salad with White Wine Vinaigrette Dressing, a Ribbon Pasta with White Cream Sauce, and our Hot Cheese Bread. Dry White Wine will Compliment! Finish Sweetly ~ Salvino's Cassata Amaretto with Pine Nuts! A Superb Dinner! Enjoy!

~ *Chapter Nine* ~

Vegetable Entrees &
Vegetable Side Dishes

Pages 195 ~ 215

Eggplants Parmesan
Vegetarian Style & Meat Style

Melanzanes Parmesana ~ Verdura e Carne

Our Mama Lena's Eggplants Parmesan ~ Both Vegetarian Style & Meat Style ~ were among the most popular dishes served at Mama Lena's Italian Kitchen Restaurant for over 14 years. Our Vegetarian Style Eggplant Parmesan was Guests' All~Time Favorite Vegetarian Entree! Our Meat Style Eggplant Parmesan is a bit richer ~ the more Classic Version. Both Styles of our Eggplants Parmesan were so much in demand, we served both styles during our very special Annual Eggplant Festival. During the Month of October every year, at Mama Lena's, we had an Eggplant Festival, and we served various Eggplant dishes as Main Entrees, or with Entrees, for the entire Festival Month. It was very entertaining for us and for our Guests! Now, we happily share with you Both Styles of Mama Lena's Eggplants Parmesan!   Enjoy!

Ingredients   Serves 4~6

The		
Fresh Eggplants	2	**Eggplants (Fresh) (Medium~Size)**
	1	**Cup of Olive Oil**
	2	**Pinches of Salt**
	2	**Pinches of Pepper**
	2	**Pinches of Sugar (Granulated)**
The		
Parmesan Layers	1/2	**Lb. of Mozzarella Cheese (Sliced Thin)**
	1	**Cup of Parmesan Cheese (Coarsely Grated)**
	1/2	**Lb. of Fresh Mushrooms**
		(Saute In A Little Butter First) ~ <u>OR</u> ~
	1	**Small Can of Sliced Mushrooms**
		(Drain of Liquid)
The		
Meat Mixture	1	**Lb. of Chuck Beef Steak (Ground Medium)**
	2	**Large Eggs (Lightly Beaten)**
	1	**Cup of Mama Lena's Bread Crumbs**
		(Italian Seasoned) (See Recipe ~ Chapter Ten)
	2	**Pinches of Parsley**
	2	**Pinches of Salt <u>And</u> 2 Pinches of Pepper**
The		
Tomato Sauce	1	**Recipe of Mama Lena's "Quick" Basic Tomato Sauce**
		(See Recipe ~ Chapter Five)
The Garnish	1/4	**Cup of Parmesan Cheese (Grated)**
	1/4	**Bunch of Fresh Parsley**

Preparation ~ Eggplants Parmesan ~ Vegetarian Style & Meat Style

**The
Fresh Eggplants
~ Prepare ~**

1. Wash Eggplants Carefully. Trim Top & Bottom Stems.
   Do Not Peel The Eggplants.
2. Cut Across The Width of The Eggplants, and
   Make 1/2" Thick Circle Slices.
3. In an Extra Large Skillet, Heat Olive Oil on Medium.
4. Saute Eggplants, Until Lightly Browned on Both Sides.
5. Drain & Cool on doubled Paper Towels. Save Pan & Oil.
6. Season Eggplants with Salt, Pepper & Sugar. Let Cool.

**The
Tomato Sauce
~ Prepare ~**

1. Prepare Mama Lena's "Quick" Basic Tomato Sauce Recipe.
   (See Recipe ~ Chapter Five)

**The
Ground Meat Mixture
~ Prepare ~**

1. In a Bowl, Combine Ground Chuck & Eggs. Mix Well.
2. Add Bread Crumbs, Salt, Pepper & Parsley. Mix Well.
3. In The Same Skillet, Heat The Olive Oil to Medium.
4. Add Meat Mixture, and Saute Until Thoroughly Browned.
5. In a Strainer, Drain The Meat of All Oil. Discard The Oil.
   Set The Meat Mixture Aside to Cool.

**The
Eggplants Parmesan
~ Baking ~**

1. In a Deep Decorative Baking Dish, Layer As Follows:
   ~ Hot Tomato Sauce (1 Cup) ~ Pour Across Bottom.
   ~ One Layer of Eggplant ~ Set on The Sauce.
   ~ Meat Layer ~ Evenly Place on Top of Eggplant.
   ~ Mozzarella Cheese Layer ~ To Top The Meat Layer.
   ~ Mushrooms Top The Mozzarella Cheese Layer.
2. For Meat Style Eggplant, Repeat in Order All Above Steps
3. For Vegetarian Eggplant, You Omit The Meat Layers.
4. Top The Second Layer with All Remaining Tomato Sauce.
5. Sprinkle Top Evenly with Grated Parmesan Cheese.
6. Seal The Pan Airtight with Foil.
7. Bake in a Preheated 325 Degree Oven for 30 Minutes.
   Keep The Pan Sealed, Until Ready to Serve.

Serving Suggestion

Serve The Baked Eggplant Parmesan from The Decorative Baking Dish. (When using a Roaster Pan to Bake, Carefully Transfer The Eggplant Parmesan to a Heated Serving Platter). Lightly sprinkle Top with Parmesan Cheese. Place Parsley Sprigs to Nicely Garnish. Accompany with a Caesar Salad & Dressing, a Basket of warm Italian Bread. Dry Red Wine compliments Meat~Style Eggplant Parmesan, and a Dry White Wine for The Vegetarian~Style. Finish Sweetly with Mama Lena's Sweet Cream Cannoli & Cappuccino!   Enjoy!

Peppers, Baked
Stuffed with Sausage

Pepe Al Forno Ripieno Salsicce

Mama Lena's Baked Stuffed Peppers with Sausage not only make a colorful and an appetizing presentation, but also an absolutely delicious Entree. We enjoyed making this wonderful recipe so much, because we knew it not only looked delightful and smelled delightful ~ it tasted delightful, too! And the Pretty Mixed Peppers, with their Tops, make it a very Happy Dish! This flavorful and satisfying dish with our Special Filling was a true Mama Lena's Favorite! This Dish always warmed the Hearts of our Guests on those Windy Chicago Evenings! We know it will warm your Heart, too! Enjoy!

Ingredients   Serves 4 ~6

The Mixed Peppers	6	Peppers (Large & Wide in Size) (2 Green, 2 Red and 2 Yellow)
	2	Pinches of Salt (For Boiling Water)
	18	Toothpicks
The Sausage Mixture	1	Lb. of Italian Sausage (Sweet, Mild Or Hot, As You Prefer)
	2	Tablespoons of Butter (Sweet & Lightly Salted)
	3	Tablespoons of Olive Oil
	1	Small Onion (Finely Chopped)
	2	Cloves of Garlic (Minced)
	1/4	Cup of Celery (Finely Chopped)
The Rice Mixture	1	Cup of White Rice (Cooked)
	1	Cup of Mama Lena's Bread Crumbs (Italian Seasoned) (See Recipe ~ Chapter Ten)
	1	Pinch of Salt
	2	Pinches of Pepper
	3	Pinches of Parsley
	1/4	Cup of Pine Nuts
	1/2	Cup of Cream Sherry (Add a Little at a Time)
The Tomato Sauce	3	Cups of Mama Lena's "Quick" Basic Tomato Sauce (See Recipe ~ Chapter Five)
The Garnish	1/4	Cup of Romano Cheese (Grated)
	1/4	Bunch of Fresh Parsley

Preparation ~ Peppers, Baked ~ Stuffed with Sausage

**The
Mixed Peppers
~ Prepare ~**

1. Cut Across Near Top of Peppers, Leaving Stems Attached.
2. Trim Stems & Discard Seeds. Wash & Dry on Paper Towels.
3. Fill an 8 Qt. Pan to Half with Water. Add The Salt, and
   Bring Water to a Boil. Turn Off Heat.
4. Set Peppers with The Tops into Boiled Water. Cover Pan.
   Allow Peppers to Steam for 3 Minutes.
5. Remove The Peppers from the Water. Set Aside to Cool.

**The
Sausage Mixture
~ Prepare ~**

1. In Large Skillet, Heat Butter on Medium until Melted.
   Add The Olive Oil. Heat and Stir In.
2. Saute The Onions and The Celery for About 3 Minutes.
3. Add The Garlic, and Saute for 1 Minute More.
4. Remove The Onions, Celery & Garlic with a Slotted Spoon.
   Set Them Aside.
5. Leave The Olive Oil in Skillet to Brown The Sausage.
6. Slit into Casing around Sausage. Remove and Discard It.
   On Medium, Saute Loose Meat 5 Minutes, Until Browned.
7. To The Browned Sausage, Add The Onions, Celery & Garlic.
   Mix Well. Cover Pan. Remove from Heat.

**The Rice Mixture
~ Prepare ~**

1. In a Large Bowl, Place The Cooked Rice, Bread Crumbs,
   Salt, Pepper, and Parsley. Mix Together Well.
2. With a Slotted Spoon, Remove Sausage, Onion, Celery &
   Garlic from Skillet. Mix In Well with The Rice Mixture.
3. Add Cream Sherry, A Little At A Time, to The Firm Mixture.
4. Add The Pine Nuts. Mix Again. If Needed, Add a Bit More
   Cream Sherry. The Mixture should be Moist, But Firm.

**The
Finishing Steps**

1. Stuff Each Pepper with The Sausage & Rice Mixture.
2. Cover Each Pepper with Their Stemmed Tops, and
   Hold in Place with Toothpicks.
3. Pour 1 Cup of Mama Lena's Tomato Sauce on Bottom of a
   Large Roaster Pan. Set The Peppers Upright in Pan.
4. Cover The Peppers, with 2 Cups More of The Tomato Sauce.
5. Cover Roaster Pan Airtight with Foil. Bake in a
   Preheated 325 Degree Oven for 20~30 Minutes.

Serving Suggestion

On Heated Decorative Platter, Spoon some Sauce across The Platter.   Then Arrange The Baked Stuffed Peppers with Their Tops. Remove All Toothpicks. Spoon More Sauce over The Peppers. Sprinkle Lightly with Romano Cheese. Garnish with Parsley Sprigs. Serve with Mama Lena's Italian & Antipasto Salad Supreme, Hot Cheese Bread and a Red Wine. At Mama Lena's, our Baked Stuffed Peppers were always served Hot, but Mama & Salvino personally loved the Peppers Chilled. "If" you have any left, try that the next day!   Enjoy!

Artichokes,
Sicilian Olive Filling

Carciofi Ripieno Siciliano Olives

Mama Lena's Artichokes with Sicilian Olive Filling is a Delicious Dish that was a very special favorite of our Guests. Our Filling, made with the Sicilian Olives and other very delicious and tasty ingredients, adds a very complimentary blend of flavors to the most revered Artichoke. Most Italians hold the Artichoke in high esteem, and it was especially so for Grandpa Matteo, who knew all his vegetable products so well. Grandma Anna's unique Filling using Sicilian Olives truly pays homage to their upbringing in Sicily, where the Sicilian Olives grow plentifully. Follow our Treasured Recipe carefully, and you will find it as easy to experience the Great Delight of The Artichoke, as our Mama Lena's Guests did!   Enjoy!

Ingredients   Serves 4~6

The Artichokes	8	Artichokes (Medium~Size)
		(Two Stages ~ First Cook Them ~ Then Steam Them)
	3	Pinches of Salt
		(2 Pinches for First Cook ~ 1 Pinch for Steaming)
	1/2	Cup of Dry White Wine (1/4 Cup ~ Each Cooking Time)
	10	Cups of Water (8 Cups for First Cook ~ 2 Cups for Steaming)
To Saute	1/2	Cup of Olive Oil
The		
Sicilian Olive	3	Cloves of Garlic (Minced)
Filling	1	Large White Onion (Finely Chopped)
	1/4	Cup of Celery (Finely Chopped)
	12	Dried Sicilian Black Olives (Pitted & Cut into Slivers)
	1/4	Lb. of Italian Salami (Remove Skin & Finely Chop)
	1	Pinch of Salt
	1	Pinch of Black Pepper
	1	Pinch of Oregano
	1	Pinch of Parsley
	1/4	Cup of Sweet Vermouth
	1/4	Cup of Parmesan Cheese (Grated)
	1	Cup of Mama Lena's Bread Crumbs (Italian Seasoned)
		(See Recipe ~ Chapter Ten)
The Garnish	1/4	Cup of Romano Cheese (Grated)
	2	Lemons (Cut into Thin Slices)
	1/4	Bunch of Fresh Parsley

Preparation ~ Artichokes, Sicilian Olive Filling

The Artichokes
~ Clean ~

1. Trim Artichoke Stems so they are Flat Across.
   This allows The Artichokes to Stand Upright.
   Remove Any Damaged Outer Leaves. Discard Them.
2. Use a Sharp Knife. Trim Off 1" of Artichoke Leaf Tips.
   (Lay Artichoke on Side to Trim). Discard The Tips.
3. Rinse The Artichokes Very Well with Cool Water.

The Artichokes
~ Cook ~

1. In an 8 Qt. Pan, Combine 8 Cups of Lukewarm Water,
   1/4 Cup of Dry White Wine and 2 Pinches of Salt.
2. On Medium High, Bring Water to a Boil. Reduce Heat.
3. Set Artichokes into Water Mix, So They Stand Upright.
4. Cover Pan. Simmer 25 Minutes. Remove Pan from Heat.
5. Allow Artichokes to Cool by Setting Upside Down in a
   Colander. Artichokes will also Drain Properly.
6. With a Teaspoon, Remove The Choke, which is
   Just Above The Artichoke Heart.

The
Filling Mixture
~ Prepare ~

1. In a Large Skillet, Heat 1/2 Cup of Olive Oil to Medium.
2. Add Chopped Onions. Saute The Onions for 2~3 Minutes.
   Add The Garlic, and Saute for 1 Minute More.
3. Add The Sicilian Black Olives, Celery, and Salami.
   Stir In with Onions & Garlic. Saute 3 Minutes More.
4. Add Salt, Pepper, Oregano & Parsley. Mix In Well.
5. Next, Add The Sweet Vermouth to Mixture. Stir In Well.
   Remove Pan from Heat. Allow The Mixture to Cool.
6. Sprinkle Bread Crumbs & Parmesan Cheese into Mixture.
   Mix Well. Set Aside, Until Ready to Fill Artichokes.

The Artichokes
~ Fill & Steam ~

1. Set The "Cooled" Artichokes on Wax Paper.
2. Spoon Prepared Filling into The Artichoke Centers, and
   In Between The Artichoke Leaves. Be Generous.
3. In The 8 Qt. Pan ~ Now, Add 2 Cups Fresh Water,
   1/4 Cup of Dry White Wine, and 1 Pinch of Salt.
4. On Medium~High Heat, Bring The Liquid to a Boil.
   Then Reduce Heat to a Simmer.
5. Place Stuffed Artichokes, Standing Upright, into Water.
6. Cover Pan. Simmer for 30 Minutes, Until Outer Leaves
   are Tender to Touch. Remove from Water to Serve!
7. See The Next Page for Serving & Eating Suggestions

Preparation ~ Artichokes, Sicilian Olive Filling

Serving Suggestions for The Stuffed Artichokes

Stand The Steamed Filled Artichokes Upright on a Heated Decorative Platter. Sprinkle Lightly over The Tops with Romano Cheese. Place Lemon Slices and Parsley Sprigs for a Nice Garnish. Serve with a Lettuce & Tomato Salad and Asiago Cheese Dressing, our Vermicelli Pasta with The Marinara Sauce, and A Basket of Delicious Hot Cheese Bread. White Wine or Rose Wine would be The Perfect Compliment. You are in for a Very Delicious and Wonderful Treat! Grandpa Matteo and our Mama Lena's Guests would truly agree! Enjoy!

Helpful Tips for Eating The Artichoke

At Mama Lena's Italian Kitchen, Salvino told our Guests that The Only Way to Properly Eat The Artichoke was to "Think Only of Enjoying It." The Artichoke Has To Be Eaten by Hand. Sometimes, Guests think more of eating by hand than of truly enjoying This Dish. Help your Guests to Enjoy with These Tips ~

~ **The Artichoke is Eaten in This Order ~**

> First ~ The Filling on Leaves ~&~ The Plump Bottom Part of Leaves
> Last ~ The Heart of The Artichoke ~&~ The Loose Filling

~ **Guests Do Eat The Leaves "By Hand" ~ Detach One Leaf At a Time.**

~ **Place The Bottom of Leaf, Near The Artichoke Stem, On The Teeth ~**

> Scrap the Plump Portion of The Leaf with Teeth.
> (This Allows Guests to get All the Filling from The Leaf ~ And ~
> Enjoy The Wonderful Flavor of The Plump Part of Lower Leaf ~
> Discard The Rest of The Leaf).

~ **The Artichoke Heart ~&~ The Loose Filling is "Eaten by Fork."**

"If" you have any Artichokes left after your Dinner, be sure to try The Artichoke the way Grandpa preferred it ~ "Chilled" the Next Day. You will notice how the flavors have set into The Filled Artichoke ~ Grandpa's way is a great way to have The Artichoke for a Lunch Dish! Our Wish is That Our Recipe is Delightful to You, and That Preparing Artichokes and Eating The Delicious Artichoke will Now be Delightful to You, too! Enjoy!

Mama Lena's
Roasted Sweet Peppers

Mama Lena's Arrostito Pepe

*Mama Lena's Roasted Sweet Peppers is A Dish you will want to have for Just Everything!
As A Side Dish, It Stands on Its Own! It Very Delightfully Enhances Any Entree or Pasta!
And, It makes Every Sandwich a Special Feast! Mama Lena's Roasted Sweet Peppers is
Truly one of our Most Delicious and Most Versatile Dishes! This is a "Fun" Vegetable Dish.
Start right now, and have some "Fun" with This Very Special Mama Lena's Dish! Enjoy!*

Ingredients   **Serves 4~6**

The Peppers	6	**Mixed Peppers (Extra~Large & Wide~Size Peppers)**
		(2 Green, 2 Red and 2 Yellow)
	2	**Pinches of Salt**
	2	**Pinches of Red Pepper Flakes (Crushed)**
The Sauce	4	**Tablespoons of Butter (Sweet & Lightly Salted)**
	1/2	**Cup of Olive Oil**
	1/8	**Cup of Sugar (Brown)**
	1	**Cup of Cream Sherry**
The Garnish	1/4	**Cup of Romano Cheese (Finely Grated)**

Preparation ~ Mama Lena's Roasted Sweet Peppers

The Peppers	1.	**Mixed Peppers ~ Remove Cores & Seeds, and Discard.**
~ Prepare ~	2.	**Cut The Mixed Peppers into Quarter Sections.**
	3.	**Season The Peppers with Salt and Red Pepper Flakes.**
The Sauce	1.	**In a Small Saucepan, Melt The Butter on Medium Heat.**
	2.	**Add The Olive Oil. Stir In, Until Blended and Hot.**
	3.	**Stir In Brown Sugar for About 2 Minutes, Until Dissolved.**
	4.	**Reduce The Heat to Low. Stir In The Cream Sherry.**
	5.	**Cover Pan. Simmer for 3 Minutes. Remove from Heat.**
The Peppers		
~ Bake ~	1.	**In a Small Roaster Pan, Spoon 1/3 of The Sauce**
		Across The Bottom of The Roaster.
	2.	**Place The Peppers Over The Bottom Layer of Sauce.**
	3.	**Spoon The Remaining 2/3 of The Sauce Over Each Pepper.**
	4.	**Seal The Baking Pan Airtight with Foil.**
	5.	**Roast Peppers in Preheated 350 Degree Oven 20 Minutes.**
Garnish Dish	1.	**Serve on a Platter & Sprinkle Lightly with Cheese. Enjoy!**

Asparagus & Sicilian Olives, Sauteed in Garlic Butter

Asparagi Siciliano Olives
Aglio Burro

Our Mama Lena's Asparagus & Sicilian Olives in Garlic Butter is such a Unique Tasting Vegetable Dish. It's a sort of delicacy of its own. We always served this with delicate Entrees as well ~ a Chicken or Veal Entree, or one of our Pastas with the Cream Sauces and some of Mama's warm Italian Bread for This Wonderful Sauce. A Dry White Wine is a Compliment to This Dish. Your guests will be treated to a Delightful Dish of great tastes and appearance also! Our Guests would just be singing! We know you and your family will, too, as you serve This Very Delicious Mama Lena's Vegetable Side Dish!. Enjoy!

Ingredients   Serves 4~6

The Fresh Asparagus	2	Lbs. of Fresh Asparagus (Medium~Size Firm Stalks)
	3	Pinches of Salt (For The Water)
	1/4	Lb. of Butter (Sweet & Lightly Salted)
	3	Tablespoons of Olive Oil
The Sicilian Olives	1/2	Lb. of Black Olives (Sicilian Dry Olives) (Whole & Not Pitted)
	2	Cloves of Garlic (Slivered)
	1/8	Cup of Pine Nuts
The Seasonings	2	Pinches of Black Pepper *(Optional ~ 1 Pinch of Cayenne Pepper, Or Red Pepper Flakes, If You Prefer Spicy Hot)
The Garnish	1/8	Cup of Parmesan Cheese (Grated)

Preparation ~ Asparagus & Sicilian Olives, Sauteed in Garlic Butter

The
Fresh Asparagus
~ Prepare ~

1. Wash The Asparagus in Cool Water. Snap Off Ends of The Asparagus. Scrape off Scales and Discard.
2. Fill a Large Sauce Pan to One~Half Full. Add 1 Pinch of Salt and Bring to a Full Boil.
3. Add The Asparagus to Boiling Water, and Immediately Reduce Heat. Cover and Cook The Asparagus, Until Just Tender, for About 7~10 Minutes. Drain in a Colander.
4. Arrange The Asparagus on a Decorative Serving Platter. Place Platter in a "Warm" Oven, while Preparing Olives and Butter Garlic Sauce.

The
Sicilian Olives
~ Saute ~

1. In a Skillet, Heat The Butter on Medium Heat. Add The Olive Oil to The Melted Butter, and Bring Them to a Sizzle.
2. Add The Sicilian Olives to The Sizzling Oil & Butter. Saute Olives 1~2 Minutes, Until Olives Plump Up.
3. Add The Garlic and The Pine Nuts, and Stir In with The Olives. Saute for 1 Minute More. Cover Pan and Remove from Heat.

The
Asparagus, Olives & Sauce
~ Combine & Serve ~

1. Take The Asparagus & The Platter from Oven.
2. Season The Asparagus with Black Pepper.
3. Arrange Sicilian Olives with The Asparagus.
4. Drizzle The Butter Garlic Sauce with The Pine Nuts Evenly Over The Asparagus and Sicilian Olives.
5. Sprinkle Lightly with The Parmesan Cheese.

Serving Suggestion

Serve Immediately and Hot on your Decorative Platter for The Very Best Taste Possible! Accompany with a Delicious Mama Lena's Entree of your Choice ~ This Very Special Vegetable Dish compliments any Mama Lena's Veal Dish. Also, be sure to serve with our Very Specially Baked Herb Potatoes, for an even nicer compliment to The Dinner. For a Very Sweet Finish, try some Mama Lena's Anisette & Vanilla Biscotti and Coffee. You will be Delighted with This Vegetable Dish and This Dinner, too! Enjoy!

Italian Green Beans, Onions & Tomatoes, Baked in Romano Cheese

Italiano Verde Fagiolini Cipolla Pomodoro Romano

As we share our Mama Lena's Italian Green Beans, Onions & Tomatoes Baked in Romano Cheese, we can still see Mama sitting at the kitchen table, checking the Italian Beans and trimming them. Mama personally loved This Dish. She grew up on the Fresh Vegetables from Grandpa's Wagon and favored many vegetables, but we remember her love of This Dish in particular. We have an idea Grandma Anna kept her daughter busy with those Italian Green Beans when she was a little girl ~ and it brought Mama good memories! This is a Dish we always enjoyed serving ~ it made us Smile. Our Mama Lena's Guests Always Smiled for This Very Special Dish, too! We can see You Smiling now! Enjoy!

Ingredients   Serves 4~6

Italian Green Beans	1~1/2	Lbs. of Italian Green Beans (Whole String~Bean Style)
	2	Pinches of Salt (Add to Boiling Water)
	1	Pinch of Cayenne Pepper (Add to Boiling Water)
The Red Onion	1	Medium Red Onion (Sliced into Thin Rings)
	1	Pinch of Oregano
	2	Tablespoons of Olive Oil
The Tomatoes	2	Large Fresh Tomatoes (Diced)
	2	Pinches of Garlic Salt
	2	Pinches of Black Pepper
	2	Pinches of Crushed Red Pepper
	4	Tablespoons of Olive Oil
The Sicilian Olives	1/2	Cup of Black Sicilian Olives (Whole & Unpitted)
	2	Tablespoons of Olive Oil
	2	Pinches of Sugar (Granulated)
Olive Oil	1	Cup of Olive Oil (For Baking)
Romano Cheese	14	Extra~Thin Slices of Romano Cheese (For Baking)
The Garnish	1/4	Cup of Romano Cheese (Finely Grated)
	1	Lemon (Slice into Thin Rounds)

Preparation ~ Italian Green Beans, Onions & Tomatoes

**The
Italian Green Beans**

1. Wash The Italian Beans. Break off The End Tips.
2. Bring 1 Quart of Water to a Full Boil, and
    Add Salt and Cayenne Pepper to Boiling Water.
3. Add The Italian Green Beans. Reduce Heat to Medium.
4. Cover Pan. Cook 10 Minutes, Until Beans are Just Al Dente.
5. Remove Pan from Heat. Drain Beans in Colander. Set Aside.
6. Once The Beans have Cooled, Slice Them in Halves.

**The
Sliced Red Onions**

1. Mix The Sliced Red Onions Rings with The Olive Oil.
2. Sprinkle The Red Onion with Oregano. Set Aside.

**The
Fresh Tomatoes**

1. Season The Tomatoes with The Garlic Salt,
    Black Pepper and Red Pepper Flakes.
2. Blend The Mixture with Olive Oil. Set It Aside.

**The
Sicilian Olives**

1. Pour 2 Tablespoons of Olive Oil and 2 Pinches of Sugar
    Over The Black Sicilian Olives.
2. Mix The Olives, Oil & Sugar Very Well. Set Aside.

**The Finished Dish
~ Combine & Bake ~**

1. In a Roaster Pan, Arrange Ingredients as Follows:
    Pour 1/4 Cup Olive Oil Evenly Across The Bottom.
    Half ~ Red Onions Slices ~ Place Over The Oil
    Half ~ Italian Green Beans ~ Place Over Onions
    Half ~ Seasoned Tomatoes ~ Place Over Green Beans
    Half ~ Sicilian Olives ~ Place Over Tomatoes
    6 Slices of Romano Cheese ~ Place on Top
    Drizzle 1/4 Cup of Olive Oil to Top All Evenly.
2. Repeat Layer, Starting with The Red Onions, and
    Then The Beans, Tomatoes & Olives.
3. Top Again ~ Final Topping is 8 Slices of Romano Cheese,
    And "1/2" Cup of Olive Oil to Top All.
4. Seal The Roaster Pan Airtight with Foil.
5. Bake in Preheated 350 Degree Oven for 25 Minutes.

Serving Suggestion

Carefully Spoon The Baked Vegetables into a Deep Heated Decorative Platter. Then, Sprinkle Lightly with Romano Cheese. Place The Lemon Slices around The Dish to Garnish Nicely. This Delicious Vegetable Dish is a compliment to any of Mama Lena's Entree of your choice. We often served This Special Dish with our Chicken Entrees ~ The Italian Green Beans and Chicken Entrees were both Mama's Personal Favorites. If Mama liked it, we were sure our Guests would, too! Serve along with our Parsley Cheese Potatoes and Herbs & Spices Bread. To Sweetly Finish, try our Cassata ~ Amaretto with Pine Nuts and a Cappuccino for Dessert. This is a Dinner of Memories & Delight! Think of Mama Lena & Grandma and Smile! Enjoy!

Herb Potatoes, Specially Baked

Patatas Erbe Specialita

Our Mama Lena's Special Baked Herb Potato has a Great Taste and a Great Look, too! This Very Appetizing Recipe is the handiwork of Salvino's creativity. It's Just Delicious! Mama said, "You can give Salvino Any Potato, and he will create A Festive Dish from it." And that was Perfectly Fine with our Mama Lena's Guests who loved to see These Delightful and Specially Baked Herb Potatoes arrive next to their Evening's Entree Dish! This Very Special Potato bursts with great tastes and dresses up every Dinner, too! Salvino really loves This Dish, too!   Enjoy!

Ingredients   **Serves 4~6**

The **White Potatoes**	2~3	**Lbs. of White Russet Potatoes** **(8 Small, Or 6 Medium~Size Potatoes)**
The **Special Mixture**	1/4	**Lb. of Butter (Sweet & Lightly Salted)**
	2	**Cloves of Garlic (Finely Minced)**
	1	**Medium Onion (Grated)**
	1/4	**Cup of Romano Cheese (Grated)**
The Cream	1	**Cup of Half & Half Cream**
The **Bread Crumbs**	1/2	**Cup of Mama Lena's Bread Crumbs (Italian Seasoned)** **(See Recipe ~ Chapter Ten)**
The **Seasonings**	4	**Pinches of Salt**
	3	**Pinches of Black Pepper**
	2	**Pinches of Marjoram**
	2	**Pinches of Tarragon**
	2	**Pinches of Chives**
	1	**Pinch of Cayenne Pepper**
The Garnish	1/4	**Cup of Romano Cheese (Grated)**
	1	**Tablespoon of Parsley Flakes (Mix into The Cheese)**
	1/4	**Bunch of Fresh Parsley**

Preparation ~ Herb Potatoes ~ Specially Baked

The Potatoes
~ Clean & Boil ~

1. Wash The Potatoes Well. Clean & Trim Skin of Any Spots.
2. Leave The Full Potato Skins On for Cooking.
3. In a Large Pan, Fill Water to Half, and Bring to a Boil.
   Reduce The Heat to Medium.
4. Set Whole Potatoes into Water. Cover The Pan.
5. Cook The Potatoes for 35 Minutes. Remove from The Pan.
6. Puncture Potatoes with a Fork to Release Steam.
7. First, Cool Potatoes Completely.
8. Peel The Outer Skins Off. Cut Potatoes Into Small Cubes.

The Mixture
~ Blending ~

1. In a Large Mixmaster Bowl, Blend Potatoes & Butter,
   On Medium Speed, for About 2 Minutes.
2. Add The Garlic, Grated Onions & Romano Cheese.
   Blend Together for 1 Minute More.
3. On Low Speed, Slowly, Add The Half & Half Cream,
   Until The Entire Mixture is Blended and Soft.
4. Add In The Seasonings of Salt, Black Pepper,
   Marjoram, Tarragon, Chives, and Cayenne Pepper.
5. Slowly, Add Bread Crumbs on Low Speed Also,
   Until The Mixture is Firm but Moist.

The Potatoes
~ Baking ~

1. Line a Large Deep Baking Sheet with Parchment Paper.
2. Using an Ice Cream Scoop, Scoop Potatoes from Mixture.
3. Place Potatoes on The Parchment Paper, About 2" Apart.
4. Place Foil, in a Tent Fashion, over The Baking Sheet to
   Protect Potatoes from Browning Too Fast.
5. Bake in a Preheated 325 Degree Oven for 10 Minutes.
6. Then, Remove Foil. Broil Potatoes for About 2-3 Minutes,
   Until The Potatoes are Just Golden Brown.
   Watch The Broiling Carefully.

Serving Suggestion

Place The Specially Baked Herb Potatoes on a Warm Decorative Platter. Sprinkle Lightly with The Mixed Romano Cheese & Parsley Flakes. Garnish Nicely with Parsley Sprigs. This Special Potato Compliments Everything! Serve with a Favorite Mama Lena's Entree, Caesar Salad, a Ribbon Pasta with our Marinara Sauce and our Tomato Cheese Bread. Anisette & Vanilla Biscotti and Coffee for a Sweet Finish. It's Time for You to Experience A Great Dinner, and a Delicious & Pretty Potato, just the way Salvino makes it!   Enjoy!

Potatoes, Parsley Cheese, Sauteed in Olive Oil

Patata Prezzemolo Asiago Olio

Our Parsley Cheese Potatoes ~ Crisp, Breaded Potatoes~ are another Salvino Specialty. They are Attractive and Delicious! These Tasty Potatoes were a favorite of our Guests, and also of Mama and Papa, who loved them served many ways. Our two favorite ways to serve The Parsley Cheese Potatoes at Mama Lena's were as a Side Dish to an Entree, Or as an Appetizer, using our Asiago Cheese Dressing as a Delightful Dip! Whatever way we served These Crisp & Delicious Potatoes, they would disappear just as soon as they arrived in our Dining Room! We think you will use This Special Recipe often!   Enjoy!

Ingredients   Serves 4~6

The White Potatoes	3	Lbs. of White Russet Potatoes (Medium~Size)
The Breading	3	Cups of Mama Lena's Bread Crumbs (Italian Seasoned) (See Recipe ~ Chapter Ten)
	1/2	Cup of Asiago Cheese (Grated)
	1	Pinch of Garlic Salt
	2	Pinches of Red Pepper Flakes (Crushed)
	4	Pinches of Parsley
The Egg Mixture	4	Large Eggs (Lightly Beaten)
	2	Pinches of Salt
	2	Pinches of Red Pepper Flakes (Crushed)
To Saute	1/4	Lb. of Butter (Sweet & Lightly Salted)
	1	Cup of Olive Oil
The Side Sauce	1	Recipe of Mama Lena's Asiago Cheese Dressing (See Recipe ~ Chapter Three) (Use as A Dip, Or A Topping Sauce)
The Garnish	1/4	Cup of Asiago Cheese (Grated)
	1/4	Bunch of Fresh Parsley

Preparation ~ Potatoes, Parsley Cheese ~ Sauteed in Olive Oil

The Potatoes
~ Pre-Bake ~

1. *Wash The Potatoes Well, and Dry with Paper Towels.*
2. *Leave The Potatoes Whole. Puncture Them with a Fork to Allow Steam to Escape.*
3. *Rub The Potato Skins, with a Little Olive Oil, To Keep The Potatoes Tender,*
4. *Set The Potatoes on a Large Baking Sheet.*
5. *Bake in Preheated 400 Degree Oven for 50~60 Minutes.*
6. *Allow The Potatoes to Cool Completely.*
7. *Cut Each Potato Lengthwise into 4 Even Quarters.*

The Potatoes
~ Bread ~

1. *In a Large Bowl, Beat The Eggs, The Salt and The Red Pepper Flakes.*
2. *In Another Bowl, Blend The Bread Crumbs, Asiago Cheese, Garlic Salt, Red Pepper Flakes and Parsley.*
3. *Dip Each Potato Quarter in Egg Mixture, and then Dip Into Breading Mixture.*
4. *Set on Paper Towels to Dry for About 10 Minutes.*

The Potatoes
~ Saute ~

1. *In a Large Skillet, Heat The Butter to a Melt on Medium. Add in The Olive Oil. Turn Heat to Medium High.*
2. *Saute The Potatoes, Until Golden Brown on Every Side.*
3. *Set on Paper Towels to Drain.*

The
Sauteed Potatoes
~ Bake ~

1. *Set The Sauteed Potatoes on a Baking Sheet, Lined with Parchment Paper.*
2. *Bake The Potatoes in a Preheated 350 Degree Oven, About 5 Minutes to Crisp Potatoes Nicely. These Potatoes are Best When Served Immediately. (If you Need a Few Minutes, Turn Off The Oven and Leave The Potatoes in The Oven, Until Ready to Serve).*

Serving Suggestion

Arrange The Crisped Potatoes on a Warmed Decorative Platter. When Serving The Parsley Cheese Potatoes as An Appetizer, Sprinkle Them Lightly with Grated Asiago Cheese and Garnish with Parsley Sprigs. Accompany with a Bowl of Mama Lena's Asiago Cheese Dressing on the Side to Dip Potatoes. When Serving The Crisped Potatoes as A Side Dish to a Dinner Entree, Drizzle Asiago Cheese Dressing over The Parsley Cheese Potatoes, and then Sprinkle Lightly with Grated Asiago Cheese. Garnish with Parsley Sprigs. Always Serve The Crisped Potatoes Hot for Best Taste! Just Great Tasting Treats! Enjoy!

Spinach, Tomato & Green Olives, Baked in Cream Sherry Sauce

Spinaci Pomodoro Verde Olives Shere

At Mama Lena's, we loved to serve our very special Spinach, Tomato & Green Olives Baked In Cream Sherry Sauce. What a Wonderful Medley of Delightful Tastes! And as we believe all dishes should have a wonderful eye appeal, This Special Mama Lena's Vegetable Dish makes the Top of the List in Presentation! We especially enjoyed serving This Dish with our delicate Fish and Seafood Entrees to bring The Special Color needed to accompany those Dishes. Also, The Rich Taste of The Spinach and Olives and The Spicy Taste of The Tomato seemed to add just the right balance to any Dinner! Mama Lena's Guests just loved this one! The Sauce from This Special Dish is a Very Delicious Treat, too! Enjoy!

Ingredients   Serves 4~6

The Fresh Spinach	1	Lb. of Fresh Spinach Leaves (Whole)
	3/4	Cup of Water (To Boil)
	1	Pinch of Salt (To Boil)
	1	Tablespoon of White Vinegar
	2	Pinches of Sugar
To Saute	3	Tablespoons of Butter (Sweet & Lightly Salted)
	1/4	Cup of Olive Oil
	2	Cloves of Garlic (Slivered)
	1	Large Onion (Finely Chopped)
The Fresh Tomatoes	3	Large Tomatoes (Cut into 4 Even Slices Each) (Makes A Total of Twelve 1/2" Slices)
	2	Pinches of Salt
	2	Pinches of Pepper
The Green Pimento Olives	1	Dozen Large Green Pimento Olives (Chopped)
The Sherry Sauce	1~1/2	Cups of Cream Sherry
The Topping	1/2	Cup of Mama Lena's Bread Crumbs (Italian Seasoned) (See Recipe ~ Chapter Ten)
	1/2	Cup of Parmesan Cheese (Grated)
The Garnish	1/4	Cup of Asiago Cheese (Grated)
	1/4	Bunch of Fresh Parsley

Preparation ~ Spinach, Tomato & Green Olives ~ Cream Sherry Sauce

**The
Fresh Spinach
~ Prepare ~**

1. Place The Fresh Spinach under Cool Water and Rinse Well.
   Drain The Spinach in a Colander. Do Not Pat Dry
   Trim Off Stems and Any Damaged Parts.
2. In a Large Saucepan, Bring 3/4 Cup of Water and
   The Salt to a Full Boil. Stir In The Vinegar & Sugar.
   Reduce The Heat to Medium.
3. Add The Fresh Spinach to The Liquid. Cover Pan.
   Allow The Spinach to Steam for 5 Minutes.
4. Drain in a Colander. Set The Steamed Spinach Aside.
   Discard The Water Mixture.

**The
Tomatoes & Olives
~ Prepare ~**

1. In a Large Skillet, Heat The Butter on Medium.
   Add The Olive Oil.
2. Add The Chopped Onions. Saute for About 2 Minutes.
3. Add The Garlic, and Saute Together for 1 Minute More.
4. Remove Garlic & Onions, with a Slotted Spoon. Set Aside.
   Save The Oil for The Tomatoes & Olives.
5. Season The Tomatoes with Salt & Pepper, and
   Add Sliced Tomatoes To The Hot Butter & Oil.
   Saute The Tomatoes on Each Side for 1/2 Minute.
6. Add The Green Olives to The Butter, Oil & Tomatoes.
   Saute All for 1 Minute More. Remove Pan from Heat.

**The Finished Dish
~ Combine & Bake ~**

1. In a Large Roaster Pan, Pour 1 Cup of Cream Sherry
   Across The Bottom of The Pan.
2. Arrange The Spinach Leaves over The Cream Sherry.
3. Spoon The Sauteed Onions & Garlic Over The Spinach.
4. Place The Tomatoes & Olives And The Butter & Oil on Top.
5. Sprinkle Entire Top with Seasoned Bread Crumbs.
6. Drizzle 1/2 Cup of Cream Sherry Over Bread Crumbs.
7. Sprinkle The Top Evenly with Parmesan Cheese.
8. Seal Roaster Pan Airtight with Foil.
9. Bake in a Preheated 325 Degree Oven for 15 Minutes.

Serving Suggestion

Serve in a Deep Heated Decorative Serving Bowl. Arrange The Spinach Leaves with The Tomatoes & Green Olives in The Bowl. Mix The Sauce of Sherry, Butter, Oil, Bread Crumbs & Cheese in The Pan. Drizzle The Sherry Sauce Over The Spinach, Tomatoes & Green Olives. Sprinkle Lightly The Entire Top of Dish with Asiago Cheese. Place Parsley Sprigs to Garnish. Serve with your Favorite Mama Lena's Entree, our Parsley Cheese Potatoes, and some warm Mama Lena's Italian Bread for this Outstanding Sauce.! You will love This Dish! Enjoy!

Zucchini, Breaded,
Served with Orange Sauce

Zucchini Fritto Bene Aranci

"Treats Beyond Compare!" That's how our Mama Lena's Guests described our delicious "Breaded Zucchini With Orange Sauce." This marvelous Mama Lena's Recipe was the work of Mama and Salvino.   Mama always loved to prepare and eat The Zucchini, and Salvino, who loved creating Sauces, perfected The Orange Sauce with a Dazzling and Delicious Effect!   Our Guests received a Great Treat the day they tasted This Lovely Dish! When Salvino asked them if they liked The New Dish, they delightfully named The Dish, "Treats Beyond Compare!" You and your family can now delight in our Mama Lena's "Treats Beyond Compare" just as our Guests did! We always double This Tasty Recipe, as This Delicious Dish disappears so very quickly!   Enjoy!

Ingredients   Serves 4~6

The Fresh Zucchini	2	Lbs. of Fresh Zucchini (4 Slices per Zucchini = 24) (Buy 6 Evenly ~ Shaped Small Individual Zucchini)
	3	Pinches of Salt
	2	Pinches of Pepper
	2	Pinches of Sugar (Granulated)
The Seasoned Breading	2	Cups of Mama Lena's Bread Crumbs (Italian Seasoned) (See Recipe ~ Chapter Ten)
	2	Tablespoons of Fresh Orange Rind (Finely Grated)
	1/4	Cup of Romano Cheese (Finely Grated)
	3	Large Eggs (Lightly Beaten) (To Dip & Coat Zucchini)
To Saute	1	Cup of Olive Oil
The Fresh Orange Sauce	2	Cups of Fresh Orange Juice
	2	Tablespoons of Fresh Orange Rind (Finely Grated)
	1	Cup of Sugar (Granulated)
	1/2	Cup of Sugar (Brown)
	1	Teaspoon of Lemon Extract ~ **OR** ~
	4	Drops of Fresh Lemon Juice
	2	Tablespoons of Cornstarch
The Garnish	1/4	Cup of Romano Cheese (Finely Grated)
	1/4	Bunch of Fresh Parsley
	1	Orange (Cut into Very Thin Slices)

Preparation ~ Zucchini, Breaded ~ Served with Orange Sauce

The
Fresh Zucchini
~ Prepare ~

1. Trim Each Zucchini of Ends & Damaged Parts. Rinse Well.
2. Slice Each Zucchini Lengthwise into 4 Long Even Slices.
3. Season Zucchini, Both Sides, with Salt & Pepper & Sugar.

The
Fresh Zucchini
~ Bread ~

1. Blend 2 Cups of Mama's Italian Seasoned Bread Crumbs
   with Fresh Orange Rind & Romano Cheese. Mix Well.
2. Dip Zucchini Slices into Lightly Beaten Eggs.
3. Bread The Zucchini with Seasoned Crumbs, Coating Well.
4. Set on Paper Towels to Dry for About 5 Minutes.

The
Fresh Zucchini
~ Saute ~

1. In an Extra~Large Skillet, Heat The Olive Oil to Medium.
2. Saute The Breaded Zucchini Slices, Until Golden Brown
   On Both Sides. Allow to Drain on Paper Towels.

The
Fresh Orange Sauce
~ Prepare ~

1. In a Large Sauce Pan, Mix Orange Juice, Orange Rind and
   Cornstarch. With a Whisk, Blend Well, Until Smooth.
2. Add In Granulated Sugar, Brown Sugar & Lemon Extract.
   Blend Again with Whisk, Until Smooth.
3. Heat Ingredients on Low Heat, Stirring Constantly,
   Until Smooth and Warm. About 2~3 Minutes.
4. Turn Heat to Medium. Bring Sauce to a Full Boil,
   Stir Constantly. As Sauce Begins Boil, Reduce Heat.
5. Simmer The Sauce for 5 Minutes. Stir Constantly.
   Cover Pan. Remove The Sauce from Heat.
6. The Sauce Should be a Thin, Smooth Clear Texture.
   This Sauce Can Be Served Warm or Chilled!

Serving Suggestion

Serve The Zucchini on a Warmed Decorative Platter with a Serving Bowl of Orange Sauce (Warm or Chilled) to Spoon on Individually. Or, Serve on a Warm Platter with Warm Orange Sauce Drizzled over The Breaded Zucchini. Either way, Lightly Sprinkle Romano Cheese over The Zucchini. Place The Parsley Sprigs & Orange Rounds to Nicely Garnish! This Dish makes a Delicious Treat & Delightful Presentation! Serve as A Side Dish to a Mama Lena's Entree, or alone as A Special Treat or Appetizer with a White or Rose Wine! Mama & Papa and all our Guests would love to join you for This Special Treat! Enjoy!

~ Chapter Ten ~
Homemade Bread

Pages   217 ~ 235

Mama Lena's Bread Dough &
Tips for Baguettes, Loaf & Round~Style Breads

Pane Italiano ala Mama Lena

Our Mama Lena's Bread Dough is our Great Basic Dough that was carefully taught to Mama by her Mother, Grandma Anna. Mama used the recipe to bake about 10 Loaves of Bread two or three times a week for her family when her children were just growing up. All the kids used to watch for the pans of bread to come hot out of the oven. We kids could hardly wait! And, At Mama Lena's Italian Kitchen, our Guests would be waiting for the Breads to come hot out of the oven just like we did! There's just nothing like the wonderful smell and taste of Homemade Bread in the home waiting for your family and guests! We know once you try it, you will love making and serving Mama's Delicious Homemade Italian Bread! Enjoy!

Ingredients   Makes 2 Loaves

The Yeast Mix

1	Package of Active Dry Yeast
1/2	Cup of Warm Water (110 ~ 115 Degrees)
2	Teaspoons of Sugar

The Flour Mix

6	Cups of All~Purpose Flour
	(You May Use 1/2 Cup More or 1/2 Cup Less)
1	Tablespoon of Salt
1~2	Cups of Warm Water
	(1 Cup First, Then Add By Tablespoon)
2	Tablespoons of Pure Olive Oil
	(Mix Last ~ Into Dough for Flavor and Texture)

The Extra Items

1/4	Cup of Pure Olive Oil (To Rub on Bowl & Baking Pans)
1/2	Cup of Extra Flour (To Dust The Pans)

Preparation ~ Mama Lena's Bread Dough & Tips

The Yeast Mix

1. In a Glass Container (8 Oz.), Mix The Sugar and The Warm Water (110 ~115 Degrees, By Thermometer).
2. Sprinkle The Yeast on Top of The Sugar & Water, and Allow Yeast to Dissolve into Water. Then, Stir Gently.
3. Cover Container. Let The Yeast Rise to Double (10~12 Minutes). (Yeast is Ready when Doubled & Top has a Foam Dome).

Preparation ~ Mama Lena's Bread Dough & Tips

The Bread Dough
~ Mixing ~

1. *In a Large Bowl, Sift 3 Level Cups of The Flour,*
   Together with 1 Tablespoon of Salt.
2. *By Hand, Blend In 1 Cup of Warm Water (110~115 Degree)*
   Until The Flour, Salt and Water are Mixed Well.
3. *Add The Risen Yeast to The Mixture, and Blend in Well.*
   (Your Mixture is Very Loose and Soft Now).
4. *One Cup At A Time, Add The Extra Flour, Mixing in Well.*
   If Dough gets Dry, Add More Warm Water, By Tablespoon.
   (Stop Adding The Extra Flour or Water, when
   The Dough is a Soft, but Firm and Smooth Ball,
   And Falls Away from The Side of The Mixing Bowl).
5. *Rest The Dough ~ Place The Dough on a Floured Surface.*
   Place a Mixing Bowl Over The Dough, and
   Allow The Dough to Rest This Way for 10 Minutes.
6. *Then, Work in The 2 Tablespoons of Olive Oil for Flavor & Texture.*
7. *Knead The Dough ~ Fold The Dough over Toward You and*
   Gently Push The Dough Away with Heel of Your Hand.
   Then, Turn The Dough a Quarter Turn to The Right,
   and Repeat Action ~ Push Into Dough and Turn Dough,
   in an Easy Gentle Rhythm, for About 5 to 8 Minutes.
   (You want a Soft Dough that is Silky Smooth & Elastic).

First Rise
For The Dough

1. *Select a Deep Bowl that The Dough will fill to 1/2, and*
   Then You will know when The Dough has Doubled in Size.
2. *Rub The Inside of The Bowl with Olive Oil.*
   Set The Dough into The Oiled Bowl,
   Then Turn Dough Over in The Bowl, so Oiled Side is Up.
3. *Cover The Top of The Bowl Loosely with Wax Paper,*
   To Keep The Dough from Sticking.
4. *Then, Cover with a Thin White Terry Kitchen Towel, so*
   Dough is Draft~free, but can Breathe.
5. *Place The Covered Bread in a Warm, Draft~free Area to*
   Rise for 2 Hours ~ Dough should Top Bowl & Be Doubled.

Select
The Bread Style

1. *Poke Two Fingers into The Dough. If Indentations Remain,*
   The Dough is Properly Doubled and Risen.
2. *Punch The Dough Down to get All The Air Out of The Dough.*
3. *Knead The Dough for 3 Minutes More on a Floured Surface.*
4. *Cut and Shape The Dough, According to Style You Select ~*
   Baguette Style ~ Loaf Style ~ Round Style.
5. *A Helpful Tip ~ As you are Shaping Your Dough, and*
   If The Dough is Being Resistant, Just Set It Aside,
   Cover It ~ and ~ Let it Rest & Relax for 5 Minutes!
   (The Bread Directions Continue ~ Next Page)

Preparation ~ Mama Lena's Bread Dough & Tips

Cutting And Shaping The Breads

Baguette~Style Bread
~ Cut The Dough into 2 Equal Dough Balls.
~ Roll Each Dough Ball into 14" x 8" Rectangle Pieces.
~ With Fingers on The 14" Side, Tightly Roll Each
    Rectangle Piece into a Long Slender Loaf.
~ Pinch Ends and Edges to Seal. Turn Seam Side Down.
~ Make 3 Diagonal Cuts (2") on Each Bread Top.
~ Place Loaves on a Baking Sheet (15~1/2 x 12),
    Which has been Lightly Oiled & Dusted.

Loaf~Style Bread
~ Cut The Dough into 2 Equal Dough Balls.
~ Roll Each Dough Ball into 16" x 9" Rectangle Pieces.
~ With Fingers on the 9" Side, Tightly Roll
    Each Rectangle into 2 Medium Loafs.
~ Turn Seamed Side Down ~ Tuck Ends Under Loaves.
~ Place Loafs into 2 Loaf Pans (9 x 5 x 3),
    Which are Lightly Oiled & Dusted.

Round~Style Bread
~ Cut The Dough into 2 Equal Dough Balls.
~ Gently Roll Each Dough Ball to a 9" Round.
~ Cut 3 Slits Into The Bread Tops (2" Slits).
~ Place Loafs in 2 Round Pans (9" Size),
    Which are Lightly Oiled & Dusted.

Second Rise For The Dough
1. Cover The Dough with Wax Paper and A Towel to Rise Again.
2. Place The Dough in a Draft~free, Warm Area, and
    Let Rise for 1~1/2 Hours More, Or Until Doubled in Size.

Baking The Bread
1. Preheat The Oven to 400 Degrees. Place Bread in Oven,
    on The Second Shelf from The Bottom of The Oven.
    * After 5 Minutes* ~ Reduce The Heat to 350 Degrees.
    Bake The Bread for 1 Hour More at 350 Degrees.
2. For a Very Crusty Bread, Remove Pans from The Oven at
    Final 10 Minutes of Baking, Brush The Tops with Water.
    Return The Pans to The Oven for Final 10 Minutes of Baking.
3. Cool Breads on Wire Racks. Seal Airtight & Do Not Refrigerate.
4. To Freeze Bread for Up to 2 Months, Seal Airtight in Plastic.

Serving Suggestion

At Mama Lena's, we served our Guests "All" of The Special Bread Recipes in This Chapter. But, as Children, This Bread was the Only Bread we knew ~ And Mama served This Bread Hot Out of The Oven with Olive Oil & Grated Cheese on It! Yum, Yum! Now, try Your Fresh Baked Bread this way, and You will be thanking Mama & Grandma just like we did! Enjoy!

Traditional Thin~Crusted Pizza

Traditione Pizza

Mama Lena's was a Dinner Restaurant, so the Traditional Thin Crusted Pizzas were served only for the Private Parties. Occasionally, we surprised our Guests by serving Small Squares of the Thin Pizza as Appetizers before the Evening's Meal. But that was only if we had made them Fresh that afternoon when some Family or Friends stopped by. Salvino would make several pizzas just for our Mama Lena's Guests to have that evening. Our Dinner Guests were always thrilled and appreciated the Surprise Treat and Tastes! There's no mistaking how delicious they really are ~ Favorites of Mama and Papa ~ so we had to share this Special Recipe with you for your family and guests, too!   Enjoy!

Ingredients   Makes Two 12" Pizzas

The Yeast Mix	2	**Packages of Active Dry Yeast**
	1	**Cup of Warm Water (110~115 Degrees)**
	2	**Teaspoons of Sugar**
The Flour Mix	5	**Cups of All~Purpose Flour**
		(You May Use 1/2 Cup More Or 1/2 Cup Less)
	1	**Tablespoon of Salt**
	2	**Tablespoons of Olive Oil**
	2	**Tablespoons of Milk**
	1~1/2	**Cup of Warm Water**
		(Use 1 Cup First ~&~ Then Add, By Tablespoon)
The Basic Topping		*** Basic Tomato~Cheese Topping* (Covers Two Thin Pizzas)**
	2	**Cups of Italian Plum Tomatoes, Crushed in Puree**
		(Drain Off All Juice) (Do Not Use Juice)
	2	**Pinches Each of Salt, Pepper, Basil, and**
		Oregano and Parsley (To Season Tomatoes)
	2	**Cups of Mozzarella Cheese (Shredded)**
	1/4	**Cup of Olive Oil**
The Optional Toppings		*** Optional Toppings* (Covers Two Tomato~Cheese Pizzas)**
	1~1/2	**Lbs. of Italian Sausage**
		(Mild, Sweet, Or Hot, As Preferred)
		(Remove Casing First & Break Up Sausage ~
		Make 30 Small Flat Pieces of Loose Sausage)
	2	**Cans (8 Oz. Each) of Sliced Mushrooms**
		(Drain Off All Juice) (Do Not Use Juice)
The Baking Pans	2	**Pizza Pans (12" Rounds) (Heavy Aluminum)**
		(The Pizza Directions Continue ~ Next Pages)

Preparation ~ Traditional Thin~Crusted Pizza

The Yeast Mix

1. In a Glass Container (16 Oz.~Size), Mix The Sugar and Warm Water (110~115 Degrees, By Thermometer).
2. Sprinkle The Yeast on Top of The Sugar and Water. Allow The Yeast to Dissolve into Water. Then, Stir In.
3. Cover Container. Let Yeast Rise to Double (15 Minutes). (Yeast is Ready When It Has Doubled, and The Yeast Top has a Foam Dome).

The Pizza Dough ~ Mixing ~

1. In a Large Bowl, Mix Together 4 Cups of Flour and Salt.
2. Move The Flour & Salt to Sides, Making a Well in Center.
3. Pour Risen Yeast, 2 Tablespoons of Milk, and 1 Cup of Warm Water and Olive Oil into Well Center.
4. Bring The Flour & Salt into the Liquid Center, and Mix with a Wooden Spoon, Until Well Blended.
5. Add More Water ~OR~ Add More Flour, By Tablespoon, To Balance The Dough Texture. (You want a Very Soft, Pliable Ball of Dough).
6. Knead The Dough on a Lightly Floured Surface for 5 Minutes, Until Dough is Soft and Silky Smooth. (See Kneading Instructions in Bread Dough Recipe)

The Pizza Dough ~ First Rising ~

1. Select a Deep Bowl that The Dough will Fill to 1/2, and Then you will know when Dough has Doubled in Size.
2. Rub The Inside of The Bowl with Olive Oil. Set The Dough into An Oiled Bowl. Turn Dough Over ~ Oiled Side Up.
3. Cover The Top of Bowl Loosely with Wax Paper, To Keep Dough from Sticking.
4. Cover Wax Paper with a Thin White Terry Kitchen Towel, So Dough is Draft~free, but can Breathe.
5. Let Dough Rise for 2 Hours, Or Until Doubled in Size.
6. Poke Two Fingers into The Dough. If Indentations Remain, The Dough Has Properly Risen and Doubled.
7. Punch The Dough Down to Get All the Air Out of Dough.
8. Knead Dough for 3 Minutes. Let Dough Rest for 5 Minutes.

The Pizza Dough ~ Shaping ~

1. Cut The Dough into 2 Equal Dough Balls.
2. Stretch Each Dough Ball by Hand First Into A Flat Round.
3. Next Roll Dough with Rolling Pin to a 13~14" Round.
4. Place Each Dough on a Lightly Oiled 12" Round Pan.
5. Carefully Curl Dough In, making a Good Edge to Fit Pan.

Preparation ~ Traditional Thin~Crusted Pizza

**The
Pizza Dough
~ Second Rising ~**

1. Brush The Dough Lightly with The Olive Oil.
2. Cover The Dough with Wax Paper and a Thin Terry Towel.
3. Set The Dough in a Warm, Draft~free Spot.
4. Allow The Dough to Rise Again for 30 Minutes More.

**Top The Pizza Dough with Tomato-Cheese Only ~OR ~
Top with One or Two of Optional Ingredients
(Sausage and Mushrooms)**

**The Risen Pizzas
~ Topping ~**

1. Brush a Little More Olive Oil on Top of The Dough.
   Spread The Olive Oil Just Up To The Curled Edge.
2. Spread Equal Amounts of The Seasoned Tomatoes
   onto The Two Rolled and Risen Doughs.
3. If You are also Using Mushrooms on Top,
   Place on The Mushrooms Over The Tomatoes Now.
4. If You are also Using Sausage on Top, Then
   Place 15 Flat Pieces on Each Pizza Dough Now.
5. Arrange The Shredded Mozzarella Across The Tops,
   After the Last Basic or Optional Ingredient is On.
6. Carefully, and Lightly, Drizzle Pizza Tops with Olive Oil.

**The Topped Pizzas
~ Baking ~**

1. Bake in a Preheated 425 Degree Oven for 20~25 Minutes,
   Until The Dough is a Medium Golden Brown.
   (Bake on The Third Shelf from The Bottom).
2. Cool 5 Minutes. Cut & Serve. Crusty & Delicious!

Serving Suggestion

Serve Nicely on a Round Decorative Platter. Using a Kitchen Scissors or a Pizza Cutter, Cut The Traditional Thin~Crusted Pizza into Attractive Pieces. For Buffets, we served on Large Round Platters or Cutting Boards for a Nice Presentation! Accompany with our Italian Salad & Dressing Supreme, Sicilian Black Olives and Sliced Fontinella Cheese. Select a Soft or Dry Red Wine or a Rose Wine to simply serve with This Delicious Pizza. This will make an Italian Feast! You just made a Great Treat for your family and guests! Mama Lena & Papa Frank would have loved to join you for this Favorite Treat of Theirs ~ They would say to you, "Buona, Buona, Buona!"   Enjoy!

Sicilian Pizza & Focaccio
Old~World Style

Siciliano Pizza e Focaccio

Our Mama Lena's Sicilian Pizza and Focaccio reflect the Old~World Sicilian Way to make Pizza and Focaccio ~ A Thick, Bready Baked Dough ~ topped with our Sicilian Toppings which are Very Light, but Tasteful and Unique Coverage for This Very Excellent Dough. The Sicilian Pizza and The Sicilian Focaccio were Special Favorites of our Mama Lena's Guests for years. Mama just loved making and having these treats, too! Sicilian Pizza we cut into Large Squares, and Sicilian Focaccio into Pie Slices and served them as Bread at Mama Lena's. Our Guests were always thrilled when these arrived in their Baskets. We know you will find the same happy response from your family and guests, as you make and serve Mama's Classic Sicilian Pizza and Focaccio! Enjoy!

Ingredients

Makes 1 Sicilian Pizza, ~OR~ 2 Focaccio Breads

The Yeast Mix	2	**Packages of Active Dry Yeast**
	1	**Cup of Warm Water (110 ~115 Degrees)**
	2	**Teaspoons of Honey**
The Flour Mix	6	**Cups of All~Purpose Flour** *(You May Need 1/2 Cup More, Or 1/2 Cup Less)*
	1/4	**Cup of Olive Oil**
	1	**Tablespoon of Salt**
	1~2	**Cups of Milk (Bring Milk to Room Temperature)** *(Use 1 Cup First and Then Add By Tablespoons)*
The Toppings	1	**Set of Topping Ingredients, Per Topping Recipe** *(See Mama Lena's Toppings That Follow)*
The Baking Pans	1	**Baking Sheet (18" x 12") for Sicilian Pizza**
	2	**Baking Round Pans (9") for Sicilian Focaccio**

Preparation ~ Sicilian Pizza & Focaccio, Old~World Style

The Yeast Mix	1.	**In a Glass Container (16 Oz. Size), Mix The Honey and The Warm Water (110~115 Degrees, By Thermometer).**
	2.	**Sprinkle The Yeast on Top of The Honey and Water, and Allow The Yeast to Dissolve into Water. Then, Stir In.**
	3.	**Cover Container. Let Yeast Rise to Double (15 Minutes).** *(The Yeast is Ready When It Has Doubled, and The Yeast Top has a Foam Dome).*

Preparation ~ Sicilian Pizza & Sicilian Focaccio ~ Old~World Style

The Sicilian Dough
~ Mixing ~

1. In a Large Bowl, Mix The Salt and Just 5 Cups of Flour.
2. Move The Flour & Salt to The Sides of The Bowl, and
    Make a Well in The Center of The Bowl.
3. Pour The Risen Yeast, 1 Cup of Milk, and
    1/4 Cup of Olive Oil into The Center Well.
4. Bring The Flour and The Salt into The Liquid Center.
    Mix with a Wooden Spoon, Until Well Blended.
5. If Needed, Add More Milk or More Flour, By Tablespoon,
    Until The Dough is Very Soft and Very Pliable.
    (The Dough Should Fall Away From Side of Bowl).
6. Knead Dough on a Lightly Floured Surface for 5 Minutes,
    Until The Dough is Soft and Silky Smooth.

The Sicilian Dough
~ First Rising ~

1. Select a Deep Bowl that The Dough will fill to 1/2, and
    Then, you will know when Dough has Doubled in Size.
2. Rub The Inside of The Bowl with The Olive Oil.
    Set Dough Into Bowl and Turn It Over ~ Oiled Side Up.
3. Cover The Top of The Bowl Loosely with Wax Paper,
    To Keep The Dough From Sticking.
4. Then Cover with a Thin White Terry Kitchen Towel, so
    The Dough is Draft~free, but can Breathe.
5. Let Dough Rise for 2 Hours. It should be Doubled in Size.
6. Poke Two Fingers into The Dough. If Indentations Remain,
    The Dough Has Properly Risen and Doubled.
7. Punch The Dough Down to Get All the Air Out of Dough.
8. Knead for 3 Minutes. Let Dough Rest for 5 Minutes.

The Sicilian Dough
~ Cut & Shape ~

1. After First Rising, Cut & Shape Sicilian Dough as Follows:
    * Sicilian Pizza *
    ~ Pat Down The Entire Ball of Dough on Floured Surface.
    ~ Stretch and Roll The Dough to 18" x 12" Rectangle Piece.
    ~ Place The Dough into One Pan (18" x 12" Size),
        Which has been Lightly Oiled.

    * Sicilian Focaccio *
    ~ Divide Dough into 2 Equal Dough Balls.
    ~ Stretch and Roll The Dough to Fit The 9" Round Pans.
    ~ Place The Dough Into Two Lightly Oiled 9" Round Pans.

The Sicilian Dough
~ Second Rising ~

1. Brush Either Style of Dough Lightly with Oil. Cover with
    Wax Paper and a Towel.   Set in a Draft~free Spot.
2. Allow The Dough to Rise 1~1/2 Hours More, Until Doubled.
    (The Sicilian Pizza Toppings Continue ~ Next Page)

Preparation ~ Sicilian Pizza & Sicilian Focaccio ~ Old~World Style

* Sicilian Pizza *
Topping

1	Large Can of Plum Tomatoes, Crushed in Puree (Drain Off All Liquid) (Do Not Use Liquid)
2	Pinches Each of Salt, Pepper, Basil & Oregano (To Season & Mix Into The Plum Tomatoes)
2	Lb. Piece Mozzarella Cheese (Cut to Small Cubes)
1/4	Cup of Olive Oil (Carefully Drizzle On)
1/2	Cup of Romano Cheese (Grated) (Use Very Last)

Optional Ingredients

1	Lb. of Italian Sausage (Sweet, Mild, Or Hot) ~ Remove Casing First ~ Break Up Sausage ~ Make 20 Small, Flat Pieces of Sausage ~
20	Anchovy Fillets (One 3 Oz. Jar) ~ Drain Off Salt ~ Rinse Well ~ Cut 10 Filets into 20 Halves ~

Top The Sicilian Pizza

1. In a Large Bowl, Combine The Plum Tomatoes (No Liquid) And The Salt, Pepper, Basil and Oregano. Mix Well.
2. Cut The Mozzarella Cheese into Small Cubes, and Press The Cubes into The Inside of The Dough.
3. If using Anchovies, Press The Anchovies Into Dough Now.
4. Spoon Seasoned Tomatoes on Dough, Except for 1/4" Rim.
5. If using Sausage, Place 3" Apart on The Tomatoes Now.
6. Drizzle Olive Oil over The Top of The Seasoned Tomatoes.
7. Sprinkle Top Lightly with Grated Romano Cheese.

* Sicilian Focaccio *
Topping

2	Cups of Roasted Red Peppers (Drain Off Juice)
1/3	Cup of Olive Oil (Brush Top First & Drizzle Later)
2	Pinches Each of Salt and Garlic Powder
4	Pinches Each of Oregano and Red Pepper Flakes
1/2	Cup of Parmesan Cheese (Coarsely Grated)

Top The Sicilian Focaccio

1. Poke Several Rows of Holes into The Dough in A Pattern.
2. Brush The Tops of The Dough Lightly with Olive Oil.
3. Insert The Red Peppers into The Patterned Dough Holes.
4. Combine The Salt, Garlic Powder, Oregano, and Red Pepper Flakes. Sprinkle onto The Dough Tops.
5. Now, Sprinkle Lightly with The Grated Parmesan Cheese.
6. Lightly Drizzle The Olive Oil across The Seasoned Tops.

Baking Sicilian Pizza ~ OR ~ Sicilian Focaccio

1. Bake in a Preheated 400 Degree Oven for 45~55 Minutes. (Place Pans on Third Shelf Up from Bottom of Oven).
2. Watch Bake Time ~ Depends on Your Oven & Baking Pans ~ Dough is Finished when Golden Brown & Baked Through.
3. Cool 5 Minutes. Cut Sicilian Pizza into Nice Squares, and Sicilian Focaccio into Pie Slices. Just Delicious! Enjoy!

Garlic & Sweet Onion Bread

Pane Aglio Dolci Cipolla Italiano

Our Mama Lena's Garlic and Sweet Onion Bread is a Tasty and Delicious Bread loved by our Guests for years, especially Those Lovers of Garlic! It also was Papa Frank's favorite. Papa Frank always had This Great Bread with our Tomato, Scallion & Red Onion Salad. We told our Mama Lena's Italian Kitchen Guests about Papa Frank's choice and they agreed with him, so we tried to serve this Delicious Bread any time we served that Salad! We are sure you are going to agree with Papa, too!   Enjoy!

Ingredients   Serves 2~3

1	Loaf of Italian Bread ~ Baguette Style
	(See Recipe ~ Chapter Ten) ~OR~ (Purchase At The Market)
1/2	Cup of Olive Oil
3	Tablespoons of Butter (Sweet & Lightly Salted)
2	Large Red Onions (Sliced Very Thin)
2	Cloves of Garlic (Minced)
3	Pinches of Sugar (Granulated)
1/4	Cup of Romano Cheese (Grated)
1	Kitchen Towel (A Thin Terry Towel is Best)

Preparation ~ Garlic & Sweet Onion Bread

Saute The Topping

1. In a Large Skillet, Heat The Olive Oil on Medium High.
2. Add Sliced Onions. Saute for About 4 Minutes.
3. Add The Garlic, and Saute Together for 1 Minute More.
4. Place The Butter on Top of The Onions & Garlic.
   Then, Sprinkle The Butter with 3 Pinches of Sugar.
   Once Butter & Sugar Melts, Stir into Onions & Garlic.
5. Remove from Heat. Cover Pan. Let Mixture Set Up 15 Minutes.

Top & Bake The Bread

1. Cut Italian Baguette Bread along One Side & At Each End,
   Lengthwise, so Bread has a Hinge on Other Side.
2. Spoon The Sauteed Mixture Evenly to Cover The Bread Bottom.
3. Sprinkle with Romano Cheese. Close The Bread.
4. Place Loaf on a Baking Sheet Lined with Parchment Paper.
5. Place a Damp Kitchen Towel over The Filled Loaf.
6. Heat in a Preheated 350 Degree Oven for 15 Minutes, Or
   Until Towel is Bone Dry. Remove The Pan from The Oven.
7. Slice The Bread, with a Serrated Knife, into 1~1/2 " Slices.
8. Serve Immediately in a Bread Basket. Use a Cloth Napkin
   To Keep Bread Hot. Makes a Nice Presentation! Enjoy!

Herbs & Spices Bread

Pane Erbe Condimento Italiano

Our Mama Lena's Herbs & Spices Italian Bread is a Lovely Bread Rich in Many Flavors. It is a Compliment to Any Mama Lena's Dinner. Mama Lena's Italian Kitchen Guests loved the way we served it at the Restaurant, or it can be made a Spicier Way, by adding Red Pepper Flakes ~ That's how Mama made it for Grandpa! The Results are Just Great Either way! This Delicious Bread is also lovely as a Snack by itself. Enjoy!

Ingredients   Serves 2~3

1	Loaf of Italian Bread ~ Baguette Style
	(See Recipe ~ Chapter Ten) ~ <u>OR</u> ~ (Purchase At The Market)

3/4	Cup of Olive Oil
4	Tablespoons of Butter (Sweet & Lightly Salted)
2	Pinches of Basil <u>and</u> 3 Pinches of Black Pepper
3	Pinches of Fennel <u>and</u> 1 Pinch of Rosemary (Ground)
3	Pinches of Oregano <u>and</u> 3 Pinches of Parsley
1	Pinch of Sage <u>and</u> 1 Pinch of Marjoram
1	Pinch of Thyme <u>and</u> 2 Pinches of Red Pepper Flakes
	*(If You Prefer Spicier)
3/4	Cup of Mixed Grated Cheese
	(Romano Cheese & Parmesan Cheese)
1	Kitchen Towel (A Thin Terry Towel is Best)

Preparation ~ Herbs & Spices Bread

Grind & Saute The Herbs

1. Combine All Herbs & Spices and Grind To Extra~Fine Texture. (Grind in A Bowl, Or In a Pepper Mill).
2. In a Small Sauce Pan, Melt The Butter on Medium High Heat. Blend in The Olive Oil. Bring The Butter & Oil to a Sizzle.
3. Add The Ground Herbs & Spices. Mix with the Butter & Oil.
4. Remove from The Heat. Cover Pan. Let Stand for 15 Minutes.

Top & Bake The Bread

1. Cut Italian Baguette Loaf along One Side & At Each End, Lengthwise, so Bread has a Hinge on Other Side.
2. Spread The Bread Open. Evenly Spoon Mixture on Both Sides.
3. Sprinkle with The Mixed Grated Cheese. Close The Bread.
4. Place The Loaf on Baking Sheet Lined with Parchment Paper.
5. Place a Damp Kitchen Towel over The Loaf.
6. Heat in a Preheated 350 Degree Oven for 15 Minutes, Or Until Towel is Bone Dry. Remove The Pan from The Oven.
7. Slice The Bread, with a Serrated Knife, into 1~1/2" Slices.
8. Serve Immediately in a Bread Basket. Use a Cloth Napkin To Keep Bread Hot. Makes a Nice Presentation! Enjoy!

Hot Cheese Bread

Pane Formaggi Pepe Italiano

Our Mama Lena's Hot Cheese Bread was a Delightfully Zesty and Tasty Compliment to our Mama Lena's Dinners. It is so simple to prepare, but with the right ingredients and attention to preparation, it just becomes A Feast in itself! The Delicious Hot Cheese Bread was served to Mama Lena's Guests with their Dinner or as an Appetizer before Dinner, and at Private Parties! Any Time, Any Way ~ This Bread is a Very Special Treat! Enjoy!

Ingredients   Serves 2~3

1   **Loaf of Italian Bread ~ Baguette Style**
     (See Recipe ~ Chapter Ten) ~OR~ (Purchase At The Market)

1/2   **Cup of Olive Oil**
3   **Tablespoons of Butter (Sweet & Lightly Salted)**
4   **Pinches of Red Pepper Flakes**
1~1/2   **Cups of Mozzarella Cheese (Coarsely Grated)**

1   **Kitchen Towel (A Thin Terry Towel is Best)**

Preparation ~ Hot Cheese Bread

Saute
The Topping
1. **In a Small Sauce Pan, Melt The Butter on Medium, and Blend in The Olive Oil. Bring The Butter & Oil to a Sizzle.**
2. **Add The Red Pepper Flakes. Stir In for 1 Minute.**
3. **Remove from Heat. Cover Pan. Let Mixture Set for 15 Minutes.**

Top & Bake
The Bread
1. **Cut Italian Baguette Bread along One Side & At Each End, Lengthwise, so The Bread has a Hinge on Other Side.**
2. **Spread Bread Open. Spoon Sauteed Red Pepper Mixture Evenly on Both Sides of The Bread.**
3. **Sprinkle with Grated Mozzarella Cheese. Close The Bread.**
4. **Place The Loaf on a Baking Sheet Lined with Parchment Paper.**
5. **Place a Damp Kitchen Towel Over The Loaf.**
6. **Heat in a Preheated 350 Degree Oven for 15 Minutes, Or Until Towel is Bone Dry. Remove Pan from The Oven.**

Slice & Serve
The Bread
1. **Slice The Bread, with a Serrated Knife, into 1~1/2" Slices.**
2. **Serve Immediately in a Bread Basket. Use a Cloth Napkin To Keep Bread Hot. Makes a Nice Presentation! Enjoy!**

Mama Lena's
Tomato Cheese Bread

Pane Pomodoro Formaggi Italiano

Our Mama Lena's Tomato Cheese Bread was The All~Time Favorite Bread for our Guests. This Very Special Recipe, created by Salvino, is a Simply Delightful and Delicious Bread, using our Homemade Bread and Tomato Sauce Recipes in a Special Way. While studying in Chicago, Salvino's Friend, Larry Comella, who is also of Italian heritage and lives in New Jersey, spent a good deal of time at Mama Lena's and noticed something important ~ Mama Lena's Guests just loved dipping our Breads into our Sauces~ So, why not try them baked together! Salvino has always thanked Larry for his insight on the most~loved of The Mama Lena's Breads! This is a Very Special Mama Lena's Treasure! Enjoy!

Ingredients   **Serves 2~3**

1	Loaf of Italian Bread ~ Baguette Style
	(See Recipe ~ Chapter Ten) ~<u>OR</u>~ (Purchase At The Market)
1/4	Cup of Olive Oil (To Brush Bread)
1/8	Cup of Oregano (Sprinkle Over The Olive Oil)
1~1/2	Cups of Mama Lena's "Quick" Basic Tomato Sauce
	(See Recipe ~ Chapter Five)
1/2	Cup of Parmesan Cheese (Coarsely Grated)
1	Kitchen Towel (A Thin Terry Towel is Best)

Preparation ~ Mama Lena's Tomato Cheese Bread

1. Cut Italian Baguette Bread along One Side and At Each End,
        Lengthwise, so The Bread has a Hinge on The Other Side.
2. Spread The Bread Open. Brush The Olive Oil on "Both" Inner Sides.
3. Sprinkle The Oregano over The Olive Oil on The Bread.
4. If you are not making Sauce Fresh, Then Be Sure to Warm It First.
        Gently Spread Warm Sauce on "Bottom Portion Only " of Bread.
5. Sprinkle All of The Parmesan Cheese over The Tomato Sauce.
6. Carefully, Close The Top of The Bread Over The Bottom of Bread.
7. Place The Loaf on a Baking Sheet Lined with Parchment Paper.
8. Cover Loaf with a Damp Kitchen Towel.
9. Heat in a Preheated 350 Degree Oven for 15 Minutes, or
        Until The Towel is Bone Dry. Remove The Bread from The Oven.
10. Slice The Bread, with a Serrated Knife, into 1~1/2" Slices.
11. Serve Immediately in a Decorative Basket. Use a Cloth Napkin
        To Keep Bread Hot. Tastes Great & Looks Lovely, too! Enjoy!

Bread Crumbs
Plain or Italian Seasoned

Pane Barbi ~ Semple Italiano Condito

Our Mama Lena's Bread Crumbs make the Difference in Our Dishes for us! Just try them! You'll see how much more Taste, Body and Freshness our Homemade Bread Crumbs add to a Dish. To prepare The Bread Crumbs, Save all your Drying Bread ~ especially your Homemade Mama Lena's Bread! Prepare Plain or Italian Seasoned Styles. You will see it's worth the effort for Great Results! Mama always made Fresh Bread Crumbs! Enjoy!

Ingredients   Makes 2 Cups

Plain Style   1   Loaf of Italian Bread (2~3 Days Old)
                          (Or Other Various Dry Breads, Comprising 1 Loaf)

Italian Seasoned   1   Loaf of Italian Bread (2~3 Days Old)
Style

                       2   Pinches of Salt   2   Pinches of Black Pepper
                       2   Pinches of Parsley   1   Pinch of Onion Powder
                       2   Pinches of Basil   1   Pinch of Garlic Powder
                       2   Pinches of Oregano   1   Pinch of Thyme
                       1   Pinch of Rosemary (Ground)

                       1/3 Cup of Parmesan Cheese (Grated)
                            (Add Cheese to Bread Crumbs, Just Prior to Use)

Preparation ~ Bread Crumbs ~ Plain Or Italian Seasoned

Plain   1. Cut The Bread into Pieces, and Spread Out on a Baking Sheet.
Style   2. Bake in 200 Degree Oven, Until Bread is Very Dry and Very Crisp.
             3. Completely Cool The Baked Bread.
             4. Grate with a Hand Grater onto Wax Paper. Set a Top Sheet of
                Wax Paper Over Crumbs and Roll them Flat with Rolling Pin.
             5. May Also Grate The Bread in an Electric Blender or Food Processor.
             6. Strain The Grated Crumbs through a Strainer.
             7. Store in Airtight Container. Refrigerate, Or Freeze for 2 Months.

Italian
Seasoned 1. Follow Directions # 1 through # 6 for Plain~Style Bread Crumbs..
Style   2. Blend The Grated Bread Crumbs, with All Seasonings, Except
                The Grated Cheese, which is Added Only Just Prior to Use.
             3. Store The Seasoned Bread Crumbs in an Airtight Container.
             4. Refrigerate or Freeze Airtight for 2 Months.
             5. You won't regret making Mama Lena's Bread Crumbs!
             6. Remember to Add Grated Cheese Just Prior to Use. Enjoy!

Bread Sticks
Plain, Garlic, Salted & Seeded Styles

Grissini Varieto

Our Mama Lena's Bread Sticks are a Delicious Delight for any meal. They are very easy to make and can be made in any of our four varieties, Plain, Garlic, Salted & Seeded Styles. Mama Lena's Bread Sticks go well with Salads, Soups, and Appetizers, and really dress up your Table! They also make Great Snacks! You will just love this Delightful Recipe! Enjoy!

Ingredients   Makes 3 Dozen

The	1	**Tablespoon of Active Dry Yeast**
Yeast Mix	1/2	**Cup of Warm Water (110~115 Degrees)**
	1	**Teaspoon of Honey**
The		
Flour Mix	2	**Cups of All~Purpose Flour**
	2	**Pinches of Salt**
	1/2	**Cup of Warm Water**
For		
Variations	1/2	**Cup of Caraway, Poppy, Or Sesame Seeds, ~ OR ~**
	1/4	**Cup of Red Pepper Flakes, ~ OR ~**
	1	**Shaker of Regular, Coarse , Garlic, Or Onion Salt**
		(Use to your Preference)

Preparation ~ Bread Sticks ~ Plain Style

The
Yeast Mix

1. *In a Glass Container (8 Oz.), Stir 1 Teaspoon of Honey into 1/2 Cup of Warm Water (110~115 Degrees).*
2. *Sprinkle 1 Tablespoon of Active Dry Yeast on Top. Let Yeast Dissolve into Water & Honey. Then, Stir In.*
3. *Cover Container. Let The Yeast Rise for 10~12 Minutes. (Yeast is Ready when Doubled & Top has a Foam Dome).*

The
Flour Mix

1. *In a Medium Bowl, Sift 2 Cups of Flour and 2 Pinches of Salt. Keep 1/2 Cup of Warm Water on The Side.*
2. *When The Yeast has Risen Completely, Add The Yeast to The Sifted Flour & Salt. Blend Together by Hand.*
3. *If Dough is Too Dry, Add 1 Tablespoon of Warm Water, At A Time, Until Dough is Smooth and Pulls Away from Side of The Bowl.*
4. *Lightly Flour your Counter. Place Dough on The Floured Surface. Knead The Dough for 10 Minutes, Until a Silky Smooth Ball.*
5. *Using a Mellon Scoop, Scoop out 3 Dozen Mellon~Sized Balls of Dough from the Large Ball of Kneaded Dough.*
6. *With your Fingers, Roll Each Mellon~Sized Ball of Dough into a Thin Strip like a Pencil ~ About 8" Long.*

Preparation ~ Bread Sticks ~ Plain, Garlic, Salted & Seeded Styles

Dough Sticks Are Now Prepared As "Plain" Bread Sticks ~
To Make The Garlic, Salted or Seeded Variations
Proceed As Follows ~

The
Variation Styles
~ Prepare ~

1. *Finish Rolling Dough Balls into Thin Plain Dough Sticks.*
2. *Brush Each Dough Stick Very Lightly With Olive Oil.*
3. *Lightly Sprinkle The Oiled Dough Sticks on*
    Both Sides with The Indicated Amounts of
    Any One of The Following Ingredients ~

    ~ SALT ~ Regular, Coarse, Garlic, Or Onion
    ~ SEEDS ~ Carraway, Poppy, Or Sesame Seeds ~
    ~ RED PEPPER FLAKES ~ For Lovers of Hot & Spicy!

The
Bread Stick Dough
~ Rising ~

1. *Line Two Baking Sheets with Parchment Paper, Or*
    Lightly Grease Two Baking Sheets.
2. *Carefully, Place Each Rolled Dough Stick on*
    The Baking Sheets, About 1~1/2" Apart.
3. *Cover The Dough Sticks with Wax Paper and a Tea Towel.*
    Let Dough Rise in a Warm Place for About 30 Minutes.
    Then Remove The Tea Towel and The Wax Paper.

The
Bread Stick Dough
~ Baking ~

1. *Bake in a Preheated 400 Degree Oven for 6 to 8 Minutes*
    on One Side. Take Out, and Gently Roll Sticks Over.
2. *Bake Again for 6 Minutes More, Until Lightly Browned.*
    (Watch During This Second Stage of Baking,
    That Bread Sticks Do Not Bake Too Long.
    The Bread Sticks should be Just Light Brown).
3. *Cool Bread Sticks Completely, for About 10 Minutes.*
4. *Serve As Soon As Bread Sticks are Cooled & Crisp!*
5. *To Store, Seal in an Airtight Container. Do Not Refrigerate.*

Serving Suggestion

Arrange Bread Sticks in a Lovely Napkined Basket, Or Stand Up in a Large Open Vase for a Nice Touch! Serve The Bread Sticks with any Mama Lena's Soups, Salads or Entrees. These Delicious Bread Sticks compliment All Dishes, and make a Delightful Addition to your Table. These Tasty Treats are Everyone's Favorites ~ Better Make a Double Recipe! Enjoy!

Crisp Croutons
Plain or Garlic Crisp Styles

Crostino ~ Semple Aglio

As our Fresh Homemade Bread Crumbs added taste, body and freshness to Every Dish,
Our Freshly Baked Crisp Croutons add a Very Delightful Taste to our Salads & Soups!
There is nothing like a Fresh Airy & Crunchy Crouton to Dress Up the Dish & Taste Buds!
Mama Lena's Guests loved "Both" The Plain & The Garlic Styles!   You will, too!   Enjoy!

Ingredients   Serves 6~8

The Plain Croutons	1/2	Loaf of Italian Bread (2~3 Days Old)
		(Cut into 8 Slices ~ Then Cube into 1/2" Cubes)
	4	Tablespoons of Olive Oil
	3	Tablespoons of Butter (Sweet & Lightly Salted)
The Garlic Croutons	1/2	Loaf of Italian Bread (2~3 Days Old)
		(Cut into 8 Slices ~ Then Cube into 1/2" Cubes)
	5	Tablespoons of Olive Oil
	4	Tablespoons of Butter (Sweet & Lightly Salted)
	3	Cloves of Garlic (Minced)

Preparation ~ Crisp Croutons ~ Plain Crisp Or Garlic Crisp Styles

The Plain Croutons

1. In a Large Skillet, Melt The Butter on Medium High.
   Blend The Olive Oil In. Bring Butter & Oil to a Sizzle.
2. Add The Cubed Bread, which you Cut as Indicated Above.
   Saute Bread Cubes, Until Golden Brown on All Sides.
3. Remove from Pan with Slotted Spoon to Drain Off Liquid.
4. Drain and Dry on Paper Towels. Cool Completely.
5. Then, Store in a Uncovered Bowl, Until Ready to Use.

The Garlic Croutons

1. In a Large Skillet, Melt The Butter on Medium High.
   Blend The Olive Oil In. Bring Butter & Oil to a Sizzle.
2. Add The Minced Garlic. Saute for 1~2 Minutes.
3. Add The Cubed Bread, which you Cut as Indicated Above.
   Saute Bread Cubes in The Garlic and Oil & Butter,
   Until Golden Brown on All Sides.
4. Remove from Pan with Slotted Spoon to Drain off Liquid.
5. Drain and Dry on Paper Towels. Cool Completely.
6. Then, Store in an Uncovered Bowl, Until Ready to Use.
   These Crisp Croutons are Just Delicious! Enjoy!

Miniature Italian Toasts

Crostini Per Antipasto

Our Mama Lena's Miniature Italian Toasts are So Delicious when served with our Variety of Appetizer Spreads in Chapter One! The Toasts are also great to serve with Any of our Mama Lena's Salads, Soups and Pastas, when you want something different, attractive, and very crunchy tasting! At Mama Lena's we used our Delicious Crisp Miniature Toasts in many different ways, and every time they were gladly welcomed by our lovely Guests! We know you will find This Recipe one you can depend on for your family and guests, too! These Treats are Just Delightful and So Very Tasty & Versatile, too!   Enjoy!

Ingredients   Makes 3 Dozen

2   Loafs of Italian Bread ~ Baguette Style
           (See Recipe ~ Chapter Ten) ~OR~ (Purchase At The Market)

1/2   Cup of Pure Olive Oil
1/2   Cup of Romano Cheese (Grated)

Preparation ~ Miniature Italian Toasts

1. **Slice Each Loaf of Bread into 18 Even Slices, About 3/4" Wide,
          Yielding About 36 Slices from The 2 Loaves.**
2. **Line Two Baking Sheets with Parchment Paper or Foil.**
3. **Place The Bread Slices on a Wax Paper on Your Table, and
          Lightly Brush The Breads on One Side with Olive Oil.**
4. **Place The Breads on The Lined Baking Sheets with Oiled Side Up.**
5. **Broil Side 1 on The Second Shelf from Broiler, About 1 Minute, Or
          Until Side 1 Tops are Toasted a Light Brown.**
6. **As soon as Breads Turn Light Brown, Remove The Pans from Oven.**
7. **Turn Breads Over to Side 2. Lightly Brush The Tops with Olive Oil.**
8. **Return The Pans to Broiler   Broil Side 2 for About 1 Minute, Or
          Until Side 2 is Toasted Light Brown. Remove Pans from Oven.**
9. **Sprinkle Lightly with Grated Romano Cheese. Serve Immediately !**

Serving Suggestion

Serve The Miniature Italian Toasts with one of Mama Lena's Delicious Appetizer Spreads. You may also use the Toasts to accompany one of our Mama Lena's Salads, Soups or Pastas! And, we loved to serve The Toasts when family or friends would stop to visit while we were cooking. We would present The Toasts and tasty sliced Cheeses & Wine. These Mama Lena's Miniature Italian Toasts are Just Delicious with Everything!   Enjoy!

~ Chapter Eleven ~
Sweet Desserts

Pages 237 ~ 259

Mama Lena's
Sweet Cream Sicilian Cannoli

Cannoli Dolci Krema Siciliano

Mama Lena's Sweet Cream Sicilian Cannoli is a Sweet Recipe special to us for many reasons. It delighted Mama Lena's Guests for years, and personally entertained us with its history. Mama used to tell us that when she was a little girl she would always be waiting impatiently for a chance to taste the Cannoli. As Grandma Anna prepared the Cannoli, she would occupy her daughter with stories of how the Cannoli originated in Sicily. And, when we were children and waiting impatiently for the Cannoli, Mama would occupy us with Grandma's stories that she lovingly remembered. At Mama Lena's Italian Kitchen, as Salvino filled and finished preparing The Cannoli on our Stage and before our Guests, he would tell the delightful stories of Mama & Grandma and The Family waiting to taste the Delicious Cannoli! Now, It's Time for You to Taste Mama Lena's Sweet Cream Sicilian Cannoli, too!   Enjoy!

Ingredients   Serves 14~20

~ The Cream Filling ~

2   Lbs. of Fresh Ricotta Cheese
1   Cup of Confectioner's Sugar
1/2 Oz. of Anisette Liqueur, ~OR~
1   Teaspoon of Anise Extract
1   Pinch of Cinnamon
1/2 Cup Semi~Sweet Chocolate Chips
3/4 Cup of Candied Citron Fruit
      (Finely Chopped)

~ The Tube Shells ~

2   Cups of All~ Purpose Flour (Sifted)
2   Tablespoons of Crisco Shortening
1   Pinch of Salt
1   Pinch of Sugar
1   Pinch of Cinnamon
1   Teaspoon of Honey
3/4 Cup of Amaretto Liqueur
1   Large Egg (Lightly Beaten)
      * (Use As A Pastry Sealer) *

~ Additional Ingredients ~

6   Cups of Vegetable Oil (To Fry Shells)
1   Shaker of Confectioner's Sugar (Dress Sprinkle Shells)
4   Oz. Fresh Pistachio Nuts (Chopped) (Final Dress Sprinkle)

~ Equipment to Prepare Shells ~

20 Round Metal Tubes To Wrap Shell Dough for Frying
      (Available in Gourmet Shops)
1   Large Deep Pan for Frying Shells
1   Thermometer for Frying
1   Round and Flat Perforated Spoon To Pick Up Shells
1   Cooling Rack For The Shell
1   Large Spatula (1" Size), Or A Large Butter Knife

238

Preparation ~ Mama Lena's ~ Sweet Cream Sicilian Cannoli

The
Sweet Cream Filling
~ Prepare ~

1. *Drain All Liquid from The Ricotta Cheese, and Discard.*
2. *In a Large Bowl, Combine The Ricotta Cheese (Drained),*
   The Confectioner's Sugar, Anisette, and Cinnamon.
   Blend All on Low Speed for 5 Minutes, Until Smooth.
3. *Citron Fruit ~ Fold In, with A Spatula, Until Well Mixed.*
4. *Chocolate Chip Pieces ~ Gently Fold In, with A Spatula.*
5. *Seal The Filling Airtight. Refrigerate The Filling,*
   Until Ready to Use to Fill The Cannoli Shells.
   The Filling Texture will Remain Firm for 3 days.
   (Use in 3 Days, Or Seal Well & Freeze for 6 Weeks).
6. *This Filling Recipe is Enough To Fill 16~20 Shells, and*
   Leaves Enough to Fill Extra Shells or Fill A Cake.

The
Cannoli Shell Dough
~ Prepare ~

1. *In a Large Bowl, Combine The Flour, Shortening, Salt,*
   Sugar, Cinnamon, and Honey. Mix Together Well.
2. *Add The Amaretto Liqueur. Blend Into The Dough Mixture.*
3. *By Hand, Shape The Dough into a Firm and Smooth Ball.*
4. *Knead The Dough on a Lightly Floured Surface,*
   For About 3~5 Minutes.
5. *Shape The Dough Again into a Smooth Ball.*
6. *Place in a Bowl. Cover The Dough with Plastic Wrap.*
   Refrigerate for 1 Hour to Chill The Dough.

Cannoli Shell Dough
~ Cut & Shape ~

1. *After 1 Hour, Place The Dough on a Lightly Floured Surface.*
2. *Section The Dough into Four (4) Equal Pieces, and*
   Roll Each Piece to 1/4" Thick, Making 4 Dough Sheets.
3. *Cut 4 Equal Squares (4" Square) from Each Dough Sheet.*
   This gives you 16 Pieces of Pastry Dough for Shells.
4. *With any Extra Dough, Shape into a Ball and Roll It Out.*
   Cut Out a Few More 4" Squares for Extra Shells.
5. *Place Each Tube Diagonally Across*
   Each 4" Square of Dough, and
   Wrap The Dough Square Around the Tube.
   Overlap Two Points of Dough in the Middle of Tube.
   Curl The Excess Dough at Tube Ends Outward.
6. *Wash The Beaten Egg Across The Middle Points of Dough*
   To Seal and Secure The Dough on The Tube.
7. *Line Up The Dough~Wrapped Tubes to Begin Frying.*
   (The Cannoli Directions Continue ~ Next Page)

Preparation ~ Mama Lena's ~ Sweet Cream Sicilian Cannoli

**The
Cannoli Shells
~ Frying ~**

1. Fill The Deep Frying Pan with All The Vegetable Oil.
    Heat The Oil to 375 Degrees on Thermometer, Or
    Until The Oil Bubbles Briskly, About 3 Minutes.
    (The Oil must be Hot to Crisp The Shells Nicely).
2. Carefully, Place 2~3 Cannoli Shells, At A Time, Into The Oil.
    Fry Shells, Until Just Golden Brown and Crispy.
3. Gently, Lift Each Shell Out of Oil with a Flat Slotted Spoon,
    Allowing The Oil to Drain Off of Each Shell.
4. Carefully, Place Each Shell on a Rack to Cool. Cool Completely.
5. To Remove The Shells, Very Gently Slide The Shells from Tubes.
6. To Dry The Shells ~ And ~ For a Nice Crispy Effect ~
    Place Shells Back on The Cooling Rack for 1 Hour More.
7. To Keep The Shells Very Crispy for 3 days ~
    Place Shells Between Loose Wax Paper and Store in Dry Spot.
8. To Keep The Shells for Several Weeks ~
    Store Them in Sealed Cookie Tins in Layers of Wax Paper.

> *   Shells are Never Filled, Until Ready to Serve.
> Shells become Soggy when Filled Too Early, And
> Cream Filling Loses Its Flavor and Texture   *

**The
Shells & Filling
~ Combine ~**

1. Place One Shell in Your Left Hand, and Fill with Your Right Hand.
    Scoop Up Some Filling, (Use Spatula or Butter Knife), and
    Fill One End of The Shell to The Middle and Out to The End.
    Then, Turn The Shell and Fill The Other End Same Way.
2. As you Fill Each Cannoli Shell, Place it on A Decorative Tray
    Until All The Shells are Filled and Nicely Lined Up.
3. Sprinkle Confectioner's Sugar Lightly over Tops of The Shells.
4. Lastly, Sprinkle Fresh Pistachio Nuts, by Hand,
    Onto The Cream Filling at Each End of The Shells.

Serving Suggestion

Mama Lena's Sweet Cream Sicilian Cannoli presents a Fabulous~Looking, Delectable Dessert to serve your family or guests for their individual selection. Without a doubt, this was the Most Popular Dessert we served at our Mama Lena's Italian Kitchen throughout the years. This Sweet Cream Sicilian Treat ~ Mama's favorite since childhood, a Family favorite and The Preferred Favorite of our lovely Mama Lena's Guests will soon become your very own favorite! We send you Sweet Tidings as you prepare This Mama Lena's Special Treasure!   Enjoy!

Cream Puffs ~ Amaretto ~ ala Madonna

Amaretto Zeppole ala Madonna

Mama Lena's Cream Puffs, Amaretto, are Lightly Crisp and Sweet Delightful Desserts. Filled with our Special Variation Ricotta Cheese Fillings of Candy, Fruit, Nuts or Wine, These Sweet Treats thrilled our Guests whenever we served them! We very much enjoyed This Special Recipe also, because we had an opportunity to use many different Fillings Salvino created. Each time we served our Delicious Amaretto Cream Puffs, the Puffs had a Different Ricotta Filling and made our "Traditional Favorite" a new Surprise to our Guests! This Very Special Sweet Recipe really pleased our Guests! You will be pleased, too! Enjoy!

Ingredients   Makes 12~14 Puffs

1	Cup of Flour (All~Purpose) (Sifted)
1	Tablespoon of Amaretto Liqueur
	(May Substitute 1 Teaspoon of Almond Extract)
4	Large Eggs (Lightly Beaten)
1	Cup of Water (Hot)
1/2	Cup of Butter (Sweet & Lightly Salted)
1	Pinch of Salt And 1 Pinch of Sugar (Granulated)
1/4	Cup of Confectioner's Sugar (For Final Sprinkling)
1	Recipe of Mama Lena's Ricotta Cheese Cream Puff Filling
	(See Recipe ~ Chapter Eleven)

Preparation ~ Cream Puffs, Amaretto

1. **In a Large Sauce Pan, Combine The Water, Butter, Salt and Sugar.**
   Mix All Ingredients Together, and Bring to a Boil.
2. **Reduce Heat to Low. Add The Flour. Stir In Quickly with a**
   Wooden Spoon, Until Mixture Leaves Side of Pan and Forms a Ball.
3. **Remove Pan from Heat. Add Lightly Beaten Eggs, A Little At A Time.**
   Beat Eggs into Flour Mixture, Until Mixture is Smooth and Glossy.
4. **Add The Amaretto Liqueur, and Beat In Well.**
5. **Immediately, Drop The Mixture, By Heaping Tablespoonfuls,**
   Onto a Shiny Silver Cookie Sheet, Lined with Parchment Paper.
   (Space The Drops of Dough about 2~3 Inches Apart).
6. **Bake in a Preheated 400 Degree Oven for 15 Minutes.**
   Then, Lower Heat and Bake at 325 for 30 Minutes More.
   Check The Puffs to see If Finished ~ Tap Puffs for a Hollow Sound.
7. **With a Sharp Serrated Knife, Cut Off The Tops of The Puffs to**
   Allow Steam to Escape. Place Top and Bottom Puffs on Rack to Cool.
8. **Cool Completely. Remove Any Soft Dough from Inside**
   The Puff Tops or The Puff Bottoms. Discard All Soft Dough.
9. **Fill The Crispy Puffs with our Ricotta Cheese Fillings in This Chapter.**
10. **Sprinkle The Tops Lightly with Confectioner's Sugar. Delightful! Enjoy!**

Cassata ~ Amaretto ~ with Pine Nuts

Cassata Amaretto Pinola

Our Mama Lena's Cassata Amaretto with Pine Nuts was The Lovely Cake we served most often with our Ricotta Cheese Fillings. This Very Light, Delightful Cake is a Salvino Specialty. He wanted a Cake with a Fresh Delicate Flavor, but one that would stand up well with our Variety of Ricotta Cheese Fillings. Always, everything served had to be Just Right for Guests! When Salvino filled This Special Treasure with one of our Ricotta Cheese Variation Fillings, this turned out to be just the right answer for a Lovely Finish to a great Mama Lena's Dinner! Our Guests were so absolutely delighted with this Simple & Sweet, yet Very Elegant Cake!. We know your guests will be, too! Salvino is happy to share This Treasure with you! Enjoy!

Ingredients   Makes 12 Servings

The Cake Dough Mixture	6	**Large Eggs (Separate Yolks & Whites)**
		~ First ~ Egg Yolks ~ Beat Lightly with Sugar
		~ Later ~ Egg Whites ~ Beaten Stiff but Not Dry
	1~1/2	**Cups of Sugar (Granulated)**
	1~1/4	**Cups of Flour (All~Purpose) (Sifted)**
	3/4	**Teaspoon of Baking Powder (Sifted)**
The Amaretto & Orange	1	**Tablespoon of Orange Rind (Grated)**
	2	**Tablespoons of Amaretto Liqueur**
The Pine Nuts	1/4	**Cup of Pine Nuts (Crushed)**
Brush The Cake	1/4	**Cup of Amaretto Liqueur (To Brush Cooled Cake)**
Cake Filling	1	**Recipe of Mama Lena's Ricotta Cheese Cake Filling (See Recipe ~ Chapter Eleven)**
Dress The Cake	2	**Tablespoons of Confectioner's Sugar (To Dress Dust The Finished Cake Only)**
The Cake Pan	1	**Bundt Pan (10" Size) (Coat with Crisco & Flour Pan)**
The Cake Garnish	8	**Mint Leaves (For Garnish Only)**
	1	**Orange (Grated For The Rind For Garnish)**

Preparation ~ Cassata ~ Amaretto ~ with Pine Nuts

The
Baking Prepartion
Steps

1. Coat Bundt Pan with Crisco & Lightly Flour Pan. Set Aside.
2. Separate Egg Yolks and Egg Whites into "Separate" Bowls.
   (Set Egg Whites in Refrigerator for Later Use).
3. Sift Flour and Baking Powder Together. Crush The Pine Nuts.
4. Preheat Oven to 375 Degrees. Set Rack to # 2 from Bottom.

The Cake Mixture
~ Prepare ~

1. In a Large Mixer, Cream The Egg Yolks with The Sugar,
   Until Smoothly Blended and Lemon Colored.
2. Gradually Blend In The Sifted Flour & Baking Powder to
   Creamed Eggs & Sugar, Until Mixture is Very Smooth.
3. Add The Orange Rind, 2 Tablespoons of Amaretto Liqueur
   and The Crushed Pine Nuts. Blend Together Well.
4. Separately Beat Chilled Egg Whites, Until They are
   Softly Stiff Peaks. (Too Much Beating May Dry Whites).
5. Very Gently, Fold The Softly Stiffened Egg Whites into
   The Blended Cake Mixture.
6. Evenly, Pour The Finished Mixture into Prepared Bundt Pan.
7. Bake in a Preheated 375 Degree Oven for 40~45 Minutes
   on The # 2 Rack from The Bottom of The Oven.
8. When Cake is Light Brown and is Dry to a Toothpick Test,
   Remove It from The Oven.
9. Cool Cake 20 Minutes. Remove from Pan. Cool 2 Hours More.

The Baked Cake
~ Cut & Brush ~

1. With a Large Serrated Knife, Very Gently Cut Through
   The Center of Cooled Cake. Place Cut Sides Up on Rack.
2. Lightly Brush 1/4 Cup Amaretto Liqueur to Cover Cut Cakes.
   Let The Brushed Cakes Set for 30 Minutes.

The Brushed Cake
~ Filling It ~

1. Select The Filling you desire from Our Variations of
   Ricotta Cheese Cake Fillings in This Chapter.
2. On The Open Bottom Half of Cake, Gently Spoon on Filling.
   Spread Evenly. Carefully Place Top of Cake Back On.
   Your Beautiful Cake is Ready for Garnish & Serving!

Serving Suggestion

Lightly Powder A Cake Platter with Confectioner's Sugar. Place The Brushed, Filled Cake onto Platter. Carefully, Pre~slice The Cake for Serving Convenience. Lightly Dust Top of The Cake with Confectioner's Sugar. Then Lightly Sprinkle Top with Grated Orange Rind, and Place Mint Leaves to Dress Finish The Cake and Platter. If Serving Fruit with The Cake, have a Decorative Bowl and Ladle to Serve The Fruit. When having a Sit~Down Dinner, Serve This Lovely Cake with Fruit & Confectioner's Sugar on Individual China Plates. Serve either way ~ Salvino's Cassata ~ Amaretto will always be a Divine Finish to your Dinner! Enjoy!

Cassata ~ Chocolate & Vanilla Cake ~ Vanilla Rum Sauce

Cassata Ciocolata Vaniglia Rum

Mama Lena's Chocolate Vanilla Rum Cassata was the Very Sweet Creation of Salvino. Most Italians love Rum Cakes, and he always favored Vanilla Cakes while Margo favored Chocolate Cakes, so he set out to make a Beautiful and a Delicious Cake that represented all three delicious flavors. Salvino then created This Exquisite Sauce which he does so wonderfully. This Very Special Cassata is a delightful blend of many lovely flavors, and Salvino's captivating Vanilla Rum Sauce and some Shaved Chocolate truly compliment it! Our Guests absolutely loved This Sweet Delight & The Sweet Presentation, too! Enjoy!

Ingredients   *Makes 12 Servings*

The Chocolate Mixture		
	1/2	Cup of Cocoa Powder (Sifted)
	1	Teaspoon of Baking Powder (Sifted)
	1/4	Cup of Butter (Sweet & Lightly Salted)
	1/2	Cup of Sugar (Granulated)
	1/4	Cup of Milk (Whole)
	1	Teaspoon of Rum Extract

The Vanilla Mixture		
	3	Cups of Flour (All~Purpose) (Sifted)
	1	Teaspoon of Baking Powder (Sifted)
	4	Eggs (Large)
	2	Cups of Sugar (Granulated)
	1	Cup of Butter (Sweet & Lightly Salted)
	1	Cup of Milk (Whole)
	2	Teaspoons of Vanilla Extract
	1	Teaspoon of Rum Extract

The Vanilla Rum Sauce		
	1	Cup of Heavy Cream
	1	Cup of Sugar (Granulated)
	1/2	Cup of Butter (Sweet & Lightly Salted)
	1	Teaspoon of Vanilla Extract
	1	Teaspoon of Rum Extract

The Chocolate Shavings		
	1	Lb. Piece of Semi~Sweet Chocolate (Whole)

Spumoni Ice Cream	1/2	Gallon of Spumoni Ice Cream

Preparation ~ Cassata ~ Chocolate & Vanilla Cake ~ Vanilla Rum Sauce

**The
Chocolate Mixture**

1. *In a Sauce Pan, Heat The Butter on Medium to a Melt.*
2. *Add Sugar. Stir Until Completely Dissolved into Butter.*
3. *Add The Sifted Cocoa and The Baking Powder.
    Stir Well, Until Blended into The Butter & Sugar.*
4. *Gradually, Add Milk, Stirring Constantly to Keep Smooth.*
5. *Lastly, Add 1 Teaspoon of Rum Extract. Blend Well.*
6. *Remove from Heat. Allow to Cool.*

**The
Vanilla Mixture**

1. *In a Large Mixmaster Bowl, Cream The Eggs, Sugar,
    Butter, and Milk to a Smooth Texture.*
2. *Gradually, Add In The Sifted Flour and Baking Powder
    Until The Mixture is Very Smooth.*
3. *Add The 2 Teaspoons of Vanilla Extract and
    The 1 Teaspoon of Rum Extract. Blend Into Mixture.*
4. *Pour 2/3 of The Vanilla Mixture into a Separate Bowl.*

**The Complete Cake
~ Combine & Bake ~**

1. *To Remaining 1/3 of Vanilla Mixture in The Mixmaster,
    Add All of The Chocolate Mixture.
    Blend on Medium, Until This Mixture is Very Smooth.*
2. *Grease and Flour your Bundt Pan.*
3. *Start Pouring Alternate Layers of The Vanilla Mixture and
    The Chocolate Mixture into The Prepared Bundt Pan.*
4. *Bake in a Preheated 350 Degree Oven for 1 Hour.*
5. *Set Pan on a Wire Rack to Cool for 15 Minutes.*
6. *Invert Cake onto Wire Rack. Cool for 15 Minutes More.*

**The
Vanilla Rum Sauce**

1. *In a Sauce Pan, Heat The Butter on Medium to a Melt.*
2. *Add The Sugar. Stir Constantly, Until Well Blended.*
3. *Reduce The Heat to Low. Add In The Heavy Cream.
    Stir Constantly, Until Smooth. Turn Heat to Simmer.*
4. *Add The Vanilla & Rum Extracts, and
    Simmer for About 5 Minutes, Stirring Constantly.*
5. *Remove from Heat. Cover Pan. Allow The Flavors to Set.*
6. *Serve The Vanilla Sauce at Room Temperature.*

**The
Chocolate Shavings**

1. *Make Shavings, By Using The Shaving Side of A Grater.
    Or, Make Chocolate Curls by using a Paring Peeler
    to Shave Chocolate. Either Way, They Look Great!*

Serving Suggestion

Place Slices of Chocolate Vanilla Rum Cake on Large Dessert Plates. Place one Scoop of Spumoni Ice Cream on The Side of The Cake. Carefully, Spoon The Vanilla Rum Sauce over The Cake Slices and over Ice Cream. Top This Very Sweet Dish by delicately setting The Chocolate Shavings on The Cake & Ice Cream! A Truly Sweet Presentation! Enjoy!

Ricotta Cheese Fillings
for
Cakes & Cream Puffs

Ricotta Cassata Kremas Varieto

Our Mama Lena's Ricotta Cheese Cake & Cream Puff Fillings are a Lovely Variety of Luscious Fillings, created by Salvino, in Combinations of Wines, Fruits, Nuts, Candies, Extracts and Fruit Rinds. You will see, as you use Salvino's delightfully simple, but Very Delicious Recipes that you will always have a finished product you are proud of. We loved surprising our Guests with Different Fillings to our Cakes and Cream Puffs, and our Guests loved us back for These Very Sweet Surprises ~ Your family will love Your Sweet Surprises, too! Enjoy!

Ingredients			**Fills One Cake, ~ OR ~** **10 Cream Puffs**
The **Basic Filling**	3	**Cups of Fresh Ricotta Cheese** **(Drain Liquid ~ Do Not Use Liquid)**	
	1	**Pinch of Cinnamon**	
	3/4	**Cup of Confectioner's Sugar (Sifted)**	

~ *The Variations To The Basic Filling* ~

The Wines & Liqueurs
~ Use 3 Tablespoons ~
Anisette
Amaretto
Creme de Cacao
Marsala
Rum, Light or Dark
Sambucca

The Fruits
~ Use 1/4 Cup ~
Candied Citron Fruit
(Finely Chopped)

*Fresh Fruit Can be
Used Over the Cake,
Not in the Filling*

The Nuts
~ Use 1/4 Cup ~ Chopped ~
Almonds
Hazelnuts
Pecans
Pistachios
Walnuts

The Candy
~ Use 1/4 Cup ~
Chocolate Chips
Sweet or
Semi-Sweet
(Whole)

The Pure Extracts
~ Use 1 Tablespoon ~
Anise
Almond
Lemon
Rum
Vanilla

The Fruit Rinds
~ Use 1/2 Teaspoon ~
Lemon
Orange

Preparation ~ Ricotta Cheese Fillings ~ for Cakes & Cream Puffs

**The
Basic Cheese Mixture
~ Prepare ~**

1. **To Prepare The Basic Ricotta Cheese Filling ~**
   - **~ Completely Drain 3 Cups of Ricotta Cheese
     (Discard Liquid ~ Do Not Use Liquid)**
   - **~ Place The Ricotta Cheese (Drained) into A Bowl.**
   - **~ Add 1 Pinch of Cinnamon.**
   - **~ Add 3/4 Cup of Confectioner's Sugar (Sifted)**
   - **~ Blend The Mixture on Low Speed for 3~5 Minutes,
     Until The Mixture is Very Smooth.**
2. **Serve Cakes & Cream Puffs with Basic Ricotta Cheese Mix,
   Which is A Delicious Filling Just Alone ~ <u>OR</u> ~
   Add The Variations, As Follows.**

**The
Variation Fillings
~ Prepare ~**

1. **Choose 2~3 Variations or More, As You Prefer.
   Add The Variations to The Basic Mixture,
   in The Amounts Indicated on Previous Page.**
2. **One At A Time, Gently Fold In Any Selected Variations,
   Until Well Blended.**
3. **Seal The Bowl Airtight. Refrigerate The Filling
   Until Ready to Use.**
4. **If Filling is Just Refrigerated, Use It Within Three Days.
   To Freeze ~ Seal Airtight and Store for 3 Months.**
5. **When You are Ready to Use The Filling,
   Remove from Refrigerator 15 Minutes Before, and
   Bring to Room Temperature. If Frozen, Defrost First.**
6. **Before Filling The Shells, Gently Stir Filling with a Spatula,
   To Get All the Flavors Blended Well Again, and
   To Keep a Smooth Filling Texture. Try Not To Crush
   Any Variations You Added to The Basic Recipe.**

Serving Suggestions

Have a Pretty Platter and China Plates with Doilies, Confectioner's Sugar to Sprinkle the Tops and Fresh Mint Leaves to Dress Up your Presentation. Serve, as stated in our Recipes for The Amaretto Cream Puffs and The Cassata ~ Amaretto. Both Recipes are in This Chapter Eleven. We know you will love using The Variations and making Surprise Delights for your Guests as we did. You will always be pleased with the results. So, we are very certain, your family and guests will be as happy as Mama Lena's Guests were with their Surprise Treats! Enjoy!

Zabaione ~ Marsala ~ With Fresh Fruit

Zabaione Marsala Frutto

Our Mama Lena's Zabaione Marsala with Fresh Fruit is a Delicious Light Custard, prepared with Sweet Marsala Wine and Fresh Fruit. This Sweet Delight has a Lovely and Smooth Texture and is the Perfect Dessert at any time! At Mama Lena's Italian Kitchen, we loved serving our Zabaione Marsala, and our Guests just loved waiting to see how it would be presented ~ Each time was a Different Version! And, we always complimented The Marsala Custard with The Best Fruit in Season, so it was an Enchanting Surprise! We are sure you will just love the ease of preparing and serving our Very Special Recipe. This Lovely Dessert is an Absolute Delight to present to your family or guests!   Enjoy!

Ingredients   **Serves 4~6**

The Marsala Custard	6	**Eggs (Large) (Use The Yolks Only)**
	1/2	**Cup of Sugar (Granulated)**
	1/2	**Teaspoon of Vanilla Extract**
	1	**Cup of Marsala Wine (Sweet)**

| **The Fresh Seasonal Fruit** | 2 | **Cups of Any of The Following Fruits in Season ~** |

~ *Apricots ~ Pitted & Pealed ~ Cut into Quarters*
~ *Blackberries, Blueberries, Raspberries ~ Whole*
~ *Cherries ~ Pitted & Cut into Halves*
~ *Peaches ~ Pitted & Pealed ~ Cut in Slices*
~ *Pears ~ Pitted & Pealed ~ Cut in Slices*
~ *Strawberries ~ Slice into Halves ~ Our Favorite!*

| | 2 | **Tablespoons of Sugar (Granulated)** **(Add To The Fruit)** |

| **The Equipment** | 1 | **Double~Boiler Sauce Pan** |

| **The Mint Garnish** | 6 | **Sprigs of Fresh Mint** |

Preparation ~ Zabaione ~ Marsala, with Fresh Fruit

**The
Freshest Fruit
~ Prepare ~**

1. First, Prepare The Fresh Seasonal Fruit you selected.
   Rinse The Fruit Well. Drain Thoroughly.
   Then, Trim and Cut The Cleaned Fruit.
2. Place The Cleaned Fruit in a Bowl, and
   Sprinkle 2 Tablespoons of Sugar over The Fruit.
   Gently, Stir The Sugar into The Fruit.
3. Seal Bowl with The Fruit Airtight with Plastic.
   Refrigerate The Fruit, Until The Zabaione Custard
   Has Been Prepared and Is Ready to Serve.

**The
Marsala Custard
~ Prepare ~**

1. Fill The Bottom Section of a Double~Boiler Pan
   to One~Third with Water. Bring Water to a Boil.
   Then Reduce The Heat to Medium.
2. In The "Cool" Top Pan, Combine The Eggs Yolks,
   The Sugar, and The Vanilla Extract.
   Using a Medium~size Wire Whisk, Lightly Beat All,
   Until The Mixture is Smooth and Lemon Colored.
3. Slowly, Add The Sweet Marsala Wine to
   The Eggs, Sugar and Extract. Continue to
   Lightly Beat, Until Mixture is Very Smoothly Blended.
4. Now, Place This Top "Cool" Section of The Double Boiler
   Onto "Warmed" Bottom Section of Double Boiler Pan.
5. On Medium Heat, Stir The Mixture Constantly with Whisk,
   Until The Mixture is Very Smooth, Warm and Thick.
   * Do Not Let The Custard Mixture Boil *
6. Remove Pan from Heat. Serve, As In Serving Suggestions.

Serving Suggestions

When Serving The Zabaione Immediately, "Layer" The Warm Marsala Custard with The Fresh Fruit in Large Lovely Glass Goblets. Top The Custard Center with a Small Bunch of The Selected Fruit. Place a Fresh Mint Sprig in the Center of The Fruit for a Nice Garnish! When Serving Zabaione Later, Add All of The Fresh Fruit to The Goblet First. Then, Spoon All The Custard "Over" The Fresh Fruit. Completely Cover The Fresh Fruit to Keep Well. Place The Mint Sprigs on Top of The Custard. Cover Goblets with Plastic, and Refrigerate to Chill, Until Ready to Serve. Your family and guests will just love this Sweet Dessert! This Delightful Dessert is an Elegant Compliment to a Mama Lena's Dinner. Enjoy!

Sweet Dough Treats
Vegetable or Plain Styles

Sfinges Festivo ~ Verdura e Semple

Our Mama Lena's Sweet Dough Treats ~ Sfinges Festivo ~ served with The Vegetables, or Just Plain and Sweet ~ was what Mama would make for us at The Holidays when we were Children. In Italian, Sfinges are Sweet Treats! This was our "Holiday" Sweet Treat! At our Mama Lena's Italian Kitchen, we continued this Tradition at The Holiday Time, and we also often served The Sfinges Festivo throughout the year. We served Both Styles ~ The Plain Sweet Dough Treats as Dessert and The Vegetable Dough Treats as Appetizers! There's another special way to serve The Sfinges ~ Mama and Grandpa's Favorite Way ~ With Anchovies ~ Sicilian Style! Whatever Style you choose, Sfinges are always Delicious! Don't wait for The Holidays to try these Very Special Mama Lena's Sweet Treats! Enjoy!

Ingredients   Makes 3~4 Dozen

The **Yeast Mixture**	1	**Package of Active Dry Yeast**
	1/2	**Cup of Warm Water (110~115 Degrees)**
	1	**Teaspoon of Sugar (Put into Warm Water)**
The **Flour Mixture**	5	**Cups of Flour (All~Purpose) (Sifted)**
	2	**Pinches of Salt**
	1	**Cup of Warm Water (110~115 Degrees)**
For Frying	1	**Quart of Vegetable Oil for Deep Frying**
	1	**Deep~Fry Thermometer (Measure To 375 Degrees)**
The **Sugar Sprinkle**	1/4	**Cup of Sugar (Granulated)**
		(Use Colored Sugar to Make a Pretty Presentation)
The **Fresh Vegetables**	2	**Cups of Your Favorite Vegetable (Cleaned & Chopped)**
		A Medley of Fresh Vegetables ~
		Asparagus, Broccoli, Cauliflower, & Fennel Bulb
The **Anchovies**	1	**Can of Anchovies (2 Oz.)**
		(Drain of Oil and Cut Anchovies in Half)
		***(Do Not Use a Sugar Sprinkle on Anchovy Treats) ***

Preparation ~ Sweet Dough Treats ~ Vegetable Style Or Plain Style

**The
Yeast Mixture
~ Prepare ~**

1. *In a Glass Container (8 Oz.), Mix The Sugar and*
    The Warm Water (110~115 Degrees, by Thermometer).
2. *Sprinkle The Yeast on Top of The Sugar & Warm Water.*
    Allow The Yeast to Dissolve into Water. Then, Stir In.
3. *Cover Container. Let The Yeast Rise to Double, 10~12 Minutes.*
    Yeast is Ready when Doubled & Top has a Foam Dome.

**The
Dough Mixture
~ Prepare ~**

1. *Sift The Flour and Salt Together into a Large Wide Bowl.*
2. *Make a Well in Center of Flour, and Pour Risen Yeast into It.*
3. *Blend The Flour & Salt into The Yeast from The Side of Bowl.*
4. *Slowly, Add 1/2 Cup of Water, and Mix, Forming a Dough Ball.*
5. *Knead The Dough for About 5 Minutes, and*
    Slowly Add Other 1/2 Cup of Water, As You Knead Dough.
    This Dough should be Very Soft & Sticky.
    (Tips on Kneading ~Chapter Ten ~ Bread Dough Recipe)
6. *Oil a Deep Bowl that is Double the Size of The Dough.*
    Place The Sticky Ball of Dough into The Bowl.
    Turn The Dough Over ~ So The Oiled Side is Up.
7. *Cover The Dough with Wax Paper. Cover Bowl with Tea Towel.*
    Place The Covered Dough in a Warm, Draft~free Area .
    Let Dough Rise, Until Doubled for 1 to 2 Hours.

**The
Fresh Vegetables
~ Prepare ~**

1. *Rinse The Fresh Vegetables Well, and*
    Break Broccoli & Cauliflower into Small Flowerets.
    Chop The Asparagus & Fennel Bulb into 1" Pieces.
2. *Set Vegetables in Boiling Water for 3 Minutes. Drain Well.*
    Place on Paper Towels to Dry, Until Ready to Use.

**The Dough Treats
~ Frying ~**

1. *Heat Vegetable Oil in a Deep Frying Pan to 375 Degrees.*
2. *For The Plain Sweet Treats, "Pinch" Out a Piece of Dough*
    (Flour Your Fingers to Keep from Sticking).
    Drop The Dough into Oil to Fry. All Shapes are Just Fine!
3. *For The Vegetables Treats, First Press Vegetables into Dough.*
    Then "Pinch" Them Out, and Drop into The Oil.
4. *Fry Only 4 Pieces at a Time ~ The Dough Expands in Frying.*
5. *Use A Slotted Spoon to Turn Dough for Even Browning.*
6. *When Dough is Golden Brown, Remove It from The Oil.*
7. *Set Golden Brown Sweet Treats on Paper Towels to Drain.*
8. *For Anchovy Treats, Press Anchovies into Risen Dough,*
    "Pinch" Out and Drop into Oil. (Do Not Sugar Sprinkle)

**Sprinkle & Serve
"Sweet Treats"**

1. *Sprinkle The Dough Treats Lightly with Colored Sugar!*
    Serve Your Sweet Dough Treats Immediately!
    Mama Lena would be Proud of You and
    Your "Sfinges Festivo!" Enjoy!

251

Biscotti ~ Anisette & Vanilla ~ Toasted Dessert Slices

Anisette e Vaniglia Biscotti

Mama Lena's Anisette & Vanilla Toasted Dessert Slices were a Favorite Dessert Cookie at our Restaurant. They were served to our Guests with Hot Coffee, the way Mama enjoyed them. This Sicilian Treat originated with Grandma, so Mama grew up loving it. Grandma Anna and Mama used these as Teething Bars for the children, so Grandpa or Papa Frank wouldn't have to rub our gums with their Homemade Wine, the second favorite Sicilian remedy for Teething! The Most Traditional Use, of course, is as The Dessert Slice ~ the way our Guests loved them! And, Mama personally loved this cookie so much, you could find her enjoying them on any day of the year in her afternoon "Cookie Break." You'll love this Mama Lena's Delight, too! Make One Half Anisette and One Half Vanilla for Variety! Enjoy!

Ingredients   Makes 36 Cookies

The Cookie Dough		
3	Cups of Flour (All~Purpose) (Sifted)
1	Tablespoon of Baking Powder (Sifted)
2	Pinches of Salt (Sifted)
5	Egg Whites (Large) (Beaten to Stiff Peaks)
1	Cup of Sugar (Granulated)
5	Egg Yolks (Large) (Lightly Beaten & Folded In Slowly)

The Flavorings

2	Tablespoons of Anisette Liqueur ~ **OR** ~
1	Tablespoon of Anise Extract (For The Anisette Biscotti)
2	Tablespoons of Pure Vanilla Extract (For The Vanilla Biscotti)

The Special Additions

1/4	Cup of Pine Nuts (Whole)
1/4	Cup of Pistachio Nuts (Buy Shelled & Chopped)
1/4	Cup of Candied Citron Fruit * (Optional) *

Mama Lena's Used The Citron Fruit at Holiday Time, Making The Biscotti Slices More Festive~

252

Preparation ~ Biscotti ~ Anisette & Vanilla ~ Toasted Dessert Slices

The Egg & Sugar Mixture

1. Using an Electric Mixer, Beat The Egg Whites to Soft Peaks.
2. Gradually, Add Sugar to The Whites, Until Peaks Stiffen.
3. Separately, Lightly Beat The Egg Yolks with a Whisk.
4. Using a Spatula, Fold in The Egg Yolks to The Stiffened Egg Whites & Sugar. Fold Gently, Until Well Blended.

The Dry Ingredients

1. Sift Together The Flour, Salt, and Baking Powder.
2. Add Sifted Flour Mixture, 1 Cup At A Time, to Egg Mixture.
3. Fold In Each Cup with The Spatula, Until Completely Blended to a Smooth and Pliable Mixture.
4. Lastly, Gently Fold in The Nuts, Until Well Mixed.
5. For Holidays to Use Citron Fruit, Gently Fold in Now.

Anisette or Vanilla Flavorings

1. For Half & Half, Separate Mixture Evenly into Two Bowls. In One Bowl, Add 1 Tablespoon of Anisette, ~ OR ~ 1/2 Tablespoon of Anise Extract. In The Other Bowl, Add 1 Tablespoon of Vanilla Extract. Blend Each.
2. To Make Only One Flavor, Just Double Above Amounts.

The Cookie Dough ~ Shaping ~

1. Remove The Dough from Bowl. Cut Dough into 4 Equal Pieces.
2. Gently Roll Each Dough Piece to 1" Thickness.
3. With Hands, Shape Each Dough Piece to The Size of 10" Long X 3" Wide X 1" High.
4. Nicely Smooth The Four (4) Long Biscotti Loaves.

The Cookie Dough ~ First Bake ~

1. Line your Two Cookie Sheets with Parchment Paper.
2. Evenly Space Two Biscotti Loaves on Each Lined Sheet.
3. Preheat The Oven to 375 Degrees.
4. Bake 20~25 Minutes, Until Center is Dry to Toothpick Test.
5. Cool Well on a Wire Rack for 30 Minutes.

The Baked Cookie ~ Second Bake ~

1. Using a Sharp Serrated Knife, Cut 3/4" Slices from The Biscotti Loaves ~ Yielding about 9 Slices per Loaf.
2. On 2 New Cookie Sheets (Do Not Line or Grease Sheets), Place The Cut Biscotti Slices on Their Sides.
3. Preheat The Oven Again, To 350 Degrees This Time.
4. Bake Two Trays of Sliced Biscotti Until Brown ~ 3 Minutes.
5. Take The Trays from Oven. Turn The Biscotti Slices Over. Place Trays Back in Oven to Crisp for 3 Minutes More.
6. Cool on Wire Rack. Store Airtight 2 Weeks. Freeze 3 Months.

Serving Suggestion

On A Large Decorative Platter with White Doilies or A Large Basket with A Cloth Napkin,, Arrange The Delightful and Very Delicious Anisette & Vanilla Dessert Slices. Just like Mama, many Guests like to "Dunk" The Biscotti, so serve "Hot" Coffee or Cappuccino! Enjoy!

Chocolate Spice Cookies

Papa's Favorite

Ciocolata Dolce Biscotti

Mama's Wonderful Chocolate Spice Cookies were Papa Frank's All~Time Favorite Sweet. Mama always made sure he had his very own supply each Christmas! Actually, Mama liked These Sweet Cookies, too, because they were also good for dunking in her Coffee, which was one of her favorite things to do on her Daily Cookie Breaks. By now, you must know that our Mama Lena had a Very Sweet Tooth! We always delighted in making these sweets for our Restaurant Guests, and they always delighted in having them sweetly arrive at their Tables!. This Delicious Sweet Recipe is a Very Special Recipe for Chocolate Spice Cookie & Frosting, just the way Mama always made it for Papa and Family! These are true Delectable Delights! Mama Lena's Italian Kitchen Guests really loved These Special Treats! You will, too! Enjoy!

Ingredients   **Makes 50 Cookies**

The Chocolate Spice Dough Mix	3/4	Cup of Shortening (Mama Used Crisco)
	1	Cup of Sugar (Granulated)
	2	Large Eggs (Lightly Beaten) (For Creaming)
	3	Cups of All~Purpose Flour
	3	Teaspoons of Baking Powder
	1	Teaspoon of Cinnamon
	1	Teaspoon of Cloves (To Soak in The Coffee)
	1/2	Cup of Very Strong Coffee
	1/4	Cup of Cocoa (Mama Used Hersheys)
	1	Teaspoon of Pure Vanilla Extract
	1/2	Cup of Walnuts (Very Finely Chopped)
	1	Orange (The Rind of The Orange)
The Frosting Mixture	2	Tablespoons of Milk (Whole)
	1/2	Teaspoon of Pure Vanilla Extract
	1~1/4	Cups of Confectioner's Sugar (Sifted)
	3/4	Teaspoons of Pure Lemon Extract
The Candy Sprinkles	1	Jar of Silver Beaded Candy Sprinkles (To Sprinkle on The Frosting)

Preparation ~ Chocolate Spice Cookies ~ Papa's Favorite

The Coffee & Cloves
~ Prepare ~

1. Make a Very Strong "Fresh" Coffee.
   Pour 1/2 Cup of The Hot Coffee into a Cup.
2. Add The Cloves to The Coffee, and
   Let Cloves Soak in The Coffee for 30 Minutes.
3. Strain Coffee into a New Cup. Discard The Cloves.
   (Use Only The Clove~Flavored Coffee).

The Creaming Mixture
~ Prepare ~

1. Cream Together The Shortening and The Sugar.
2. Add in The Lightly Beaten Eggs, and
   Continue to Cream, Until Mix is Very Smooth.

The Dry Ingredients
~ Combine ~

1. To Creamed Mixture, Very Gradually Add In ~
   The Flour, Baking Powder, and The Cinnamon,
   Until Very Well Mixed.
2. Add In The Cocoa and The Vanilla. Blend In Well.
3. Add In the Clove~Flavored Coffee. Blend In Well.
4. Lastly, Slowly Add in Walnuts and Orange Rind,
   Until Evenly Mixed into The Mixture.
5. Dough is Now Firm and Moist. Chill for 1 Hour.

The Cookie Dough
~ Baking ~

1. Flour a Mellon Scooper and Scoop out 50 Scoops.
   (Scoops will be 1" Round for Cookies).
2. Place The Dough Scoops on Cookies Sheets,
   Lined with Parchment Paper.
3. Bake in Preheated 375 Degree Oven, for 15 Minutes,
   Until Cookies Test As Finished with Toothpick.
4. Cool Very Completely on Wire Racks Before Frosting.

The Sweet Frosting
~ Prepare ~

1. In a Bowl, Combine The Liquids First.
   Gradually, Add in The Confectioner's Sugar
   For a Nice Smooth Frosting.
2. Frosting is Always a Matter of Balance ~
   Frosting Too Thick ~ Then A Drop More Milk.
   Frosting Too Thin ~ Confectioner's Sugar,
   A Tablespoon At A Time.
3. Place Wax Paper Under The Wire Racks, and
   Lightly Spoon Frosting on Top of Cookies.
4. Shake Silver~Beaded Sprinkles on Top of Frosting.
5. Let Frosted Cookies Set Up in a Cool Spot for 1 Hour.
6. Store in Sealed Containers Between Wax Paper.
7. Every 3~4 Days, Place a Drop of Extract into The
   Containers to Keep Cookies Fresh & Flavorful.

Serving Suggestion

The Chocolate Spice Cookies Look Lovely & Smell Lovely, too. Your family will just love them! Place Cookies on a Large White Decorative Platter with Doilies for Serving to Highlight Them. What a Special Addition to your Festive Christmas or Special Occasion Table!   Once you try these Delicious Cookies, you'll find reasons to make them often as we did at Mama Lena's! Papa would like to try the first one ~ Mama would need the second one to dunk!   Enjoy!

Fig Cookies ~ Cucidati ~

Mama's & Grandma Anna's Favorite

Cucidati Festivo e Glassatura

Here's a Special "Introduction" for our last "Sweet Desserts" Recipes. This Very Lovely and Treasured Recipe has a fine history in Sicilian Tradition, a history in Christmas Tradition, as well as a history in our Family Tradition, and in our Mama Lena's Italian Kitchen Repertoire.

Our Mama Lena's Old~World Fig Cookies & Frosting were a Special Treat that our Guests always looked forward to. A Cookie so different and so delicious, that as soon as our Guests tasted them, they would start asking for the next time we would make them. Everyone loved them so much, and they always tried to figure out the recipe! Salvino told our Guests that This Cookie Recipe was a Very Special One, one that takes effort, but is well worth the effort! And so, he told them one day we would write a Cookbook with The Cucidati ~ Here it is!

When we were children, Mama made this Very Special Treat for us only at Christmas. We were always so excited, because we were allowed to help make the Fig Cookies, as well as eat them! With Nine Children helping, it's no wonder Mama only made these once a year, as a Christmas Treat! Papa Frank had a Sausage Grinder that he clamped on the side of the Wooden Kitchen Table ~ That was long before Food Processors. The Figs, Raisins and Nuts would be ground together in this Grinder, and that was the first fight between us ~ who was going to turn the handle on the Grinder! It was Fun for Us, but a Chore of Love for Mama!

The Fig Cookies are a Sicilian Treat, with Figs growing plentifully in Sicily. This Very Special Recipe was taught to Grandma Anna by her Mother when they lived in Sicily. Then, Grandma Anna taught it to her own daughter, Mama Lena, who shared it with Her Children. So this Recipe goes back to the Old World. This Cookie was always the favorite of Mama and Grandma Anna because it came from Mama Lena's Grandmother. Mama made The Cucidati for us as children, and when we opened The Restaurant we made them together for our Mama Lena's Italian Kitchen Guests at Christmas Time. But, in time, we started making them more often during the year, because our Guests loved them so!

Now, don't you wait until Christmas to try this wonderful Treasured Recipe! We will make it easy for you to successfully prepare Mama Lena's Recipe. Once you try Mama's Cucidati, you will find so many festive occasions as reasons to make these Fig Treats again and again! From Our Hearts, The Mama Lena's Family hopes you will truly love This Treasure. Enjoy!

*F*ig *C*ookies ~ *C*ucidati ~

Ingredients   **Makes 50 Cookies**

~ Cucidati ~		
Fresh Fig Filling	1	Ring of Dried Figs (1 Lb.) (Process, Blend, Or Grind)
		~ Cut Out Cores First ~ Chop Into Small Pieces.
		~ Boil Figs 5~10 Minutes ~ Allow Figs to Cool.
		~ Drain Off Fig Juice ~ Do Not Use Fig Juice.
	2	Cups of Water (To Boil The Figs)
	1	Cup of Seedless Raisins (Grind Or Process)
	3/4	Cup of Chopped Walnuts (Grind Or Process)
	1	Large Orange (Grated) (Use Only The Rind)
	1/4	Cup of Honey
	1/4	Teaspoon of Nutmeg
	1/4	Teaspoon of Cinnamon
	1/4	Cup of Sugar (Granulated)
~ Cucidati ~		
Cookie Mixture	2~1/2	Cups of All~Purpose Flour (Sifted)
	2~1/2	Teaspoons of Baking Powder (Sifted)
	1/2	Teaspoon of Salt (Sifted)
	2	Large Eggs (Lightly Beaten) (For Creaming)
	1/2	Cup of Sugar (Granulated) (For Creaming)
	1	Teaspoon of Pure Vanilla Extract
	3	Tablespoons of Butter (Soften) (For Creaming)
	3	Tablespoons of Crisco (Soften) (For Creaming)
	1/3	Cup of Milk (Add In At The Very Last)
		(You May Need Less ~ Add A Little At A Time)
~ Cucidati ~		
Cookie Frosting	2~1/4	Cups of Confectioner's Sugar (Sifted)
	3/4	Teaspoon of Pure Vanilla Extract
	1~1/2	Teaspoons of Pure Lemon Extract
	3	Tablespoons of Milk (Add A Little At A Time)
The		
Candy Sprinkles	1	Jar of Multi~Colored Candy Sprinkles (Nonpareils)
		(To Sprinkle On The Frosting)

Preparation ~ Fig Cookies ~ Cucidati ~
Mama's & Grandma Anna's Favorite

Cucidati
~ Prepare Filling ~

1. In a Large Pan, Bring 2 Cups of Water to a Boil.
   Set The Figs (Cored & Chopped), into Boiling Water.
   Cover The Pan and Boil for 5~10 Minutes,
   Just Until The Figs are Very Tender.
2. Cool The Figs. Drain Off Liquid. Do Not Use Fig Liquid.
3. When Using ~ A Food Processor ~ OR ~ A Blender:
   Combine The Drained Figs, The Raisins & The Walnuts.
   ~ In a Processor ~ Process for 10~20 Seconds, ~ OR ~
   ~ In a Blender ~ Blend for 30~45 Seconds.
   Then, Add in The Orange Rind, The Honey,
   The Nutmeg, The Cinnamon, & The Sugar, And
   ~ Process Again ~ 10~20 Seconds, ~ OR ~
   ~ Blend Again ~ 30~45 Seconds,
   Just Until The Mixture is Very Smooth.
4. When Using ~ A Hand Grinder, Then Proceed As Follows:
   Combine The Drained Figs, Raisins and Walnuts
   ~ Grind Two Times to Get a Smooth Texture ~
   If Texture is Too Dry, Add a Few Drops of Water.
   ~ In a Large Bowl and Using an Electric Hand Mixer,
   Combine The "Ground" Figs, Raisins & Walnuts with
   The Orange Rind, Honey, Nutmeg, Cinnamon & Sugar.
   Blend for 2~3 Minutes, or Until Well Mixed

Cucidati
~ Prepare Dough ~

1. Sift The Flour, The Baking Powder & The Salt. Set Aside.
2. In A Separate Bowl, Combine The Eggs, The Sugar,
   The Vanilla, and The Softened Butter & Crisco.
   Cream Together in Electric Mixer, Until Very Smooth.
3. Gradually, Add In The Sifted Flour Mix to The Creamed Mixture,
   Blending Constantly with The Electric Mixer.
4. Lastly, Add The Milk, A Little At A Time,
   Until The Dough is Soft but Firm. Shape into a Ball.
5. Cover with Wax Paper. Refrigerate & Chill for 30 Minutes.
6. Cut The Dough Ball into 8 Separate Small Balls of Dough.
7. On a Lightly Floured Surface, Roll Each Dough Ball Out to
   A Strip about 10" Long X 4" Wide X 1/4" Thick.

Cucidati
~ Fill The Dough ~

1. Spread a Row of Filling Down Center of Each Dough Strip.
2. Starting at 10" Long Edge, Fold Dough Over The Filling
   and Roll It Closed. Seal The Edge with Water.
3. Cut Across The Filled and Rolled Dough Strip
   Diagonally Every 1" to Make Cookies.
4. Make 3 Small Slits Diagonally on Each Cookie,
   Allowing for Steam and for A Pretty Appearance, too!

Preparation ~ Fig Cookies ~ Cucidati ~
Mama's & Grandma Anna's Favorite

Cucidati
~ Baking Cookies ~

1. *Line The Cookie Sheets with Parchment Paper.*
2. *Space The Cookies at Least 1 Inch Apart from Each Other.*
3. *Bake in Preheated 375 Degree Oven for 10~15 Minutes, Or Until The Dough is Just Lightly Browned.*
4. *Cool The Cookies Thoroughly on a Wire Racks. (At Least 1 Hour of Cooling for Filled Cookies)*

Cucidati
~ Prepare Frosting ~

1. *In a Large Bowl, Sift The Confectioner's Sugar.*
2. *Add The Vanilla Extract and The Lemon Extract. Stir In.*
3. *Very Slowly, Add The Milk, As Needed, By Tablespoon. Blend Into a Firmly, Smooth Glazed Frosting.*

Cucidati
~ Frost The Cookies ~

1. *When The Cookies have Cooled for About 1 Hour, Cover Cookie Tops with The Glazed Frosting.*
2. *Immediately, Place The Multi~Colored Candy Sprinkles onto The Glazed Frosting. Arrange Attractively.*

Cucidati
~ Cool & Store Cookies ~

1. *Now, Place The Frosted Cookies on a Clean Cookie Sheets.*
2. *Set Aside in a Nice Cool, Dry Place (Do Not Stack). Allow Cookie Dough and Filling Flavors & Texture Time to Properly Set~Up, About 2~3 Hours, Before Storing The Cookies.*
3. *Then, Store The Cookies in Tightly Sealed Containers Between Loose Layers of Wax Paper.*
4. *Cucidati Cookies will stay Fresh This Way for 2 Weeks.*
5. *Every 3~4 Days, Place 1 Drop of Extract in Containers to Keep Fresh and Flavorful ~ Lemon or Vanilla!*

Serving Suggestion

The Fig Cookies ~ Cucidati ~ Have a Very Pretty Appearance. Arrange These Delightful Treats Attractively on a Decorative Platter with Doilies to Proudly Show Them Off! Your Lovely Results ~ Your Cucidati ~ Deserve a Special Place on The Table! Serve with a Nice Dessert Wine and Special Coffees and Teas. The Delicious Cucidati is a Cookie rich in History, rich in Regard, and now rich in Your Fine Efforts! Mama & Grandma Anna would be Proud of You! We Know You Will Really Love This Very Treasured Mama Lena's Sweet Treat! Enjoy!

~ Chapter Twelve ~
The Kitchen Essentials

Pages 261 ~271

~ Treasured Ingredients ~

~ Kitchen Terms ~

~ Measures & Sizes ~

~ Tips for Cooking & Baking ~

The Cheeses

At Mama Lena's Italian Kitchen, we used Imported Italian Cheeses and Domestic Cheeses. We purchased our Ricotta Fresh ~ always Fresh ~ at the Market. The Fresh Ricotta Cheese has a completely different and better taste than the preserved! Be sure to ~ Always Buy The Best Quality ~ That's what produces the Best Results! Enjoy!

~ *Our Seven Basic Cheeses* ~ *Imported & Domestic* ~

Asiago Cheese
Imported ~ From Italy ~ (Very Smooth Taste)
In our Eyes, Italy's Best Cheese
Use ~ Grated or Shaved on Entrees, Pastas, & Focaccio
Or ~ Serve in Slices on Sandwiches or for Appetizers

Fontina Cheese Or Fontinella Cheese
~ Imported Style ~ From Italy ~ (Nutty, Tangy Taste)
~ Domestic Style ~ From Wisconsin
Use ~ Medium Chunks on Antipasto, Salads and
         with Italian Bread & Olives.
Or ~ Serve in Small Chunks on Thin Pizzas & Pan Pizzas

Mozzarella Cheese
Imported & Domestic ~ (Very Mild Taste)
Use ~ Eggplant Parmesan, Lasagna and other
         Baked Pastas, and of course, on Pizzas.
         Also Sliced Thin & Served on Italian Bread.

Parmesan Cheese Reggiano
Imported from Italy ~ (Medium, Sharp Taste)
Use ~ Grated over Pastas, Soups, Vegetables,
         Main Entrees, and The Breads.
         * Also, We Mix with Our Bread Crumbs. *

Provolone Cheese
Imported, Italy ~ Domestic, Wisconsin ~ (Mildly Sharp)
Use ~ Sliced in Wedges for Antipasto Salad, and
         Cubed for Pizzas, Sliced on Sandwiches,
         and Grated or Shaved for Pastas

Ricotta Cheese
Domestic ~ Fresh ~ (Mild Italian Cottage Cheese)
Use ~ Pasta Filling for Cannelloni, Manicotti, Ravioli &
         Lasagna ~ Also in Our Velvet Cloud Sauce,
         Mama Lena's Cannoli and Our Cake Fillings

Romano Cheese
Imported from Italy ~ (Light, Tangy Taste)
Use ~ Best Use is Grated ~ It Grates & Shaves Beautifully ~
         Wonderful over Pastas, Entrees, Soups, Salads,
         and Breads. * Also, We Mix with Our Bread Crumbs.*

Note For Breadcrumbs ~ Add Grated Cheese Last and Use Immediately.
Try Half Parmesan & Half Romano Cheese Grated & Blended. Enjoy!

The Herbs & Spices

Herbs and Spices add an aromatic and flavorful taste to the food, while enhancing the natural flavors of a dish. We briefly outline some of our favorites to show which Foods we feel the specific Herbs & Spices go best with. Everyone has their favorites also to suit their taste or cooking and you'll find yours in time. Mama's favorites were ~ Basil, Cloves, Fennel, Garlic, Mint, Oregano and Parsley. Whenever possible, Mama used Fresh Herbs & Spices, but she also used Dried Herbs & Spices. Mama said to try to remember these three things~
1 ~ Chop The Fresh ~OR~ Crush The Dried Herbs & Spices Just Before Use for Best Flavors,
2 ~ Measures ~ 3 Tablespooons of Fresh Herbs & Spices ~ TO~ 1 Tablespoon of Dried, and
3 ~ Be Considerate of Guests ~ Season Food Lightly. Place Extra Seasonings on the Table, Especially the Red Peppers Flakes. Allow the guests to decide on their own preference. Then, your Meal will be Just Right for You, Your Family and Your Guests! Enjoy!

ANISE	**Desserts (A Very Delightful Addition)**
BASIL	**Sauces, Pasta, Chicken, Fish and Meat Entrees**
BAY LEAF	**Soups and Some Sauces**
CAPERS	**Sauces, Eggplant and Veal Dishes**
CELERY SALT	**Salads and Sauces and Dressings**
CHIVES	**Any Mama Lena's Recipe calling for a Fine Onion Taste or Fresh in Antipasto Dishes and as a Garnish**
CLOVES	**Fish Sauces, Vegetables and in Some Dessert Recipes**
FENNEL	**Sauces (Mainly Fish Sauces) ~ Fresh Raw in Salads**
GARLIC *	***For "Every" Italian Dish or Bread (Except Desserts) "Without Garlic, Close Any Kitchen That Cooks Italian!" *But Remember, Garlic is Supposed to "Kiss" the Pallet, Not Overwhelm It. Whether Fresh, Dried or Garlic Salt, Always Use The Garlic Gently, Gently, Gently!***
LEEK	**Soups and Some Sauces ~ Also Fresh Raw in Salads**
MARJORAM	**Meats and Many Vegetable Dishes**
MINT	**Sauces, Soups, Salads, Vegetable Dishes**
OREGANO	**Sauces, Any Entree Dish and on Some Breads and Pizzas**
PARSLEY	**Sauces, Bread Crumbs, Garnishing Dishes & Main Dishes**
ROSEMARY	**Sauces, Meat and Chicken Dishes, Breads and Focaccio**
SAGE	**Roasted Lamb, Poultry or Veal Dishes**
TARRAGON	**Sauces and Chicken & Fish Dishes**
THYME	**Meat, Fish, Chicken Dishes (A Treat on Vegetable Dishes)**
SALT*	**These Four are Most Often Overused. Be Very Careful ~**
PEPPER*	**Use Just A Pinch At A Time with These 4 Seasonings.**
CAYENNE*	**Test Taste after They Cook into Food, Or Season Lightly,**
RED PEPPER*	**And Place Them on Table for the Guests to Decide. Enjoy!**

The Pastas

At Mama Lena's Italian Kitchen, we always served Imported Pastas, finding them to have a great taste and texture for our Daily Menu. Only when we had Private Parties on Sundays, would we make our Homemade Pastas. Following are a Few Tips, as in our Chapter Four, on Pasta Preparation and Serving. Enjoy!

Preparation ~ Commercial Pastas

Boil 6 Quarts of Water, 2 Pinches of Salt & 2 Tablespoons of Olive Oil. Cook for About 10~12 Minutes for Al~Dente, Stirring Often with A Long Wooden Spoon (Metal Forks and Spoons tear the Pasta). Drain the Pasta Well in Large Colander. * Do Not Rinse Pasta with Water.* Serve Immediately with one of Mama Lena's Pasta Sauces.

To Pre~Cook the Pasta for Later Use, Finish Cooking Pasta, and Move the Pan to the Sink. Allow Cold Water to Run into Side of Pan to Cool Down Pasta. Drain Well in a Colander. Store in Airtight Containers in the Refrigerator for 2 to 3 Days. Freeze for Up to 1 Month.

Preparation ~ Homemade Pastas

Be More Careful with Homemade Pasta. This Pasta is Much More Delicate. Cooking Time for The Homemade Pasta is Also Considerably Less Than the Commercial Pasta. Make These Pastas with Semolina Flour, if you can, Or an All~Purpose Flour will be satisfactory.

Boil 6 Quarts Water, Add 2 Pinches of Salt and 2 Tablespoons of Olive Oil. *Cook Pasta Only 6~9 Minutes, to Size ~ For Thin Noodles ~ About 6 Minutes For The Cannelloni, Lasagna, Manicotti, Ravioli & Shells ~ About 9 Minutes. Watch This Pasta Very Carefully ~ Gently, Stir with a Wooden Spoon.

Note ~ Watch that you have a "Slow" Boil. We notice that Gas Stoves are easier to adjust quickly. If you are working on Electric Stove, you have to be more watchful ~ the heat adjustments take longer.

Drain The Homemade Pasta in a Plastic Colander, so Pasta doesn't tear. *Do Not Rinse Pasta* Serve Your Homemade Pasta Immediately with a Mama Lena's Sauce! Enjoy!

Serving Suggestion

We Heat our Serving Platters. Preheat the Oven to 200 Degrees ~ Set the Platter in Oven for 3 Minutes, and Then Turn Off Heat. Move Platter to Table. Place Hot Sauce on Bottom of Platter, then Pasta, then More Hot Sauce and Toss Gently. Sprinkle Pasta Lightly with Grated Cheese. Garnish and Serve. Follow These Easy Steps to be sure you are serving your Pasta Nice and Hot, and It Will Remain That Way for the Entire Meal. Enjoy!

The Olive Oils

Like Mama and Grandma for years before, at Mama Lena's Italian Kitchen, Salvino used only two Oils in all our Cooking and most of our Baking. The Two Oils were The Olive Oils ~ The Extra Virgin Olive Oils and The Pure Olive Oils. Each one has their own specific use, which we will highlight below.

The Olive Oils are pressed from Olives in various stages of ripeness. They are Wonderfully Smooth and Flavorful. Once you use the Olive Oils, you'll be so pleased with the results in how your food cooks and tastes, we think you will insist on using them always, too! Enjoy!

The Extra~ Virgin Olive Oils

Taste	**Excellent Fruity & Nutty Taste**
	(1% Acidity Level ~ Made from Unripe Olives)
Types	**Different Variations, Light or Dark ~ Buy Small Bottles, and**
	Try Out Which Variation of the Extra Virgin You Like Best.
	(The Extra Virgin Olive Oils are Very Expensive)
Uses	**On Salads, in Dressings and to Marinate Meats & Vegetables.**
	Or Drizzle Lightly Over Antipasto Raw Vegetables

The Pure Olive Oils

* Our Recipes refer to this, as "Pure Olive Oil" or just "Olive Oil" *

Taste	**Slightly Sharper Fruity Flavor**
	(Has a Higher Acidity Level and is Made from Ripe Olives)
Types	**Different Variations, Light or Dark ~ Best to Purchase Large Size**
	as it Cost Less and You Have More Uses for the Pure Olive Oil.
Uses	**For All Cooking of Entrees, for Frying, and in Making Sauces.**
	For Baking of Breads and Cakes and Dressing the Breads

*** Do Store Olive Oils in a Cool, Dark,
Dry Spot for Up to 3 Months.***
* Do Not Refrigerate the Olive Oils *

The Vinegars

Mama Lena's Italian Kitchen served some of the Best Salads and Dressings you would ever want to taste, as you will learn for yourself in this Book. And what is a Great Salad, an Antipasto or a Marinade without a lovely Wine Vinegar, made from the best grapes, so there is no bitterness!

We always purchased the "Best" Wine Vinegars ~ clear, not cloudy ~ at our Market. And we always used Red Wine or White Wine Vinegars. Though, the Balsamic Vinegar is highly regarded and more recently popular, we always found that it was best to use Balsamic Alone to enjoy the taste fully. For the results we wished to achieve, we always used a fine Red Wine or White Wine Vinegar with Extra~Virgin Olive Oils for our Recipes. So, here's a little background on The Vinegars, so you can choose for yourself. Enjoy!

The Balsamic Vinegars

      Taste   **Sweet Tasting like a Dark Syrup**

      Type   **Dark, Clear Caramel Look (Aged and Expensive)**

      Uses   **In Fish or Meat Sauces and on Hot & Cold Salads Alone**

The Red Wine Vinegars

      Taste   **Sharper Sweet~Sour Taste**

      Type   **Clear Deep Pink to Deep Red Color**
                  (Like the Color of a Rose' Wine to a Red Wine)

      Uses   **Salads, Dressings, Appetizers, and Marinades**

The White Wine Vinegars

      Taste   **Milder Sweet~Sour Taste**

      Type   **Clear Golden White Color (Like Color of a Chablis Wine)**

      Uses   **Salads, Dressings, Appetizers and Marinades**

Note * Store in a Cool, Dark, Dry Spot for Up to 3 Months *

The Wines & Liqueurs

At Mama Lena's Italian Kitchen, we used Favorite Italian Wines in our Cooking and Baking. And although, we were small in space and did not stock Wines, we allowed our Guests to bring their own Wines. Since the Menu was not known to the Guests, we would suggest the Wine that we felt would be the Best Compliment to Our Evening's Meal. We Opened All The Wines for our Guests, Chilled The Rose' and The White Wines, and personally served each Guest their Wine. The service was appreciated by Guests and also kept their "Evening Out" expenses down! We wanted to share our Wonderful Food with our Guests. We also wished to Entertain and Serve Them in every way to make Their Evening Special and Worthwhile!

We were not experts in Wine, but knew from our years of Cooking with and Enjoying a Glass of Wine with the Meal what would be Appropriate and Complimentary. We Listened Closely to What Our Guests Enjoyed, and we learned from them also, as they gave us their opinions. We Share With You Our Very Humble, But Tried & True, Knowledge of Wines! Enjoy!

The Cooking Wines and The Baking Wines

CREAM SHERRY ~ *Mama & Salvino Never Cooked with Cooking Sherry They preferred the smooth Cream Sherry Wine*
MARSALA WINES ~ *The Pride of Sicily ~ Sweet or Dry, as you Prefer*
AMARETTO LIQUEUR ~ *Lovely in our Desserts and Some Main Dishes, too*
ANISETTE LIQUEUR ~ *An Italian Tradition in Many Desserts*
VERMOUTHS ~ *Sweet or Dry, as you Prefer*

The Dinner Wines ~ The Reds, The Roses' and The Whites

The Reds BARDOLINO ~ *Dry, Ruby Red Wine*
CHIANTI ~ *Mellow Ruby Red Wine*
LAMBRUSCO ~ *Soft, Semi-Sweet Red Wine*
VALPOLICELLA ~ *A Smooth, Light Red Wine*

The Roses' VIN ROSE' ~ *Sweet, Light Rose' Wine*
RIUNITE ~ *Soft Blush Wine*
ZINFANDEL ~ *Very Dry Rose' Wine*

The Whites CHABLIS ~ *A Dry, Light White Wine*
PORTOFINO ~ *A Dry, Full Bodied White Wine*
RIESLINGS ~ *Very Light Tart or Freshly Sweet White Wines*
RIUNITE ~ *Soft White Wine*
SOAVE BIANCO ~ *Excellent Dry White Wine*

The Dessert Wines ~ The Dessert Wines and The Dessert Liqueurs

AMARETTO LIQEUER ~ *Sweet, Almond Flavor ~ Salvino's Favorite*
ASTI SPUMANTI WINE ~ *Sweet, Light, Sparkling ~ Margo's Favorite*
SWEET MARSALA WINE ~ *Sicily's Sweet & Rich ~ Mama, Papa & Family Favorite*

Mama Lena's Recipe Terms

AL DENTE ~ Cooked "Firm to the Tooth" (Pasta Not Overcooked)

ANTIPASTO ~ Italian Word for Appetizers, or Something Served "Before" the Main Meal

CLOVE ~ GARLIC ~ One Segment of the Garlic Bulb

COMBINE ~ Mix Specific Ingredients Together

CROUTONS ~ Fried Cubes of Bread (Used for Soups & Salads)

GARNISH ~ Decorating a Plate for an Attractive Finish

KNEAD ~ Rhythmic Movement of the Dough with Your Hands to Condition it for Pasta & Bread Making

MARINATE ~ Soak Meats or Vegetables in a Special Liquid to develop a Special Flavor or Tenderness

PASTA ~ Italian Word for Various Macaroni's and Spaghetti's

PREHEAT ~ Turning Oven to Recommended Temperature and Allowing It to Reach that Temperature Prior to Baking Item

PUREE ~ Reducing a Food to a Smooth Liquid

SAUTE ~ Frying by Pan for Short Period of Time (Not Deep Fry)

SIMMER ~ Cooking on the Range in the Lowest Temperature

STEAM ~ Cooking with Water & Partially Covered to Soften

TOAST ~ Browning of Breads in Oven or Toaster

TOSS ~ Lightly Lifting and Tumbling Ingredients

CRUSH ~ Pressure Press to Extract Liquid or Reduce Size
CUBE ~ Cutting Food into Small Square of 1/2" or Larger
CHOP ~ Quick Cutting of Food into Small Pieces
DICE ~ Quick Cutting of Food into Extra Small Pieces
GRATE ~ Shaving Particles from Food with a Metal Grater
MINCE ~ Cutting or Pressing Food into Extra Fine Particles
SLIVER ~ Cutting into Long, Very Thin Pieces

Measures & Can Sizes

Here's Quick References to the Measures & Can Sizes we most often refer to in our Recipes! Note also, we have included the "scientifically exact" Measurements for Pinches! However, Mama Lena's Italian Kitchen knows "A Pinch is an Individual Touch." Mama Lena had her own Individual Pinch for Cooking and Salvino has his own Individual Pinch for the Cooking. A Pinch is Your Own Touch ~ A Personal Touch ~ that You Lend to Your Cooking. That's The Beauty of Your Individual Pinch. You Personally Touch The Seasonings, Get a Feeling for The Dish, and Impart that Feeling to the Food for Just Right Results for You ~ Perfect! Enjoy!

The Measures ~ A Quick Reference

1 PINCH	~	**1/8 Teaspoon**
2 PINCHES	~	**1/4 Teaspoon**
4 PINCHES	~	**1/2 Teaspoon**
6 PINCHES	~	**3/4 Teaspoon**
8 PINCHES	~	**1 Full Teaspoon**

3 Teaspoons ~1 Tablespoon ~ 1/2 Fl. Oz.

1/8 Cup	~	**2 Tablespoons**	~	**1 Fl. Oz.**
1/4 Cup	~	**4 Tablespoons**	~	**2 Fl. Oz.**
1/3 Cup	~	**5.3 Tablespoons**	~	**3 Fl. Oz.**
1/2 Cup	~	**8 Tablespoons**	~	**4 Fl. Oz.**
3/4 Cup	~	**12 Tablespoons**	~	**6 Fl. Oz.**
1 Cup	~	**16 Tablespoons**	~	**8 Fl. Oz.**

2 Cups	~	**1 Pint**	~	**1 Pound**	~	**16 Fl. Oz.**
4 Cups	~	**2 Pints**	~	**1 Quart**	~	**32 Fl. Oz.**
8 Cups	~	**2 Quarts**	~	**1/2 Gallon**	~	**64 Fl. Oz.**
16 Cups	~	**4 Quarts**	~	**1 Gallon**	~	**128 Fl. Oz.**

At Mama Lena's Italian Kitchen, we needed and always used the Extra~Large Cans of "Full~Red ®," "Tomato Magic ®," and "7/11 ®" from Stanislaus Food Products. But our Recipes have been scaled down in this Book for your home use, so you will need to know Smaller Can Sizes. They are, as follows ~

The Common Can Sizes ~ A Quick Reference

~ For Tomato Paste ~	**~ For Plum Tomatoes ~**
	Crushed or Whole

Small	~ 6 Oz. ~ 3/4 Cup	**Medium Size**	~ 15 Oz. ~ About 2 Cups
Medium	~ 12 Oz. ~ 1~1/2 Cups	**Large Size**	~ 28 Oz. ~ About 3~1/4 Cups
Large	~ 18 Oz. ~ 2~1/4 Cups	**Extra-Large**	~ 6 Lb., 10 Oz. ~ 12~13 Cups

Cooking & Baking Temperatures

In Each Chapter Beginning and in Each Recipe, we have tried to be very, very careful to be As Clear As Possible and point out "The Details," often left out of recipes, that actually make for Successful Cooking and Baking. Now, we share a few additional General Cooking & Baking Tips that we have always found Very Helpful in achieving our Successful Cooking and Baking Results. We hope they prove as helpful to you! Enjoy!

Know Your Own Range

Gas Cooking	~	**Even Heat ~ Easier to Control**
		Temperatures Adjust Quickly
Electric Cooking	~	**Intense Heat ~ Tends to be Dryer Heat**
		Temperatures take Longer Time to Adjust
Your Own Range	~	**Follow your Range Guidebooks for the Temperatures**
		Recommended for Cooking & Baking
		Most Ranges Vary in Temperature ~ For Accuracy ~
		Check Your Own Oven Temperatures with an
		Oven Thermometer to be Able to Adjust Properly

Oven Temperatures

~	**Very Low**	~ **250 F to 275 F**
~	**Low Bake**	~ **300 F to 325 F**
~	**Moderate**	~ **350 F to 375 F**
~	**Hot Bake**	~ **400 F to 425 F**
~	**Very Hot**	~ **450 F to 475 F**
~	**Too Hot**	~ **500 F to 525 F**
~	**Broiling**	~ **550 F to 600 F**

Attention to Cooking with Foil

You will notice that many of our Recipes call for Sealing the Roaster Pan with Aluminum Foil. This does make for Beautiful Results. This is the way we cooked and baked for all the years. But you must be Very Careful ~ Always Open the Foil Cover Away From You ~ Then, the Steam will flow away from you. Just Unseal the Foil at the Far End Away From You ~ a Little at a Time ~ and the Steam will Escape Properly and Safely ~ It's Always Best To Be Careful In The Kitchen ~ Happy and Safe Cooking to You!

Kitchen Cooking & Baking Pans

A Standard Set of Pots and Pans will get you through Most Cooking Needs. We recommend an Additional 2 Skillets ~ Non-Stick, Small & Large Sizes. And for Baking, we suggest that you have on hand ~ A Bundt Pan, An Angel Food Stay~Form Pan, 2 Loaf Pans & 2 Round Pans, a Small Square and Large Square Pan & 6 Cookie Sheets in Small to Large Sizes. Also, have on hand 2~4 Wire Racks as Trivets and Cooling Racks.

Kitchen Equipment
Shopping & Recipe Advice

Kitchen Measure Cups & Measure Spoons

Have a Set of Standard Measuring Cups and Measuring Spoons on Hands, as well as a few Larger~Size Measuring Cups for larger amounts of Liquid or Dry Ingredients. Prepare your Kitchen with the Ingredients and Equipment you Need At Hand "Before" You Start!

Kitchen Mixing Bowls & Mixing Spoons

Several Sizes of Mixing Bowls ~ Get Ones With Covers, so they can be converted to Storage Containers. The Hard Plastic makes good Mixing Bowls and Good Containers, too. Large Wooden Spoons are wonderful for Mixing Ingredients and Gentle for Stirring Pasta! And we Use Two Slotted Metal Spoons ~ One Curved Spoon~Style and One Flat Style ~ Just Great!

Kitchen Mixers

Mixers are a wonderful convenience, especially in Baking. We recommend a Hand Mixer, a Full Standard Mixer and a Blender for Every Kitchen. A Food Processor is a great asset, too!

Kitchen Knives and Kitchen Scissors

It's nice to have a Full Kitchen Knife & Holder Set, but if you don't ~ Be sure you Always Have At Least 3 Good Knifes ~ A Serrated Paring Knife, a Serrated Bread Knife, a Very Sharp 12"~15" Chef's Knife for every other Kitchen Use. Kitchen Scissors are recommended.

Ingredients for Cooking & Baking

Shop Wisely, But Always Buy The Best Quality Possible in All Foods to get The Best Results!

Shopping in an Italian Store

We highly recommend that you shop, whenever possible, in an Italian Store for any of your Ingredients for Italian Cooking. First, the Ingredients you need will be readily available to you, and Second, your Recipe Results will be more authentic. Also, it's a wonderful Experience to put you in the Mood for Italian Cooking! Gourmet Shops are great choices, too!

Follow The Recipe

Our Recipes Are Our Very Special Treasures, But They Are Your Detailed Instructional Aid! Mama Lena's Advice ~ "Careful Preparation Is The Key, Even To The Most Simple Recipe!" Prepare! Carefully Read The Recipe! Buy The Best Ingredients for The Best Quality Results! Select Proper Kitchen Essentials! Watch Recipe Timing! You Will Be Successful! Enjoy!

The Contact Information Page

Most Sincere Thanks to You for Joining Us on This Very Memorable Journey into Our "Mama Lena's Italian Kitchen" and "A Pinch of This and A Pinch of That." We Hope You Enjoyed This Journey, As We Sincerely Enjoyed Sharing with You Our Lovely Story and Our Treasured Recipes in Our Story~Cookbook!

To Contact Us with Any Questions ~ Our Contact Information Is:

MarSala's Enterprises, Ltd.
Two Elm Creek Drive
Suite #501
Elmhurst, Illinois 60126

Web Site
www.MamaLenas.com
E~Mail
marsalas@mamalenas.com

Our Story~Cookbook Is A Simply Great Gift That Keeps on Giving Year After Year! As you place an Order, Please indicate if you wish any Books to be Autographed. Just Clearly Print The Names of All Persons you wish The Books Autographed To. We will be Most Happy to Accommodate You!

Send your Check or Money Order for $29.95 per Book in the USA, plus $6.00 for Priority Shipping & Handling per Book. (Illinois Residents ~ Add $2.00 Sales Tax). Canadian & International Friends ~ Send $34.95, plus $12.00 PS&H per Book. We Will Ship Your Orders Anywhere in The USA or in The World that You Request.

A Special Discount of 25% Off Retail Price Applies for Orders of 10 Books or More. When placing such an Order, send $22.50 per Book, plus $6.00 PS & H per Book. (Illinois Residents, Add Tax of $1.50 per Book). Canadian and International Orders of 10 Books or More will require $26.25 per Book, plus $12.00 PS&H per Book.

Thank you ~ Your Orders will receive Prompt Attention ~ Please Do Not Mail Cash.

Once Again, Our Most Sincere Thanks for Joining Us on This Special Journey into " Mama Lena's Italian Kitchen " and "A Pinch of This and A Pinch of That."

Enjoy!